Learning Predictive Analytics with Python

Gain practical insights into predictive modelling
by implementing Predictive Analytics algorithms
on public datasets with Python

Ashish Kumar

[PACKT] open source*
PUBLISHING   community experience distilled

BIRMINGHAM - MUMBAI

Learning Predictive Analytics with Python

First published: February 2016

Production reference: 1050216

Published by Packt Publishing Ltd.
Livery Place
35 Livery Street
Birmingham B3 2PB, UK.

ISBN 978-1-78398-326-1

www.packtpub.com

Credits

Author
Ashish Kumar

Reviewer
Matt Hollingsworth

Commissioning Editor
Kartikey Pandey

Acquisition Editor
Nikhil Karkal

Content Development Editor
Amey Varangaonkar

Technical Editor
Saurabh Malhotra

Copy Editor
Sneha Singh

Project Coordinator
Francina Pinto

Proofreader
Safis Editing

Indexer
Hemangini Bari

Graphics
Disha Haria

Kirk D'Penha

Production Coordinator
Shantanu N. Zagade

Cover Work
Shantanu N. Zagade

Foreword

Data science is changing the way we go about our daily lives at an unprecedented pace. The recommendations you see on e-commerce websites, the technologies that prevent credit card fraud, the logic behind airline itinerary and route selections, the products and discounts you see in retail stores, and many more decisions are largely powered by data science. Futuristic sounding applications like self-driving cars, robots to do household chores, smart wearable technologies, and so on are becoming a reality, thanks to innovations in data science.

Predictive analytics is a branch of data science, used to predict unknown future events based on historical data. It uses a number of techniques from data mining, statistical modelling and machine learning to help make forecasts with an acceptable level of reliability.

Python is a high-level, object-oriented programming language. It has gained popularity because of its clear syntax and readability, and beginners can pick up the language easily. It comes with a large library of modules that can be used to do a multitude of tasks ranging from data cleaning to building complex predictive modelling algorithms.

I'm a co-founder at Tiger Analytics, a firm specializing in providing data science and predictive analytics solutions to businesses. Over the last decade, I have worked with clients at numerous Fortune 100 companies and start-ups alike, and architected a variety of data science solution frameworks. Ashish Kumar, the author of this book, is currently a budding data scientist at our company. He has worked on several predictive analytics engagements, and understands how businesses are using data to bring in scientific decision making to their organizations. Being a young practitioner, Ashish relates to someone who wants to learn predictive analytics from scratch. This is clearly reflected in the way he presents several concepts in the book.

Whether you are a beginner in data science looking to build a career in this area, or a weekend enthusiast curious to explore predictive analytics in a hands-on manner, you will need to start from the basics and get a good handle on the building blocks. This book helps you take the first steps in this brave new world; it teaches you how to use and implement predictive modelling algorithms using Python. The book does not assume prior knowledge in analytics or programming. It differentiates itself from other such programming cookbooks as it uses publicly available datasets that closely represent data encountered in business scenarios, and walks you through the analysis steps in a clear manner.

There are nine chapters in the book. The first few chapters focus on data exploration and cleaning. It is written keeping beginners to programming in mind—by explaining different data structures and then going deeper into various methods of data processing and cleaning. Subsequent chapters cover the popular predictive modelling algorithms like linear regression, logistic regression, clustering, decision trees, and so on. Each chapter broadly covers four aspects of the particular model—math behind the model, different types of the model, implementing the model in Python, and interpreting the results.

Statistics/math involved in the model is clearly explained. Understanding this helps one implement the model in any other programming language. The book also teaches you how to interpret the results from the predictive model and suggests different techniques to fine tune the model for better results. Wherever required, the author compares two different models and explains the benefits of each of the models. It will help a data scientist narrow down to the right algorithm that can be used to solve a specific problem. In addition, this book exposes the readers to various Python libraries and guides them with the best practices while handling different datasets in Python.

I am confident that this book will guide you to implement predictive modelling algorithms using Python and prepare you to work on challenging business problems involving data. I wish this book and its author Ashish Kumar every success.

Pradeep Gulipalli
Co-founder and Head of India Operations - Tiger Analytics

About the Author

Ashish Kumar has a B. Tech from IIT Madras and is a Young India Fellow from the batch of 2012-13. He is a data science enthusiast with extensive work experience in the field. As a part of his work experience, he has worked with tools, such as Python, R, and SAS. He has also implemented predictive algorithms to glean actionable insights for clients from transport and logistics, online payment, and healthcare industries. Apart from the data sciences, he is enthused by and adept at financial modelling and operational research. He is a prolific writer and has authored several online articles and short stories apart from running his own analytics blog. He also works pro-bono for a couple of social enterprises and freelances his data science skills.

He can be contacted on LinkedIn at `https://goo.gl/yqrfo4`, and on Twitter at `https://twitter.com/asis64`.

Acknowledgments

I dedicate this book to my beloved grandfather who is the prime reason behind whatever I am today. He is my source of inspiration and he is the one I want to be like. Not a single line of this book was written without thinking about him; may you stay strong and healthy.

I want to acknowledge the support of my family, especially my parents and siblings. My conversations with them were the power source, which kept me going.

I want to acknowledge the guidance and support of my friends for insisting that I should do this when I was skeptical about taking this up. I would like to thank Ajit and Pranav for being the best friends one could ask for and always being there for me. A special mention to Vijayaraghavan for lending his garden for me to work in and relax post the long writing sessions. I would like to thank my college friends, especially my wing mates, Zenithers, who have always been pillars of support. My friends at the Young India Fellowship have made me evolve as a person and I am grateful to all of them.

I would like to thank my college friends, especially my wing mates, Zenithers, who have been pillars of support all throughout my life. My friends at the Young India Fellowship have made me evolve as a person and I am grateful to all of them.

I would like to extend my sincere gratitude to my faculty and well wishers at IIT Madras and the Young India Fellowship. The Tiger Analytics family, especially Pradeep, provided a conducive environment and encouraged me to take up and complete this task. I would also like to convey my sincere regards to Zeena Johar for believing in me and giving me the best learning and working opportunities, which were more than what I could have asked for in my first job.

I want to thank my editors Nikhil, Amey, Saurabh, Indrajit, and reviewer, Matt, for their wonderful comments and prompt responses. I would like to thank the entire PACKT publication team that was involved with ISBN B01782.

About the Reviewer

Matt Hollingsworth is a software engineer, data analyst, and entrepreneur. He has M.S. and B.S. degrees in Physics from the University of Tennessee. He is currently working on his MBA at Stanford, where he is putting his past experience with Big Data to use as an entrepreneur. He is passionate about about technology and loves finding new ways to use it to make our lives better.

He was part of the team at CERN that first discovered the Higgs boson, and he helped develop both the physics analysis and software systems to handle the massive data set that the Large Hadron Collider (LHC) produces. Afterward, he worked with Deepfield Networks to analyze traffic patterns in network telemetry data for some of the biggest computer networks in the world. He also co-founded Global Dressage Analytics, a company that provides dressage athletes with a web-based platform to track their progress and build high-quality training regimens.

If you are reading this book, chances are that you and him have a lot to talk about! Feel free to reach out to him at http://linkedin.com/in/mhworth or matt@mhworth.com.

www.PacktPub.com

Support files, eBooks, discount offers, and more

For support files and downloads related to your book, please visit www.PacktPub.com.

Did you know that Packt offers eBook versions of every book published, with PDF and ePub files available? You can upgrade to the eBook version at www.PacktPub.com and as a print book customer, you are entitled to a discount on the eBook copy. Get in touch with us at service@packtpub.com for more details.

At www.PacktPub.com, you can also read a collection of free technical articles, sign up for a range of free newsletters and receive exclusive discounts and offers on Packt books and eBooks.

https://www2.packtpub.com/books/subscription/packtlib

Do you need instant solutions to your IT questions? PacktLib is Packt's online digital book library. Here, you can search, access, and read Packt's entire library of books.

Why subscribe?

- Fully searchable across every book published by Packt
- Copy and paste, print, and bookmark content
- On demand and accessible via a web browser

Free access for Packt account holders

If you have an account with Packt at www.PacktPub.com, you can use this to access PacktLib today and view 9 entirely free books. Simply use your login credentials for immediate access.

Table of Contents

Preface

Social media and the Internet of Things have resulted in an avalanche of data. The data is powerful but not in its raw form; it needs to be processed and modelled and Python is one of the most robust tools we have out there to do so. It has an array of packages for predictive modelling and a suite of IDEs to choose from. Learning to predict who would win, lose, buy, lie, or die with Python is an indispensable skill set to have in this data age.

This book is your guide to get started with *Predictive Analytics using Python* as the tool. You will learn how to process data and make predictive models out of them. A balanced weightage has been given to both the statistical and mathematical concepts and implementing them in Python using libraries, such as pandas, scikit-learn, and NumPy. Starting with understanding the basics of predictive modelling, you will see how to cleanse your data of impurities and make it ready for predictive modelling. You will also learn more about the best predictive modelling algorithms, such as linear regression, decision trees, and logistic regression. Finally, you will see what the best practices in predictive modelling are, as well as the different applications of predictive modelling in the modern world.

What this book covers

Chapter 1, Getting Started with Predictive Modelling, talks about aspects, scope, and applications of predictive modelling. It also discusses various Python packages commonly used in data science, Python IDEs, and the methods to install these on systems.

Chapter 2, Data Cleaning, describes the process of reading a dataset, getting a bird's eye view of the dataset, handling the missing values in the dataset, and exploring the dataset with basic plotting using the pandas and matplotlib packages in Python. The data cleaning and wrangling together constitutes around 80% of the modelling time.

Chapter 3, Data Wrangling, describes the methods to subset a dataset, concatenate or merge two or more datasets, group the dataset by categorical variables, split the dataset into training and testing sets, generate dummy datasets using random numbers, and create simulations using random numbers.

Chapter 4, Statistical Concepts for Predictive Modelling, explains the basic statistics needed to make sense of the model parameters resulting from the predictive models. This chapter deals with concepts like hypothesis testing, z-tests, t-tests, chi-square tests, p-values, and so on followed by a discussion on correlation.

Chapter 5, Linear Regression with Python, starts with a discussion on the mathematics behind the linear regression validating the mathematics behind it using a simulated dataset. It is then followed by a summary of implications and interpretations of various model parameters. The chapter also describes methods to implement linear regression using the stasmodel.api and scikit-learn packages and handling various related contingencies, such as multiple regression, multi-collinearity, handling categorical variables, non-linear relationships between predictor and target variables, handling outliers, and so on.

Chapter 6, Logistic Regression with Python, explains the concepts, such as odds ratio, conditional probability, and contingency tables leading ultimately to detailed discussion on mathematics behind the logistic regression model (using a code that implements the entire model from scratch) and various tests to check the efficiency of the model. The chapter also describes the methods to implement logistic regression in Python and drawing and understanding an ROC curve.

Chapter 7, Clustering with Python, discusses the concepts, such as distances, the distance matrix, and linkage methods to understand the mathematics and logic behind both hierarchical and k-means clustering. The chapter also describes the methods to implement both the types of clustering in Python and methods to fine tune the number of clusters.

Chapter 8, Trees and Random Forests with Python, starts with a discussion on topics, such as entropy, information gain, gini index, and so on. To illustrate the mathematics behind creating a decision tree followed by a discussion on methods to handle variations, such as a continuous numerical variable as a predictor variable and handling a missing value. This is followed by methods to implement the decision tree in Python. The chapter also gives a glimpse into understanding and implementing the regression tree and random forests.

Chapter 9, Best Practices for Predictive Modelling, entails the best practices to be followed in terms of coding, data handling, algorithms, statistics, and business context for getting good results in predictive modelling.

Appendix, *A List of Links*, contains a list of sources which have been directly or indirectly consulted or used in the book. It also contains the link to the folder which contains datasets used in the book.

What you need for this book

In order to make the best use of this book, you will require the following:

- All the datasets that have been used to illustrate the concepts in various chapters. These datasets can be downloaded from this URL: `https://goo.gl/zjS4C6`. There is a sub-folder containing required datasets for each chapter.

- Your computer should have any of the Python distribution installed. The examples in the book have been worked upon in IPython Notebook. Following the examples will be much easier if you use IPython Notebook. This comes with Anaconda distribution that can be installed from `https://www.continuum.io/downloads`.

- The Python packages which are used widely, for example, pandas, matplotlib, scikit-learn, NumPy, and so on, should be installed. If you install Anaconda these packages will come pre-installed.

- One of the best ways to use this book will be to take the dataset used to illustrate concepts and flow along with the chapter. The concepts will be easier to understand if the reader works hands on on the examples.

- A basic aptitude for mathematics is expected. It is beneficial to understand the mathematics behind the algorithms before applying them.

- Prior experience or knowledge of coding will be an added advantage. But, not a pre-requisite at all.

- Similarly, knowledge of statistics and some algorithms will be beneficial, but is not a pre-requisite.

- An open mind curious to learn the tips and tricks of a subject that is going to be an indispensable skillset in the coming future.

Who this book is for

If you wish to learn the implementation of predictive analytics algorithms using Python libraries, then this is the book for you. If you are familiar with coding in Python (or some other programming/statistical/scripting language) but have never used or read about predictive analytics algorithms, this book will also help you. The book will be beneficial to and can be read by any data science enthusiasts. Some familiarity with Python will be useful to get the most out of this book but it is certainly not a pre-requisite.

Conventions

In this book, you will find a number of styles of text that distinguish between different kinds of information. Here are some examples of these styles, and an explanation of their meaning.

A typical code snippet would look as follows:

```
def closest_station(lat, longi):
    stations = np.array([[41.995, -87.933],
                         [41.786, -87.752]])
    loc = np.array([lat, longi])
    deltas = stations - loc[None, :]
    dist2 = (deltas**2).sum(1)
    return np.argmin(dist2)
```

The outputs of the code snippets are generally shown as the screenshots. This is how a screenshot looks:

y	0	1
education		
Basic	1133	98
High School	824	97
Illiterate	1	0
Professional Course	470	65
University Degree	1099	165
Unknown	141	26

New terms and **important words** are shown in bold. Words that you see on the screen, for example, in menus or dialog boxes, appear in the text like this: "The plot of **Monthly Income** and **Monthly Expense** for a group of 400 people."

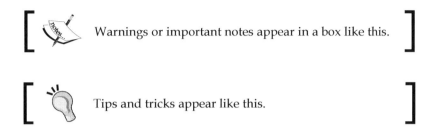

Warnings or important notes appear in a box like this.

Tips and tricks appear like this.

URLs are shown as below:

https://pypi.python.org/pypi/pip

A lot of tables have been used to summarize the results of mathematical discussions and illustrate certain concepts.

Reader feedback

Feedback from our readers is always welcome. Let us know what you think about this book — what you liked or may have disliked. Reader feedback is important for us to develop titles that you really get the most out of.

To send us general feedback, simply send an e-mail to feedback@packtpub.com, and mention the book title via the subject of your message.

If there is a topic that you have expertise in and you are interested in either writing or contributing to a book, see our author guide on www.packtpub.com/authors.

Customer support

Now that you are the proud owner of a Packt book, we have a number of things to help you to get the most from your purchase.

Downloading the example code

You can download the example code files for all Packt books you have purchased from your account at http://www.packtpub.com. If you purchased this book elsewhere, you can visit http://www.packtpub.com/support and register to have the files e-mailed directly to you.

Downloading the color images of this book

We also provide you with a PDF file that has color images of the screenshots/diagrams used in this book. The color images will help you better understand the changes in the output. You can download this file from: `http://www.packtpub.com/sites/default/files/downloads/LearningPredictiveAnalyticswithPython_ColorImages.pdf`.

Errata

Although we have taken every care to ensure the accuracy of our content, mistakes do happen. If you find a mistake in one of our books—maybe a mistake in the text or the code—we would be grateful if you would report this to us. By doing so, you can save other readers from frustration and help us improve subsequent versions of this book. If you find any errata, please report them by visiting `http://www.packtpub.com/submit-errata`, selecting your book, clicking on the **erratasubmissionform** link, and entering the details of your errata. Once your errata are verified, your submission will be accepted and the errata will be uploaded on our website, or added to any list of existing errata, under the Errata section of that title. Any existing errata can be viewed by selecting your title from `http://www.packtpub.com/support`.

Piracy

Piracy of copyright material on the Internet is an ongoing problem across all media. At Packt, we take the protection of our copyright and licenses very seriously. If you come across any illegal copies of our works, in any form, on the Internet, please provide us with the location address or website name immediately so that we can pursue a remedy.

Please contact us at `copyright@packtpub.com` with a link to the suspected pirated material.

We appreciate your help in protecting our authors, and our ability to bring you valuable content.

Questions

You can contact us at `questions@packtpub.com` if you are having a problem with any aspect of the book, and we will do our best to address it.

1
Getting Started with Predictive Modelling

Predictive modelling is an art; its a science of unearthing the story impregnated into silos of data. This chapter introduces the scope and application of predictive modelling and shows a glimpse of what could be achieved with it, by giving some real-life examples.

In this chapter, we will cover the following topics in detail:

- Introducing predictive modelling
- Applications and examples of predictive modelling
- Installing and downloading Python and its packages
- Working with different IDEs for Python

Introducing predictive modelling

Did you know that Facebook users around the world share 2,460,000 pieces of content every minute of the day? Did you know that 72-hours worth of new video content is uploaded on YouTube in the same time and, brace yourself, did you know that everyday around 2.5 exabytes (10^{18}) of data is created by us humans? To give you a perspective on how much data that is, you will need a million 1 TB (1000 GB) hard disk drives every day to store that much data. In a year, we will outgrow the US population and will be north of five times the UK population and this estimation is by assuming the fact that the rate of the data generation will remain the same, which in all likelihoods will not be the case.

The breakneck speed at which the social media and Internet of Things have grown is reflected in the huge silos of data humans generate. The data about where we live, where we come from, what we like, what we buy, how much money we spend, where we travel, and so on. Whenever we interact with a social media or Internet of Things website, we leave a trail, which these websites gleefully log as their data. Every time you buy a book at Amazon, receive a payment through PayPal, write a review on Yelp, post a photo on Instagram, do a check-in on Facebook, apart from making business for these websites, you are creating data for them.

Harvard Business Review (HBR) says "Data is the new oil" and that "Data Scientist is the sexiest job of the 21st century". So, why is the data so important and how can we realize the full potential of it? There are broadly two ways in which the data is used:

- **Retrospective analytics**: This approach helps us analyze history and glean out insights from the data. It allows us to learn from mistakes and adopt best practices. These insights and learnings become the torchbearer for the purpose of devising better strategy. Not surprisingly, many experts have been claiming that data is the new middle manager.

- **Predictive analytics**: This approach unleashes the might of data. In short, this approach allows us to predict the future. Data science algorithms take historical data and spit out a statistical model, which can predict who will buy, cheat, lie, or die in the future.

Let us evaluate the comparisons made with oil in detail:

- Data is as abundant as oil used to be, once upon a time, but in contrast to oil, data is a non-depleting resource. In fact, one can argue that it is reusable, in the sense that, each dataset can be used in more than one way and also multiple number of times.

- It doesn't take years to create data, as it takes for oil.

- Oil in its crude form is worth nothing. It needs to be refined through a comprehensive process to make it usable. There are various grades of this process to suit various needs; it's the same with data. The data sitting in silos is worthless; it needs to be cleaned, manipulated, and modelled to make use of it. Just as we need refineries and people who can operate those refineries, we need tools that can handle data and people who can operate those tools. Some of the tools for the preceding tasks are Python, R, SAS, and so on, and the people who operate these tools are called **data scientists**.

15

A more detailed comparison of oil and data is provided in the following table:

Data	Oil
It's a non-depleting resource and also reusable.	It's a depleting resource and non-reusable.
Data collection requires some infrastructure or system in place. Once the system is in place, the data generation happens seamlessly.	Drilling oil requires a lot of infrastructure. Once the infrastructure is in place, one can keep drawing the oil until the stock dries up.
It needs to be cleaned and modelled.	It needs to be cleaned and processed.
The time taken to generate data varies from fractions of second to months and years.	It takes decades to generate.
The worth and marketability of different kinds of data is different.	The worth of crude oil is same everywhere. However, the price and marketability of different end products of refinement is different.
The time horizon for monetization of data is smaller after getting the data.	The time horizon for monetizing oil is longer than that for data.

Scope of predictive modelling

Predictive modelling is an *ensemble of statistical algorithms* coded in a *statistical tool*, which when applied on *historical data*, outputs a *mathematical function* (or equation). It can in-turn be used to predict outcomes based on some inputs (on which the model operates) from the future to drive a goal in business context or enable better decision making in general.

To understand what predictive modelling entails, let us focus on the phrases highlighted previously.

Ensemble of statistical algorithms

Statistics are important to understand data. It tells volumes about the data. How is the data distributed? Is it centered with little variance or does it varies widely? Are two of the variables dependent on or independent of each other? Statistics helps us answer these questions. This book will expect a basic understanding of basic statistical terms, such as mean, variance, co-variance, and correlation. Advanced terms, such as hypothesis testing, Chi-Square tests, p-values, and so on will be explained as and when required. Statistics are the cog in the wheel called model.

Algorithms, on the other hand, are the blueprints of a model. They are responsible for creating mathematical equations from the historical data. They analyze the data, quantify the relationship between the variables, and convert it into a mathematical equation. There is a variety of them: Linear Regression, Logistic Regression, Clustering, Decision Trees, Time-Series Modelling, Naïve Bayes Classifiers, Natural Language Processing, and so on. These models can be classified under two classes:

- **Supervised algorithms**: These are the algorithms wherein the historical data has an output variable in addition to the input variables. The model makes use of the output variables from historical data, apart from the input variables. The examples of such algorithms include Linear Regression, Logistic Regression, Decision Trees, and so on.

- **Un-supervised algorithms**: These algorithms work without an output variable in the historical data. The example of such algorithms includes clustering.

The selection of a particular algorithm for a model depends majorly on the kind of data available. The focus of this book would be to explain methods of handling various kinds of data and illustrating the implementation of some of these models.

Statistical tools

There are a many statistical tools available today, which are laced with inbuilt methods to run basic statistical chores. The arrival of open-source robust tools like R and Python has made them extremely popular, both in industry and academia alike. Apart from that, Python's packages are well documented; hence, debugging is easier.

Python has a number of libraries, especially for running the statistical, cleaning, and modelling chores. It has emerged as the first among equals when it comes to choosing the tool for the purpose of implementing preventive modelling. As the title suggests, Python will be the choice for this book, as well.

Historical data

Our machinery (model) is built and operated on this oil called data. In general, a model is built on the historical data and works on future data. Additionally, a predictive model can be used to fill missing values in historical data by interpolating the model over sparse historical data. In many cases, during modelling stages, future data is not available. Hence, it is a common practice to divide the historical data into training (to act as historical data) and testing (to act as future data) through sampling.

As discussed earlier, the data might or might not have an output variable. However, one thing that it promises to be is messy. It needs to undergo a lot of cleaning and manipulation before it can become of any use for a modelling process.

Mathematical function

Most of the data science algorithms have underlying mathematics behind them. In many of the algorithms, such as regression, a mathematical equation (of a certain type) is assumed and the parameters of the equations are derived by fitting the data to the equation.

For example, the goal of linear regression is to fit a linear model to a dataset and find the equation parameters of the following equation:

$$Y = \alpha_0 + \beta_1.X_1 + \beta_2.X_2 + ... + \beta_n.X_n$$

The purpose of modelling is to find the best values for the coefficients. Once these values are known, the previous equation is good to predict the output. The equation above, which can also be thought of as a linear function of Xi's (or the input variables), is the linear regression model.

Another example is of logistic regression. There also we have a mathematical equation or a function of input variables, with some differences. The defining equation for logistic regression is as follows:

$$P = \frac{e^{a+b*x}}{1+e^{a+b*x}} = \frac{1}{1+e^{-(a+b*x)}}$$

Here, the goal is to estimate the values of a and b by fitting the data to this equation. Any supervised algorithm will have an equation or function similar to that of the model above. For unsupervised algorithms, an underlying mathematical function or criterion (which can be formulated as a function or equation) serves the purpose. The mathematical equation or function is the backbone of a model.

Business context

All the effort that goes into predictive analytics and all its worth, which accrues to data, is because it solves a business problem. A business problem can be anything and it will become more evident in the following examples:

- Tricking the users of the product/service to buy more from you by increasing the click through rates of the online ads

- Predicting the probable crime scenes in order to prevent them by aggregating an invincible lineup for a sports league
- Predicting the failure rates and associated costs of machinery components
- Managing the churn rate of the customers

The predictive analytics is being used in an array of industries to solve business problems. Some of these industries are, as follows:

- Banking
- Social media
- Retail
- Transport
- Healthcare
- Policing
- Education
- Travel and logistics
- E-commerce
- Human resource

By what quantum did the proposed solution make life better for the business, is all that matters. That is the reason; predictive analytics is becoming an indispensable practice for management consulting.

In short, predictive analytics sits at the sweet spot where statistics, algorithm, technology and business sense intersect. Think about it, a mathematician, a programmer, and a business person rolled in one.

Knowledge matrix for predictive modelling

As discussed earlier, predictive modelling is an interdisciplinary field sitting at the interface and requiring knowledge of four disciplines, such as **Statistics**, **Algorithms**, **Tools**, **Techniques**, and **Business Sense**. Each of these disciplines is equally indispensable to perform a successful task of predictive modelling.

These four disciplines of predictive modelling carry equal weights and can be better represented as a knowledge matrix; it is a symmetric 2 x 2 matrix containing four equal-sized squares, each representing a discipline.

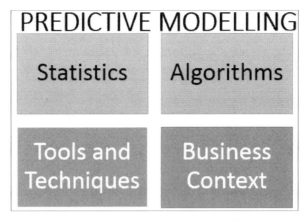

Fig. 1.1: Knowledge matrix: four disciplines of predictive modelling

Task matrix for predictive modelling

The tasks involved in predictive modelling follows the Pareto principle. Around 80% of the effort in the modelling process goes towards data cleaning and wrangling, while only 20% of the time and effort goes into implementing the model and getting the prediction. However, the meaty part of the modelling that is rich with almost 80% of results and insights is undoubtedly the implementation of the model. This information can be better represented as a matrix, which can be called a task matrix that will look something similar to the following figure:

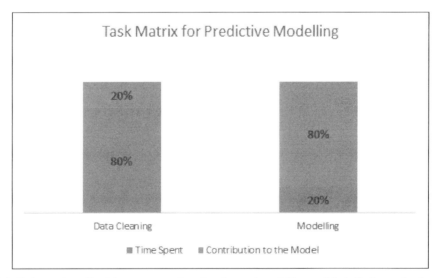

Fig. 1.2: Task matrix: split of time spent on data cleaning and modelling and their final contribution to the model

Many of the data cleaning and exploration chores can be automated because they are alike most of the times, irrespective of the data. The part that needs a lot of human thinking is the implementation of a model, which is what makes the bulk of this book.

Applications and examples of predictive modelling

In the introductory section, data has been compared with oil. While oil has been the primary source of energy for the last couple of centuries and the legends of OPEC, Petrodollars, and Gulf Wars have set the context for the oil as a begrudged resource; the might of data needs to be demonstrated here to set the premise for the comparison. Let us glance through some examples of predictive analytics to marvel at the might of data.

LinkedIn's "People also viewed" feature

If you are a frequent LinkedIn user, you might be familiar with LinkedIn's "People also viewed" feature.

What it does?

Let's say you have searched for some person who works at a particular organization and LinkedIn throws up a list of search results. You click on one of them and you land up on their profile. In the middle-right section of the screen, you will find a panel titled "People Also Viewed"; it is essentially a list of people who either work at the same organization as the person whose profile you are currently viewing or the people who have the same designation and belong to same industry.

Isn't it cool? You might have searched for these people separately if not for this feature. This feature increases the efficacy of your search results and saves your time.

How is it done?

Are you wondering how LinkedIn does it? The rough blueprint is as follows:

- LinkedIn leverages the search history data to do this. The model underneath this feature plunges into a treasure trove of search history data and looks at what people have searched next after finding the correct person they were searching for.

- This event of searching for a particular second person after searching for a particular first person has some probability. This will be calculated using all the data for such searches. The profiles with the highest probability of being searched (based on the historical data) are shown in the "People Also Viewed" section.

- This probability comes under the ambit of a broad set of rules called **Association Rules**. These are very widely used in Retail Analytics where we are interested to know what a group of products will sell together. In other words, what is the probability of buying a particular second product given that the consumer has already bought the first product?

Correct targeting of online ads

If you browse the Internet, which I am sure you must be doing frequently, you must have encountered online ads, both on the websites and smartphone apps. Just like the ads in the newspaper or TV, there is a publisher and an advertiser for online ads too. The publisher in this case is the website or the app where the ad will be shown while the advertiser is the company/organization that is posting that ad.

The ultimate goal of an online ad is to be clicked on. Each instance of an ad display is called an impression. The number of clicks per impression is called **Click Through Rate** and is the single most important metric that the advertisers are interested in. The problem statement is to determine the list of publishers where the advertiser should publish its ads so that the Click Through Rate is the maximum.

How is it done?

- The historical data in this case will consist of information about people who visited a certain website/app and whether they clicked the published ad or not. Some or a combination of classification models, such as Decision Trees, and Support Vector Machines are used in such cases to determine whether a visitor will click on the ad or not, given the visitor's profile information.

- One problem with standard classification algorithms in such cases is that the Click Through Rates are very small numbers, of the order of less than 1%. The resulting dataset that is used for classification has a very sparse positive outcome. The data needs to be downsampled to enrich the data with positive outcomes before modelling.

The logistical regression is one of the most standard classifiers for situations with binary outcomes. In banking, whether a person will default on his loan or not can be predicted using logistical regression given his credit history.

Santa Cruz predictive policing

Based on the historical data consisting of the area and time window of the occurrence of a crime, a model was developed to predict the place and time where the next crime might take place.

How is it done?

- A decision tree model was created using the historical data. The prediction of the model will foretell whether a crime will occur in an area on a given date and time in the future.

- The model is consistently recalibrated every day to include the crimes that happened during that day.

The good news is that the police are using such techniques to predict the crime scenes in advance so that they can prevent it from happening. The bad news is that certain terrorist organizations are using such techniques to target the locations that will cause the maximum damage with minimal efforts from their side. The good news again is that this strategic behavior of terrorists has been studied in detail and is being used to form counter-terrorist policies.

Determining the activity of a smartphone user using accelerometer data

The accelerometer in a smartphone measures the acceleration over a period of time as the user indulges in various activities. The acceleration is measured over the three axes, X, Y, and Z. This acceleration data can then be used to determine whether the user is sleeping, walking, running, jogging, and so on.

How is it done?

- The acceleration data is clustered based on the acceleration values in the three directions. The values of the similar activities cluster together.

- The clustering performs well in such cases if the columns contributing the maximum to the separation of activities are also included while calculating the distance matrix for clustering. Such columns can be found out using a technique called Singular Value Decomposition.

Sport and fantasy leagues

Moneyball, anyone? Yes, the movie. The movie where a statistician turns the fortunes of a poorly performing baseball team, Oak A, by developing an algorithm to select players who were cheap to buy but had a lot of latent potential to perform.

How was it done?

- Bill James, using historical data, concluded that the older metrics used to rate a player, such as stolen balls, runs batted in, and batting average were not very useful indicators of a player's performance in a given match. He rather relied on metrics like on-base percentage and sluggish percentage to be a better predictor of a player's performance.

- The chief statistician behind the algorithms, Bill James, compiled the data for performance of all the baseball league players and sorted them for these metrics. Surprisingly, the players who had high values for these statistics also came at cheaper prices.

This way, they gathered an unbeatable team that didn't have individual stars who came at hefty prices but as a team were an indomitable force. Since then, these algorithms and their variations have been used in a variety of real and fantasy leagues to select players. The variants of these algorithms are also being used by Venture Capitalists to optimize and automate their due diligence to select the prospective start-ups to fund.

Python and its packages – download and installation

There are various ways in which one can access and install Python and its packages. Here we will discuss a couple of them.

Anaconda

Anaconda is a popular Python distribution consisting of more than 195 popular Python packages. Installing Anaconda automatically installs many of the packages discussed in the preceding section, but they can be accessed only through an IDE called Spyder (more on this later in this chapter), which itself is installed on Anaconda installation. Anaconda also installs IPython Notebook and when you click on the IPython Notebook icon, it opens a browser tab and a Command Prompt.

Anaconda can be downloaded and installed from the following web address: http://continuum.io/downloads

Download the suitable installer and double click on the .exe file and it will install Anaconda. Two of the features that you must check after the installation are:

- IPython Notebook
- Spyder IDE

Search for them in the "Start" icon's search, if it doesn't appear in the list of programs and files by default. We will be using IPython Notebook extensively and the codes in this book will work the best when run in IPython Notebook.

IPython Notebook can be opened by clicking on the icon. Alternatively, you can use the Command Prompt to open IPython Notebook. Just navigate to the directory where you have installed Anaconda and then write ipython notebook, as shown in the following screenshot:

```
C:\Windows\system32\cmd.exe

Microsoft Windows [Version 6.1.7601]
Copyright (c) 2009 Microsoft Corporation.   All rights reserved.

C:\Users\ashish>ipython notebook
```

Fig. 1.3: Opening IPython Notebook

On the system used for this book, Anaconda was installed in the C:\Users\ashish directory. One can open a new Notebook in IPython by clicking on the New Notebook button on the dashboard, which opens up. In this book, we have used IPython Notebook extensively.

Standalone Python

You can download a Python version that is stable and is compatible to the OS on your system. The most stable version of Python is 2.7.0. So, installing this version is highly recommended. You can download it from https://www.python.org/ and install it.

There are some Python packages that you need to install on your machine before you start predictive analytics and modelling. This section consists of a demo of installation of one such library and a brief description of all such libraries.

Installing a Python package

There are several ways to install a Python package. The easiest and the most effective is the one using `pip`. As you might be aware, `pip` is a package management system that is used to install and manage software packages written in Python. To be able to use it to install other packages, `pip` needs to be installed first.

Installing pip

The following steps demonstrate how to install `pip`. Follow closely!

1. Navigate to the webpage shown in the following screenshot. The URL address is `https://pypi.python.org/pypi/pip`:

Downloading pip from the Python's official website

2. Download the `pip-7.0.3.tar.gz` file and unzip in the folder where Python is installed. If you have Python v2.7.0 installed, this folder should be `C:\Python27`:

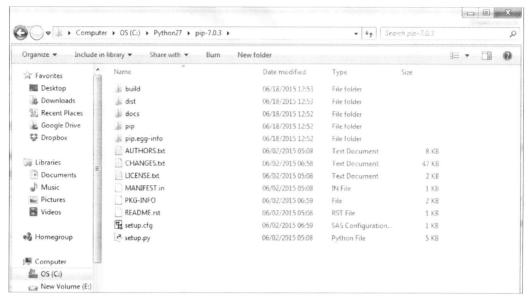

Unzipping the .zar file for pip in the correct folder

3. On unzipping the previously mentioned file, a folder called `pip-7.0.3` is created. Opening that folder will take you to the screen similar to the one in the preceding screenshot.

4. Open the CMD on your computer and change the current directory to the current directory in the preceding screenshot that is `C:\Python27\pip-7.0.3` using the following command:

   `cd C:\Python27\pip-7.0.3.`

5. The result of the preceding command is shown in the following screenshot:

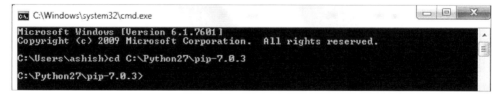

Navigating to the directory where pip is installed

6. Now, the current directory is set to the directory where setup file for `pip` (`setup.py`) resides. Write the following command to install `pip`:

   `python setup.py install`

7. The result of the preceding command is shown in the following screenshot:

Installing pip using a command line

Once `pip` is installed, it is very easy to install all the required Python packages to get started.

Installing Python packages with pip

The following are the steps to install Python packages using `pip`, which we just installed in the preceding section:

1. Change the current directory in the command prompt to the directory where the Python v2.7.0 is installed that is: `C:\Python27`.

2. Write the following command to install the package:

    ```
    pip install package-name
    ```

3. For example, to install pandas, you can proceed as follows:

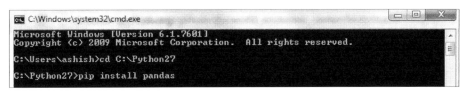

Installing a Python package using a command line and pip

4. Finally, to confirm that the package has installed successfully, write the following command:

    ```
    python  -c "import pandas"
    ```

5. The result of the preceding command is shown in the following screenshot:

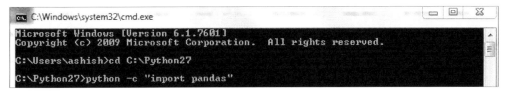

Checking whether the package has installed correctly or not

If this doesn't throw up an error, then the package has been installed successfully.

Python and its packages for predictive modelling

In this section, we will discuss some commonly used packages for predictive modelling.

pandas: The most important and versatile package that is used widely in data science domains is pandas and it is no wonder that you can see import pandas at the beginning of any data science code snippet, in this book, and anywhere in general. Among other things, the pandas package facilitates:

- The reading of a dataset in a usable format (data frame in case of Python)
- Calculating basic statistics
- Running basic operations like sub-setting a dataset, merging/concatenating two datasets, handling missing data, and so on

The various methods in pandas will be explained in this book as and when we use them.

> To get an overview, navigate to the official page of *pandas* here: http://pandas.pydata.org/index.html

NumPy: NumPy, in many ways, is a MATLAB equivalent in the Python environment. It has powerful methods to do mathematical calculations and simulations. The following are some of its features:

- A powerful and widely used a N-d array element
- An ensemble of powerful mathematical functions used in linear algebra, Fourier transforms, and random number generation
- A combination of random number generators and an N-d array elements is used to generate dummy datasets to demonstrate various procedures, a practice we will follow extensively, in this book

> To get an overview, navigate to official page of NumPy at http://www.NumPy.org/

matplotlib: matplotlib is a Python library that easily generates high-quality 2-D plots. Again, it is very similar to MATLAB.

- It can be used to plot all kind of common plots, such as histograms, stacked and unstacked bar charts, scatterplots, heat diagrams, box plots, power spectra, error charts, and so on
- It can be used to edit and manipulate all the plot properties such as title, axes properties, color, scale, and so on

 To get an overview, navigate to the official page of *matplotlib* at: `http://matplotlib.org`

IPython: IPython provides an environment for interactive computing.

It provides a browser-based notebook that is an IDE-cum-development environment to support codes, rich media, inline plots, and model summary. These notebooks and their content can be saved and used later to demonstrate the result as it is or to save the codes separately and execute them. It has emerged as a powerful tool for web based tutorials as the code and the results flow smoothly one after the other in this environment. At many places in this book, we will be using this environment.

 To get an overview, navigate to the official page of *IPython* here `http://ipython.org/`

Scikit-learn: `scikit-learn` is the mainstay of any predictive modelling in Python. It is a robust collection of all the data science algorithms and methods to implement them. Some of the features of `scikit-learn` are as follows:

- It is built entirely on Python packages like `pandas`, `NumPy`, and `matplotlib`
- It is very simple and efficient to use
- It has methods to implement most of the predictive modelling techniques, such as linear regression, logistic regression, clustering, and Decision Trees
- It gives a very concise method to predict the outcome based on the model and measure the accuracy of the outcomes

 To get an overview, navigate to the official page of `scikit-learn` here: `http://scikit-learn.org/stable/index.html`

Python packages, other than these, if used in this book, will be situation based and can be installed using the method described earlier in this section.

IDEs for Python

The IDE or the Integrated Development Environment is a software that provides the source-code editor cum debugger for the purpose of writing code. Using these software, one can write, test, and debug a code snippet before adding the snippet in the production version of the code.

IDLE: IDLE is the default Integrated Development Environment for Python that comes with the default implementation of Python. It comes with the following features:

- Multi-window text-editor with auto-completion, smart-indent, syntax, and keyword highlighting
- Python shell with syntax highlighting

IDLE is widely popular as an IDE for beginners; it is simple to use and works well for simple tasks. Some of the issues with IDLE are bad output reporting, absence of line numbering options, and so on. As a result, advanced practitioners move on to better IDEs.

IPython Notebook: IPython Notebook is a powerful computational environment where code, execution, results, and media can co-exist in one single document. There are two components of this computing environment:

- **IPython Notebook**: Web applications containing code, executions, plots, and results are stored in different cells; they can be saved and edited as and when required
- **Notebook**: It is a plain text document meant to record and distribute the result of a computational analysis

The IPython documents are stored with an extension `.ipynb` in the directory where it is installed on the computer.

Some of the features of IPython Notebook are as follows:

- Inline figure rendering of the `matplotlib` plots that can be saved in multiple formats(JPEG, PNG).
- Standard Python syntax in the notebook can be saved as a Python script.
- The notebooks can be saved as HTML files and `.ipynb` files. These notebooks can be viewed in browsers and this has been developed as a popular tool for illustrated blogging in Python. A notebook in IPython looks as shown in the following screenshot:

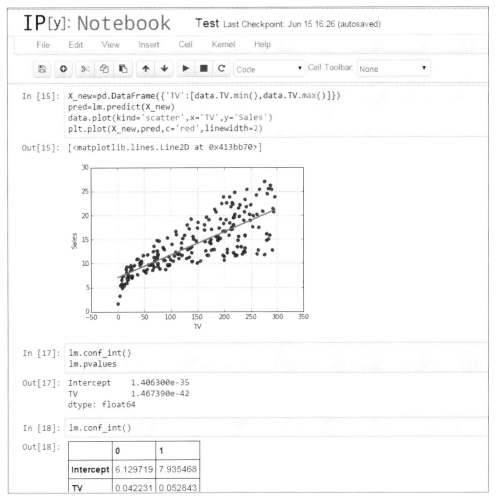

An Ipython Notebook

Spyder: Spyder is a powerful scientific computing and development environment for Python. It has the following features:

- Advanced editing, auto-completion, debugging, and interactive testing
- Python kernel and code editor with line numbering in the same screen
- Preinstalled scientific packages like NumPy, pandas, scikit-learn, matplotlib, and so on.

- In some ways, Spyder is very similar to RStudio environment where text editing and interactive testing go hand in hand:

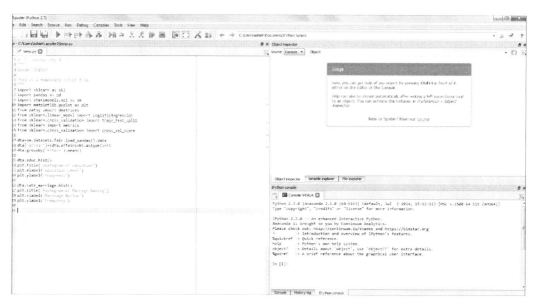

The interface of Spyder IDE

In this book, IPython Notebook and Spyder have been used extensively. IDLE has been used from time to time and some people use other environments, such as **Pycharm**. Readers of this book are free to use such editors if they are more comfortable with them. However, they should make sure that all the required packages are working fine in those environments.

Summary

The following are some of the takeaways from this chapter:

- Social media and Internet of Things have resulted in an avalanche of data.

- Data is powerful but not in its raw form. The data needs to be processed and modelled.

- Organizations across the world and across the domains are using data to solve critical business problems. The knowledge of statistical algorithms, statisticals tool, business context, and handling of historical data is vital to solve these problems using predictive modelling.

- Python is a robust tool to handle, process, and model data. It has an array of packages for predictive modelling and a suite of IDEs to choose from.

Let us enter the battlefield where Python is our weapon. We will start using it from the next chapter. In the next chapter, we will learn how to read data in various cases and do a basic processing.

2
Data Cleaning

Without any further ado, lets kick-start the engine and start our foray into the world of predictive analytics. However, you need to remember that our fuel is data. In order to do any predictive analysis, one needs to access and import data for the engine to rev up.

I assume that you have already installed Python and the required packages with an IDE of your choice. Predictive analytics, like any other art, is best learnt when tried hands-on and practiced as frequently as possible. The book will be of the best use if you open a Python IDE of your choice and practice the explained concepts on your own. So, if you haven't installed Python and its packages yet, now is the time. If not all the packages, at-least `pandas` should be installed, which are the mainstay of the things that we will learn in this chapter.

After reading this chapter, you should be familiar with the following topics:

- Handling various kind of data importing scenarios that is importing various kind of datasets (`.csv`, `.txt`), different kind of delimiters (`comma`, `tab`, `pipe`), and different methods (`read_csv`, `read_table`)
- Getting basic information, such as dimensions, column names, and statistics summary
- Getting basic data cleaning done that is removing NAs and blank spaces, imputing values to missing data points, changing a variable type, and so on
- Creating dummy variables in various scenarios to aid modelling
- Generating simple plots like scatter plots, bar charts, histograms, box plots, and so on

From now on, we will be using a lot of publicly available datasets to illustrate concepts and examples. All the used datasets have been stored in a Google Drive folder, which can be accessed from this link: `https://goo.gl/zjS4C6`.

This folder is called "Datasets for Predictive Modelling with Python". This folder has a subfolder dedicated to each chapter of the book. Each subfolder contains the datasets that were used in the chapter.

The paths for the dataset used in this book are paths on my local computer. You can download the datasets from these subfolders to your local computer before using them. Better still, you can download the entire folder, at once and save it somewhere on your local computer.

Reading the data – variations and examples

Before we delve deeper into the realm of data, let us familiarize ourselves with a few terms that will appear frequently from now on.

Data frames

A **data frame** is one of the most common data structures available in Python. Data frames are very similar to the tables in a spreadsheet or a SQL table. In Python vocabulary, it can also be thought of as a dictionary of series objects (in terms of structure). A data frame, like a spreadsheet, has index labels (analogous to rows) and column labels (analogous to columns). It is the most commonly used pandas object and is a 2D structure with columns of different or same types. Most of the standard operations, such as aggregation, filtering, pivoting, and so on which can be applied on a spreadsheet or the SQL table can be applied to data frames using methods in `pandas`.

The following screenshot is an illustrative picture of a data frame. We will learn more about working with them as we progress in the chapter:

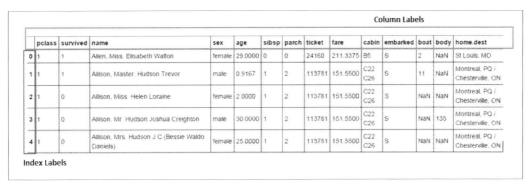

Fig. 2.1 A data frame

Delimiters

A **delimiter** is a special character that separates various columns of a dataset from one another. The most common (one can go to the extent of saying that it is a default delimiter) delimiter is a comma (,). A `.csv` file is called so because it has comma separated values. However, a dataset can have any special character as its delimiter and one needs to know how to juggle and manage them in order to do an exhaustive and exploratory analysis and build a robust predictive model. Later in this chapter, we will learn how to do that.

Various methods of importing data in Python

`pandas` is the Python library/package of choice to import, wrangle, and manipulate datasets. The datasets come in various forms; the most frequent being in the `.csv` format. The delimiter (a special character that separates the values in a dataset) in a CSV file is a comma. Now we will look at the various methods in which you can read a dataset in Python.

Case 1 – reading a dataset using the read_csv method

Open an IPython Notebook by typing `ipython notebook` in the command line.

Download the Titanic dataset from the shared Google Drive folder (any of `.xls` or `.xlsx` would do). Save this file in a CSV format and we are good to go. This is a very popular dataset that contains information about the passengers travelling on the famous ship Titanic on the fateful sail that saw it sinking. If you wish to know more about this dataset, you can go to the Google Drive folder and look for it.

A common practice is to share a variable description file with the dataset describing the context and significance of each variable. Since this is the first dataset we are encountering in this book, here is the data description of this dataset to get a feel of how data description files actually look like:

```
VARIABLE DESCRIPTIONS:
pclass              Passenger Class
                    (1 = 1st; 2 = 2nd; 3 = 3rd)
survival            Survival
                    (0 = No; 1 = Yes)
name                Name
sex                 Sex
age                 Age
sibsp               Number of Siblings/Spouses Aboard
parch               Number of Parents/Children Aboard
ticket              Ticket Number
fare                Passenger Fare
cabin               Cabin
embarked            Port of Embarkation
                    (C = Cherbourg; Q = Queenstown; S =
Southampton)
boat                Lifeboat
body                Body Identification Number
home.dest           Home/Destination
```

The following code snippet is enough to import the dataset and get you started:

```
import pandas as pd
data = pd.read_csv('E:/Personal/Learning/Datasets/Book/titanic3.csv')
```

The read_csv method

The name of the method doesn't unveil its full might. It is a kind of misnomer in the sense that it makes us think that it can be used to read only CSV files, which is not the case. Various kinds of files, including `.txt` files having delimiters of various kinds can be read using this method.

Let's learn a little bit more about the various arguments of this method in order to assess its true potential. Although the `read_csv` method has close to 30 arguments, the ones listed in the next section are the ones that are most commonly used.

The general form of a `read_csv` statement is something similar to:

```
pd.read_csv(filepath, sep=', ', dtype=None, header=None,
skiprows=None, index_col=None, skip_blank_lines=TRUE, na_filter=TRUE)
```

Now, let us understand the significance and usage of each of these arguments one by one:

- `filepath`: `filepath` is the complete address of the dataset or file that you are trying to read. The complete address includes the address of the directory in which the file is stored and the full name of the file with its extension. Remember to use a forward slash (/) in the directory address. Later in this chapter, we will see that the filepath can be a URL as well.

- `sep`: `sep` allows us to specify the delimiter for the dataset to read. By default, the method assumes that the delimiter is a comma (,). The various other delimiters that are commonly used are blank spaces ( ), tab (|), and are called space delimiter or tab demilited datasets. This argument of the method also takes regular expressions as a value.

- `dtype`: Sometimes certain columns of the dataset need to be formatted to some other type, in order to apply certain operations successfully. One example is the date variables. Very often, they have a string type which needs to be converted to date type before we can use them to apply date-related operations. The `dtype` argument is to specify the data type of the columns of the dataset. Suppose, two columns a and b, of the dataset need to be formatted to the types `int32` and `float64`; it can be achieved by passing `{'a':np.float64, 'b'.np.int32}` as the value of `dtype`. If not specified, it will leave the columns in the same format as originally found.

- `header`: The value of a `header` argument can be an `integer` or a `list`. Most of the times, datasets have a header containing the column names. The header argument is used to specify which row to be used as the header. By default, the first row is the header and it can be represented as `header =0`. If one doesn't specify the header argument, it is as good as specifying `header=0`. If one specifies `header=None`, the method will read the data without the header containing the column names.

- `names`: The column names of a dataset can be passed off as a list using this argument. This argument will take `lists` or `arrays` as its values. This argument is very helpful in cases where there are many columns and the column names are available as a list separately. We can pass the list of column names as a value of this argument and the column names in the list will be applied.

- `skiprows`: The value of a `skiprows` argument can be an `integer` or a `list`. Using this argument, one can skip a certain number of rows specified as the value of this argument in the read data, for example `skiprows=10` will read in the data from the 11th row and the rows before that will be ignored.

- `index_col`: The value of an `index_col` argument can be an `integer` or a `sequence`. By default, no row labels will be applied. This argument allows one to use a column, as the row labels for the rows in a dataset.

- `skip_blank_lines`: The value of a `skip_blank_lines` argument takes Boolean values only. If its value is specified as `True`, the blank lines are skipped rather than interpreting them as NaN (not allowed/missing values; we shall discuss them in detail soon) values. By default, its value is set to `False`.

- `na_filter`: The value of a `na-filter` argument takes Boolean values only. It detects the markers for missing values (empty strings and NA values) and removes them if set to `False`. It can make a significant difference while importing large datasets.

Use cases of the read_csv method

The `read_csv` method can be put to a variety of uses. Let us look at some such use cases.

Passing the directory address and filename as variables

Sometimes it is easier and viable to pass the directory address and filename as variables to avoid hard-coding. More importantly so, when one doesn't want to hardcode the full address of the file and intend to use this full address many times. Let us see how we can do so while importing a dataset.

```
import pandas as pd
path = 'E:/Personal/Learning/Datasets/Book'
filename = 'titanic3.csv'
fullpath = path+'/'+filename
data = pd.read_csv(fullpath)
```

For such cases, alternatively, one can use the following snippet that uses the `path.join` method in an `os` package:

```
import pandas as pd
import os
path = 'E:/Personal/Learning/Datasets/Book'
filename = 'titanic3.csv'
fullpath = os.path.join(path,filename)
data = pd.read_csv(fullpath)
```

One advantage of using the latter method is that it trims the lagging or leading white spaces, if any, and gives the correct filename.

Reading a .txt dataset with a comma delimiter

Download the `Customer Churn Model.txt` dataset from the Google Drive folder and save it on your local drive. To read this dataset, the following code snippet will do:

```
import pandas as pd
data = read_csv('E:/Personal/Learning/Datasets/Book/Customer Churn
Model.txt')
```

As you can see, although it's a text file, it can be read easily using the `read_csv` method without even specifying any other argument of the method.

Specifying the column names of a dataset from a list

We just read the `Customer Churn Model.txt` file in the last segment with the default column names. But, what if we want to rename some or all of the column names? Or, what if the column names are not there already and we want to assign names to columns from a list (let's say, available in a CSV file).

Look for a CSV file called `Customer Churn Columns.csv` in the Google Drive and download it. I have put English alphabets as placeholders for the column names in this file. We shall use this file to create a list of column names to be passed on to the dataset. You can change the names in the CSV files, if you like, and see how they are incorporated as column names.

The following code snippet will give the name of the column names of the dataset we just read:

```
import pandas as pd
data = pd.read_csv('E:/Personal/Learning/Datasets/Book/Customer Churn
Model.txt')
data.columns.values
```

If you run it on one of the IDEs, you should get the following screenshot as
the output:

```
array(['State', 'Account Length', 'Area Code', 'Phone', "Int'l Plan",
        'VMail Plan', 'VMail Message', 'Day Mins', 'Day Calls',
        'Day Charge', 'Eve Mins', 'Eve Calls', 'Eve Charge', 'Night Mins',
        'Night Calls', 'Night Charge', 'Intl Mins', 'Intl Calls',
        'Intl Charge', 'CustServ Calls', 'Churn?'], dtype=object)
```

Fig. 2.2: The column names in the Customer Churn Model.txt dataset

This basically lists all the column names of the dataset. Let us now go ahead and
change the column names to the names we have in the `Customer Churn Columns.csv` file.

```
data_columns = pd.read_csv('E:/Personal/Learning/Predictive Modeling
Book/Book Datasets/Customer Churn Columns.csv')
data_column_list = data_columns['Column_Names'].tolist()
data=pd.read_csv('E:/Personal/Learning/Predictive Modeling Book/Book
Datasets/Customer Churn Model.txt',header=None,names=data_column_list)
data.columns.values
```

The output after running this snippet should look like the following screenshot (if
you haven't made any changes to the values in the `Customer Churn Columns.csv`
file):

```
array(['A', 'B', 'C', 'D', 'E', 'F', 'G', 'H', 'I', 'J', 'K', 'L', 'M',
        'N', 'O', 'P', 'Q', 'R', 'S', 'T', 'U'], dtype=object)
```

Fig. 2.3: The column names in the Customer Churn Columnsl.txt dataset which have been passed
to the data frame data

The key steps in this process are:

- Sub-setting the particular column (containing the column names) and
  converting it to a list—done in the second line
- Passing the `header=None` and `names=name of the list` containing
  the `column names(data_column_list in this case)` in the
  `read_csv` method

If some of the terms, such as sub-setting don't make sense now, just remember that
it is an act of selecting a combination of particular rows or columns of the dataset.
We will discuss this in detail in the next chapter.

Case 2 – reading a dataset using the open method of Python

pandas is a very robust and comprehensive library to read, explore, and manipulate a dataset. But, it might not give an optimal performance with very big datasets as it reads the entire dataset, all at once, and blocks the majority of computer memory. Instead, you can try one of the Python's file handling methods—open. One can read the dataset line by line or in chunks by running a `for` loop over the rows and delete the chunks from the memory, once they have been processed. Let us look at some of the use case examples of the `open` method.

Reading a dataset line by line

As you might be aware that while reading a file using the `open` method, we can specify to use a particular mode that is read, write, and so on. By default, the method opens a file in the read-mode. This method can be useful while reading a big dataset, as this method reads data line-by-line (not at once, unlike what pandas does). You can read datasets into chunks using this method.

Let us now go ahead and open a file using the `open` method and count the number of rows and columns in the dataset:

```
data=open('E:/Personal/Learning/Predictive Modeling Book/Book
Datasets/Customer Churn Model.txt','r')
cols=data.next().strip().split(',')
no_cols=len(data.next().strip().split(','))
```

A couple of points about this snippet:

- `'r'` has been explicitly mentioned and hence the file will be opened in the read mode. To open it in the write mode, one needs to pass `'w'` in place of `'r'`.

- The `next` method navigates the computer memory to the line next to the header. The `strip` method is used to remove all the trailing and leading blank spaces from the line. The `split` method breaks down a line into chunks separated by the argument provided to the `split` method. In this case, it is `','`.

Finding the number of the rows is a bit tedious, but here lies the key trick to reading a huge file in chunks:

```
counter=0

main_dict={}
for col in cols:
    main_dict[col]=[]
```

Basically, we are doing the following two tasks in the preceding code snippet:

- Defining a `counter` variable that will increment its value by `1` on passing each line and hence will count the number of rows/lines at the end of the loop

- Defining a dictionary called `main_dict` with column names as the keys and the values in the columns as the values of the dictionary

Now, we are all set to run a `for` loop over the lines in the dataset to determine the number of rows in the dataset:

```
for line in data:
    values = line.strip().split(',')
    for i in range(len(cols)):
        main_dict[cols[i]].append(values[i])
    counter += 1

print "The dataset has %d rows and %d columns" % (counter,no_cols)
```

The explanation of the code-snippet is as follows:

1. Running a `for` loop over the lines in the dataset and splitting the lines in the values by `','`. These values are nothing but the values contained in each column for that line (row).

2. Running a second `for` loop over the columns for each line and appending the column values to the `main_dict` dictionary, which we defined in the previous step. So, for each key of the `main_dict` dictionary, all the column values are appended together. Each key of the `main_dict` becomes the column name of the dataset, while the values of each key in the dictionary are the values in each column.

3. Printing the number of rows and columns of the dataset that are contained in counter and `no_cols` respectively.

The `main_dict` dictionary, in a way, contains all the information in the dataset; hence, it can be converted to a data frame, as we have read already in this chapter that a `dictionary` can be converted to a data frame using the `DataFrame` method in pandas. Let us do that:

```
import pandas as pd
df=pd.DataFrame(main_dict)
print df.head(5)
```

This process can be repeated after a certain number of lines, say 10000 lines, for a large file; it can be read in and processed in chunks.

Changing the delimiter of a dataset

Earlier in this chapter, we said that juggling and managing delimiters is a great skill to master. Let us see one example of how we can change the delimiter of a dataset.

The `Customer Churn Model.txt` has comma (',') as a delimiter. It looks something similar to the following screenshot:

```
KS,128,415,382-4657,no,yes,25,265.100000,110,45.070000,197.400000,99,16.780000,244.700000,
OH,107,415,371-7191,no,yes,26,161.600000,123,27.470000,195.500000,103,16.620000,254.400000
NJ,137,415,358-1921,no,no,0,243.400000,114,41.380000,121.200000,110,10.300000,162.600000,1
OH,84,408,375-9999,yes,no,0,299.400000,71,50.900000,61.900000,88,5.260000,196.900000,89,8.
OK,75,415,330-6626,yes,no,0,166.700000,113,28.340000,148.300000,122,12.610000,186.900000,1
AL,118,510,391-8027,yes,no,0,223.400000,98,37.980000,220.600000,101,18.750000,203.900000,1
MA,121,510,355-9993,no,yes,24,218.200000,88,37.090000,348.500000,108,29.620000,212.600000,
MO,147,415,329-9001,yes,no,0,157.000000,79,26.690000,103.100000,94,8.760000,211.800000,96,
LA,117,408,335-4719,no,no,0,184.500000,97,31.370000,351.600000,80,29.890000,215.800000,90,
WV,141,415,330-8173,yes,yes,37,258.600000,84,43.960000,222.000000,111,18.870000,326.400000
```

Fig. 2.4: A chunk of Customer Churn Model.txt dataset with default delimiter comma (',')

Note that, any special character can be a delimiter. Let us change the delimiter to a 'slash t' ('/t'):

```
infile='E:/Personal/Learning/Datasets/Book/Customer Churn Model.txt'
outfile='E:/Personal/Learning/Datasets/Book/Tab Customer Churn Model.
txt'
with open(infile) as infile1:
  with open(outfile,'w') as outfile1:
    for line in infile1:
      fields=line.split(',')
      outfile1.write('/t'.join(fields))
```

This code snippet will generate a file called `Tab Customer Churn Model.txt` in the specified directory. The file will have a `'/t'` delimiter and will look something similar to the following screenshot:

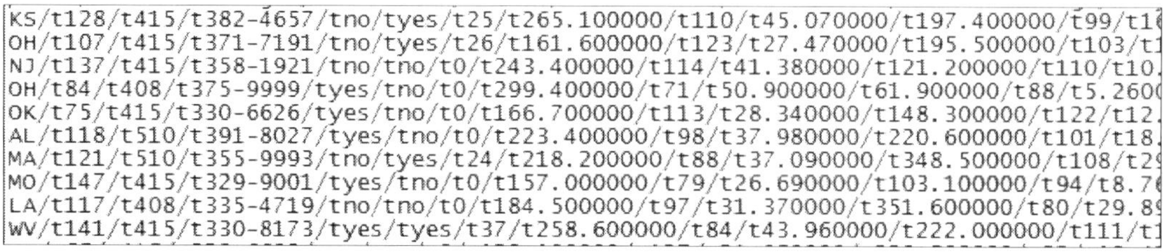

```
KS/t128/t415/t382-4657/tno/tyes/t25/t265.100000/t110/t45.070000/t197.400000/t99/t1(
OH/t107/t415/t371-7191/tno/tyes/t26/t161.600000/t123/t27.470000/t195.500000/t103/t1
NJ/t137/t415/t358-1921/tno/tno/t0/t243.400000/t114/t41.380000/t121.200000/t110/t10.
OH/t84/t408/t375-9999/tyes/tno/t0/t299.400000/t71/t50.900000/t61.900000/t88/t5.2600
OK/t75/t415/t330-6626/tyes/tno/t0/t166.700000/t113/t28.340000/t148.300000/t122/t12.
AL/t118/t510/t391-8027/tyes/tno/t0/t223.400000/t98/t37.980000/t220.600000/t101/t18.
MA/t121/t510/t355-9993/tno/tyes/t24/t218.200000/t88/t37.090000/t348.500000/t108/t29
MO/t147/t415/t329-9001/tyes/tno/t0/t157.000000/t79/t26.690000/t103.100000/t94/t8.76
LA/t117/t408/t335-4719/tno/tno/t0/t184.500000/t97/t31.370000/t351.600000/t80/t29.89
WV/t141/t415/t330-8173/tyes/tyes/t37/t258.600000/t84/t43.960000/t222.000000/t111/t1
```

Fig. 2.5: A chunk of Tab Customer Churn Model.txt with changed delimiter ('/t')

The code snippet can be explained as follows:

1. Creating two variables called `infile` and `outfile`. The `infile` variable is the one whose delimiter we wish to change and `outfile` is the one in which we will write the results after changing the delimiter.

2. The `infile` is opened in the read mode, while `outfile` is opened in the write mode.

3. The lines in the `infile` are split based on the existing delimiter that is `','` and the chunks are called fields. Each line will have several fields (equal to the number of columns).

4. The lines in the `outfile` are created by joining the fields of each line separated by the new delimiter of our choice that is `'/t'`.

5. The file is written into the directory specified in the definition of the `outfile`.

To demonstrate this, the `read_csv` method, as described earlier, can be used to read datasets that have a delimiter other than a comma, we will try to read the dataset with a `'/t'` delimiter, we just created:

```
import pandas as pd
data=pd.read_csv('E:/Personal/Learning/Predictive Modeling Book/Book
Datasets/Tab Customer Churn Model.txt',sep='/t')
```

Case 3 – reading data from a URL

Several times, we need to read the data directly from a web URL. This URL might contain the data written in it or might contain a file which has the data. For example, navigate to this website, `http://winterolympicsmedals.com/` which lists the medals won by various countries in different sports during the Winter Olympics. Now type the following address in the URL address bar: `http://winterolympicsmedals.com/medals.csv`.

A CSV file will be downloaded automatically. If you choose to download it manually, saving it and then specifying the directory path for the `read_csv` method is a time consuming process. Instead, Python allows us to read such files directly from the URL. Apart from the significant saving in time, it is also beneficial to loop over the files when there are many such files to be downloaded and read in.

A simple `read_csv` statement is required to read the data directly from the URL:

```
import pandas as pd
medal_data=pd.read_csv('http://winterolympicsmedals.com/medals.csv')
```

Alternatively, to work with URLs to get data, one can use a couple of Python packages, which we have not used till now, that is `csv` and `urllib`. The readers can go to the documentation of the packages to learn more about these packages. It is sufficient to know that `csv` provides a range of methods to handle the CSV files, while `urllib` is used to navigate and access information from the URL. Here is how it can be done:

```
import csv
import urllib2

url='http://archive.ics.uci.edu/ml/machine-learning-databases/iris/
iris.data'
response=urllib2.urlopen(url)
cr=csv.reader(response)

for rows in cr:
  print rows
```

The working of the preceding code snippet can be explained in the following two points:

1. The `urlopen` method of the `urllib2` library creates a response that can be read in using the `reader` method of the `csv` library.

2. This instance is an iterator and can be iterated over its rows.

The `csv` module is very helpful in dealing with CSV files. It can be used to read the dataset row by row, or in other words, iterate over the dataset among other things. It can be used to write to CSV files as well.

Case 4 – miscellaneous cases

Apart from the standard cases described previously, there are certain less frequent cases of data file handling that might need to be taken care of. Let's have a look at two of them.

Reading from an .xls or .xlsx file

Go to the Google Drive and look for `.xls` and `.xlsx` versions of the Titanic dataset. They will be named `titanic3.xls` and `titanic3.xlsx`. Download both of them and save them on your computer. The ability to read Excel files with all its sheets is a very powerful technique available in pandas. It is done using a `read_excel` method, as shown in the following code:

```
import pandas as pd
data=pd.read_excel('E:/Personal/Learning/Predictive Modeling Book/Book
Datasets/titanic3.xls','titanic3')

import pandas as pd
data=pd.read_excel('E:/Personal/Learning/Predictive Modeling Book/Book
Datasets/titanic3.xlsx','titanic3')
```

It works with both, `.xls` and `.xlsx` files. The second argument of the `read_excel` method is the sheet name that you want to read in.

Another available method to read a delimited data is `read_table`. The `read_table` is exactly similar to `read_csv` with certain default arguments for its definition. In some sense, `read_table` is a more generic form of `read_csv`.

Writing to a CSV or Excel file

A data frame can be written in a CSV or an Excel file using a `to_csv` or `to_excel` method in pandas. Let's go back to the `df` data frame that we created in *Case 2 – reading a dataset using the open method of Python*. This data frame can be exported to a directory in a CSV file, as shown in the following code:

```
df.to_csv('E:/Personal/Learning/Predictive Modeling Book/Book
Datasets/Customer Churn Model.csv'
```

Or to an Excel file, as follows:

```
df.to_excel('E:/Personal/Learning/Predictive Modeling Book/Book
Datasets/Customer Churn Model.csv'
```

Basics – summary, dimensions, and structure

After reading in the data, there are certain tasks that need to be performed to get the touch and feel of the data:

- To check whether the data has read in correctly or not
- To determine how the data looks; its shape and size

- To summarize and visualize the data
- To get the column names and summary statistics of numerical variables

Let us go back to the example of the Titanic dataset and import it again. The `head()` method is used to look at the first first few rows of the data, as shown:

```
import pandas as pd
data=pd.read_csv('E:/Personal/Learning/Datasets/Book/titanic3.csv')
data.head()
```

The result will look similar to the following screenshot:

	pclass	survived	name	sex	age	sibsp	parch	ticket	fare	cabin	embarked	boat	body	home.dest
0	1	1	Allen, Miss. Elisabeth Walton	female	29.0000	0	0	24160	211.3375	B5	S	2	NaN	St Louis, MO
1	1	1	Allison, Master. Hudson Trevor	male	0.9167	1	2	113781	151.5500	C22 C26	S	11	NaN	Montreal, PQ / Chesterville, ON
2	1	0	Allison, Miss. Helen Loraine	female	2.0000	1	2	113781	151.5500	C22 C26	S	NaN	NaN	Montreal, PQ / Chesterville, ON
3	1	0	Allison, Mr. Hudson Joshua Creighton	male	30.0000	1	2	113781	151.5500	C22 C26	S	NaN	135	Montreal, PQ / Chesterville, ON
4	1	0	Allison, Mrs. Hudson J C (Bessie Waldo Daniels)	female	25.0000	1	2	113781	151.5500	C22 C26	S	NaN	NaN	Montreal, PQ / Chesterville, ON

Fig. 2.6: Thumbnail view of the Titanic dataset obtained using the head() method

In the `head()` method, one can also specify the number of rows they want to see. For example, `head(10)` will show the first 10 rows.

The next attribute of the dataset that concerns us is its dimension, that is the number of rows and columns present in the dataset. This can be obtained by typing `data.shape`.

The result obtained is `(1310,14)`, indicating that the dataset has 1310 rows and 14 columns.

As discussed earlier, the column names of a data frame can be listed using `data.column.values`, which gives the following output as the result:

```
array(['pclass', 'survived', 'name', 'sex', 'age', 'sibsp', 'parch',
       'ticket', 'fare', 'cabin', 'embarked', 'boat', 'body', 'home.dest'], dtype=object)
```

Fig. 2.7: Column names of the the Titanic dataset

Another important thing to do while glancing at the data is to create summary statistics for the numerical variables. This can be done by:

```
data.describe()
```

We get the following result:

	pclass	survived	age	sibsp	parch	fare	body
count	1309.000000	1309.000000	1046.000000	1309.000000	1309.000000	1308.000000	121.000000
mean	2.294882	0.381971	29.881135	0.498854	0.385027	33.295479	160.809917
std	0.837836	0.486055	14.413500	1.041658	0.865560	51.758668	97.696922
min	1.000000	0.000000	0.166700	0.000000	0.000000	0.000000	1.000000
25%	2.000000	0.000000	21.000000	0.000000	0.000000	7.895800	72.000000
50%	3.000000	0.000000	28.000000	0.000000	0.000000	14.454200	155.000000
75%	3.000000	1.000000	39.000000	1.000000	0.000000	31.275000	256.000000
max	3.000000	1.000000	80.000000	8.000000	9.000000	512.329200	328.000000

Fig. 2.8: Summary statistics for the numerical variables in the Titanic dataset

Knowing the type each column belongs to is the key to determine their behavior under some numerical or manipulation operation. Hence, it is of critical importance to know the type of each column. This can be done as follows:

```
data.dtypes
```

We get the following result from the preceding code snippet:

```
pclass        float64
survived      float64
name           object
sex            object
age           float64
sibsp         float64
parch         float64
ticket         object
fare          float64
cabin          object
embarked       object
boat           object
body          float64
home.dest      object
dtype: object
```

Fig. 2.9: Variable types of the columns in the Titanic dataset

Handling missing values

Checking for missing values and handling them properly is an important step in the data preparation process, if they are left untreated they can:

- Lead to the behavior between the variables not being analyzed correctly
- Lead to incorrect interpretation and inference from the data

To see how; move up a few pages to see how the describe method is explained. Look at the output table; why are the counts for many of the variables different from each other? There are 1310 rows in the dataset, as we saw earlier in the section. Why is it then that the count is 1046 for age, 1309 for pclass, and 121 for body. This is because the dataset doesn't have a value for 264 (1310-1046) entries in the age column, 1 (1310-1309) entry in the pclass column, and 1189 (1310-121) entries in the body column. In other words, these many entries have missing values in their respective columns. If a column has a count value less than the number of rows in the dataset, it is most certainly because the column contains missing values.

Checking for missing values

There are a multitude of in-built methods to check for missing values. Let's go through some of them. Suppose you wish to find the entries that have missing values in a column of a data frame. It can be done as follows for the body column of the data data frame:

```
pd.isnull(data['body'])
```

This will give a series indicating True in the cells with missing values and False for non-missing values. Just the opposite can be done as follows:

```
pd.notnull(data['body'])
```

The result will look something similar to the following screenshot:

```
0     False
1     False
2     False
3      True
4     False
5     False
6     False
7     False
8     False
9      True
10     True
11    False
12    False
13    False
14    False
```

Fig. 2.10: The notnull method gives False for missing values and True for non-missing values

The number of entries with missing values can be counted for a particular column to verify whether our calculation earlier about the number of missing entries was correct or not. This can be done as follows:

```
pd.isnull(data['body']).values.ravel().sum()
```

The result we get is 1189. This is the same number of missing entries from the body column as we have calculated in the preceding paragraph. In the preceding one-liner, the values (`True/False`; `1/0` in binary) have been stripped off the series and have been converted into a row (using the `ravel` method) to be able to sum them up. The sum of `1/0` values (`1` for missing values and `0` for non-missing) gives the number of total missing values.

The opposite of `isnull` is `notnull`. This should give us `121` as the result:

```
pd.nottnull(data['body']).values.ravel().sum()
```

Before we dig deeper into how to handle missing data, let's see what constitutes the missing data and how missing values are generated and propagated.

What constitutes missing data?

`Nan` is the default keyword for a missing value in Python. `None` is also considered as a missing value by the `isnull` and `notnull` functions.

How missing values are generated and propagated

There are various ways in which a missing values are incorporated in the datatset:

- **Data extraction**: While extracting data from a database, the missing values can be incorporated in the dataset due to various incompatibilities between the database server and the extraction process. In this case, the value is actually not missing but is being shown as missing because of the various incompatibilities. This can be corrected by optimizing the extraction process.

- **Data collection**: It might be the case that at the time of collection, certain data points are not available or not applicable and hence can't be entered into the database. Such entries become missing values and can't be obtained by changing the data extraction process because they are actually missing. For example, in case of a survey in a village, many people might not want to share their annual income; this becomes a missing value. Some datasets might have missing values because of the way they are collected. A time series data will have data starting from the relevant time and before that time it will have missing values.

Any numerical operator on a missing value propagates the missing value to the resultant variable. For example, while summing the entries in two columns, if one of them has a missing value in one of the entries, the resultant sum variable will also have a missing value.

Treating missing values

There are basically two approaches to handle missing values: deletion and imputation. Deletion means deleting the entire row with one or more missing entries. Imputation means replacing the missing entries with some values based on the context of the data.

Deletion

One can either delete a complete row or column. One can specify when to delete an entire row or column (when any of the entries are missing in a row or all of the entries are missing in a row). For our dataset, we can write something, as shown:

```
data.dropna(axis=0,how='all')
```

The statement when executed will drop all the rows (`axis=0` means rows, `axis=1` means columns) in which all the columns have missing values (the `how` parameter is set to `all`). One can drop a row even if a single column has a missing value. One needs to specify the `how` method as `'any'` to do that:

```
data.dropna(axis=0,how='any')
```

Imputation

Imputation is the method of adding/replacing missing values with some other values such as `0`, a string, or mean of non-missing values of that variable. There are several ways to impute a missing value and the choice of the best method depends on the context of the data.

One method is to fill the missing values in the entire dataset with some number or character variable. Thus, it can be done as follows:

```
data.fillna(0)
```

This will replace the missing values anywhere in the dataset with the value `0`. One can impute a character variable as well:

```
data.fillna('missing')
```

The preceding statement will impute a `missing` string in place of NaN, None, blanks, and so on. Another way is to replace the missing values in a particular column only is as shown below.

If you select the `body` column of the data by typing `data['body']`, the result will be something similar to the following screenshot:

```
0      NaN
1      NaN
2      NaN
3      135
4      NaN
5      NaN
6      NaN
7      NaN
8      NaN
9       22
10     124
11     NaN
12     NaN
```

Fig. 2.11: The values in the body column of the Titanic dataset without imputation for missing values

One can impute zeros to the missing values using the following statement:

```
data['body'].fillna(0)
```

But after imputing `0` to the missing values, we get something similar to the following screenshot:

```
0       0
1       0
2       0
3      135
4       0
5       0
6       0
7       0
8       0
9       22
10     124
11      0
12      0
```

Fig. 2.12: The values in the body column of the Titanic dataset after imputing 0 for missing values

A common imputation is with the mean or median value of that column. This basically means that the missing values are assumed to have the same values as the mean value of that column (excluding missing values, of course), which makes perfect sense. Let us see how we can do that using the `fillna` method. Let us have a look at the `age` column of the dataset:

```
data['age']
```

```
1295    21.0
1296    27.0
1297    NaN
1298    36.0
1299    27.0
1300    15.0
1301    45.5
1302    NaN
1303    NaN
1304    14.5
1305    NaN
1306    26.5
1307    27.0
1308    29.0
1309    NaN
```

Fig. 2.13: The values in the age column of the Titanic dataset without imputation for missing values

As shown in the preceding screenshot, some of the entries in the age column have missing values. Let us see how we can impute them with mean values:

```
data['age'].fillna(data['age'].mean())
```

The output looks something similar to the following screenshot:

```
21.000000
27.000000
29.881135
36.000000
27.000000
15.000000
45.500000
29.881135
29.881135
14.500000
29.881135
26.500000
27.000000
29.000000
29.881135
```

Fig. 2.14: The values in the age column of the Titanic dataset after imputing mean for missing values

As you can see, all the NaN values have been replaced with 29.881135, which is the mean of the age column.

One can use any function in place of mean, the most commonly used functions are median or some defined calculation using lambda. Apart from that, there are two very important methods in fillna to impute the missing values: ffill and backfill. As the name suggests, ffill replaces the missing values with the nearest preceding non-missing value while the backfill replaces the missing value with the nearest succeeding non-missing value. It will be clearer with the following example:

```
data['age'].fillna(method='ffill')
```

```
1295    21.0
1296    27.0
1297    27.0
1298    36.0
1299    27.0
1300    15.0
1301    45.5
1302    45.5
1303    45.5
1304    14.5
1305    14.5
1306    26.5
1307    27.0
```

Fig. 2.15: The result of using ffill method of imputation on the age column of the Titanic dataset

As it can be seen, the missing value in row number 1297 is replaced with the value in row number 1296.

With the backfill statement, something similar happens:

```
data['age'].fillna(method='backfill')
```

```
1295    21.0
1296    27.0
1297    36.0
1298    36.0
1299    27.0
1300    15.0
1301    45.5
1302    14.5
1303    14.5
1304    14.5
1305    26.5
1306    26.5
```

Fig. 2.16: The result of using backfill method of imputation

As it can be seen, the missing value in row number `1297` is replaced with the value in row number `1298`.

Creating dummy variables

Creating dummy variables is a method to create separate variable for each category of a categorical variable., Although, the categorical variable contains plenty of information and might show a causal relationship with output variable, it can't be used in the predictive models like linear and logistic regression without any processing.

In our dataset, `sex` is a categorical variable with two categories that are male and female. We can create two dummy variables out of this, as follows:

```
dummy_sex=pd.get_dummies(data['sex'],prefix='sex')
```

The result of this statement is, as follows:

	sex_female	sex_male
0	1	0
1	0	1
2	1	0
3	0	1
4	1	0
5	0	1
6	1	0

Fig. 2.17: Dummy variable for the sex variable in the Titanic dataset

This process is called dummifying, the variable creates two new variables that take either `1` or `0` value depending on what the sex of the passenger was. If the sex was female, `sex_female` would be `1` and `sex_male` would be `0`. If the sex was male, `sex_male` would be `1` and `sex_female` would be `0`. In general, all but one dummy variable in a row will have a `0` value. The variable derived from the value (for that row) in the original column will have a value of `1`.

These two new variables can be joined to the source data frame, so that they can be used in the models. The method to that is illustrated, as follows:

```
column_name=data.columns.values.tolist()
column_name.remove('sex')
data[column_name].join(dummy_sex)
```

The column names are converted to a list and the sex is removed from the list before joining these two dummy variables to the dataset, as it will not make sense to have a sex variable with these two dummy variables.

Visualizing a dataset by basic plotting

Plots are a great way to visualize a dataset and gauge possible relationships between the columns of a dataset. There are various kinds of plots that can be drawn. For example, a scatter plot, histogram, box-plot, and so on.

Let's import the `Customer Churn Model` dataset and try some basic plots:

```
import pandas as pd
data=pd.read_csv('E:/Personal/Learning/Predictive Modeling Book/Book
Datasets/Customer Churn Model.txt')
```

While plotting any kind of plot, it helps to keep these things in mind:

- If you are using IPython Notebook, write `% matplotlib inline` in the input cell and run it before plotting to see the output plot inline (in the output cell).

- To save a plot in your local directory as a file, you can use the `savefig` method. Let's go back to the example where we plotted four scatter plots in a 2x2 panel. The name of this image is specified in the beginning of the snippet, as a `figure` parameter of the plot. To save this image one can write the following code:

```
figure.savefig('E:/Personal/Learning/Predictive Modeling Book/Book
Datasets/Scatter Plots.jpeg')
```

As you can see, while saving the file, one can specify the local directory to save the file and the name of the image and the format in which to save the image (`jpeg` in this case).

Scatter plots

We suspect the **Day Mins** and **Day Charge** to be highly correlated, as the calls are generally charged based on their duration. To confirm or validate our hypothesis, we can draw a scatter plot between Day Mins and Day Charge. To draw this scatter plot, we write something similar to the following code:

```
data.plot(kind='scatter',x='Day Mins',y='Day Charge')
```

The output looks similar to the following figure where the points lie on a straight line confirming our suspicion that they are (linearly) related. As we will see later in the chapter on linear regression, such a situation will give a perfect linear fit for the two variables:

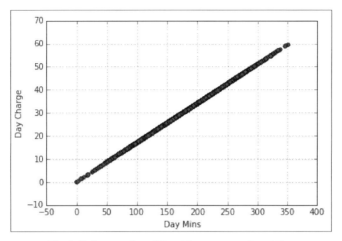

Fig. 2.18: Scatter plot of Day Charge versus Day Mins

The same is the case when we plot **Night Mins** and **Night Charge** against one another. However, when we plot Night Calls with Night Charge or Day Calls with Day Charge, we don't get to see much of a relationship.

Using the `matplotlib` library, we can get good quality plots and with a lot of flexibility. Let us see how we can plot multiple plots (in different panels) in the same image:

```
import matplotlib.pyplot as plt
figure,axs = plt.subplots(2, 2,sharey=True,sharex=True)
data.plot(kind='scatter',x='Day Mins',y='Day Charge',ax=axs[0][0])
data.plot(kind='scatter',x='Night Mins',y='Night Charge',ax=axs[0][1])
data.plot(kind='scatter',x='Day Calls',y='Day Charge',ax=axs[1][0])
data.plot(kind='scatter',x='Night Calls',y='Night Charge',ax=axs[1]
[1])
```

Here, we are plotting four graphs in one image in a 2x2 panel using the `subplots` method of the `matplotlib` library. As you can see in the preceding snippet, we have defined the panel to be 2x2 and set `sharex` and `sharey` parameters to be `True`. For each plot, we specify their location by passing appropriate values for the `ax` parameter in the `plot` method. The result looks similar to the following screenshot:

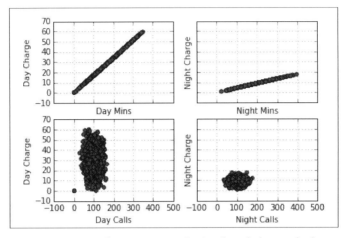

Fig. 2.19: Four plots in a 2x2 panel using the subplots method

Histograms

Plotting histograms is a great way to visualize the distribution of a numerical variable. Plotting a histogram is a method to understand the most frequent ranges (or bins as they are called) in which the variable lies. One can also check whether the variable is normally distributed or skewed on one side.

Let's plot a histogram for the `Day Calls` variable. We can do so by writing the following code:

```
import matplotlib.pyplot as plt
plt.hist(data['Day Calls'],bins=8)
plt.xlabel('Day Calls Value')
plt.ylabel('Frequency')
plt.title('Frequency of Day Calls')
```

The first line of the snippet is of prime importance. There we specify the variable for which we have to plot the histogram and the number of bins or ranges we want. The `bins` parameters can be passed as a fixed number or as a list of numbers to be passed as bin-edges. Suppose, a numerical variable has a minimum value of `1` and a maximum value of `1000`. While plotting histogram for this variable, one can either specify `bins=10` or `20`, or one can specify `bins=[0,100,200,300,...1000]` or `[0,50,100,150,200,.....,1000]`.

The output of the preceding code snippet appears similar to the following snapshot:

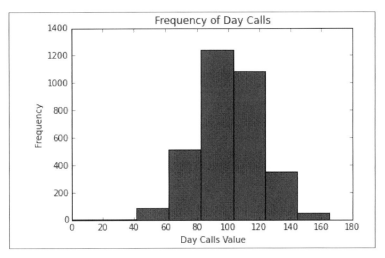

Fig. 2.20: Histogram of the Day Calls variable

Boxplots

Boxplots are another way to understand the distribution of a numerical variable. It specifies something called quartiles.

If the numbers in a distribution with 100 numbers are arranged in an increasing order; the 1st quartile will occupy the 25th position, the 3rd quartile will occupy the 75th position, and so on. The median will be the average of the 50th and 51st terms. (I hope you brush up on some of the statistics you have read till now because we are going to use a lot of it, but here is a small refresher). Median is the middle term when the numbers in the distribution are arranged in the increasing order. Mode is the one that occurs with the maximum frequency, while mean is the sum of all the numbers divided by their total count.

Plotting a boxplot in Python is easy. We need to write this to plot a boxplot for Day Calls:

```
import matplotlib.pyplot as plt
plt.boxplot(data['Day Calls'])
plt.ylabel('Day Calls')
plt.title('Box Plot of Day Calls')
```

The output looks similar to the following snapshot:

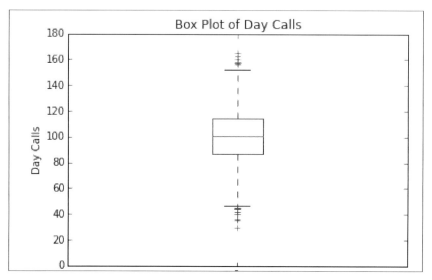

Fig. 2.21: Box Plot for the Day Calls variable

The blue box is of prime importance. The lower-horizontal edge of the box specifies the 1st quartile, while the upper-horizontal edge specifies the 3rd quartile. The horizontal line in the red specifies the median value. The difference in the 1st and 3rd quartile values is called the Inter Quartile Range or IQR. The lower and upper horizontal edges in black specify the minimum and maximum values respectively.

The boxplots are important plots because of the following reasons:

- Boxplots are potent tools to spot outliers in a distribution. Any value that is `1.5*IQR` below the 1st quartile and is `1.5*IQR` above the 1st quartile can be classified as an outlier.

- For a categorical variable, boxplots are a great way to visualize and compare the distribution of each category at one go.

There are a variety of other types of plots that can be drawn depending on the problem at hand. We will learn about them as and when needed. For exploratory analysis, these three types are enough to provide us enough evidence to further or discard our initial hypotheses. These three types can have multiple variations and together with the power of looping and panel-wise plotting, we can make the plotting; hence, the data exploration process is very efficient.

Summary

The main learning outcomes of this chapter are summarized as follows:

- Various methods and variations in importing a dataset using pandas: `read_csv` and its variations, reading a dataset using open method in Python, reading a file in chunks using the `open` method, reading directly from a URL, specifying the column names from a list, changing the delimiter of a dataset, and so on.

- Basic exploratory analysis of data: observing a thumbnail of data, shape, column names, column types, and summary statistics for numerical variables

- Handling missing values: The reason for incorporation of missing values, why it is important to treat them properly, how to treat them properly by deletion and imputation, and various methods of imputing data.

- Creating dummy variables: creating dummy variables for categorical variables to be used in the predictive models.

- Basic plotting: scatter plotting, histograms and boxplots; their meaning and relevance; and how they are plotted.

This chapter is a head start into our journey to explore our data and wrangle it to make it modelling-worthy. The next chapter will go deeper in this pursuit whereby we will learn to aggregate values for categorical variables, sub-set the dataset, merge two datasets, generate random numbers, and sample a dataset.

Cleaning, as we have seen in the last chapter takes about 80% of the modelling time, so it's of critical importance and the methods we are learning will come in handy in the pursuit of that goal.

3
Data Wrangling

I assume that by now you are at ease with importing datasets from various sources and exploring the look and feel of the data. Handling missing values, creating dummy variables and plots are some tasks that an analyst (predictive modeller) does with almost all the datasets to make them model-worthy. So, for an aspiring analyst it will be better to master these tasks, as well.

Next in the line of items to master in order to juggle data like a pro is data wrangling. Put simply, it is just a fancy word for the slicing and dicing of data. If you compare the entire predictive modelling process to a complex operation/surgery to be performed on a patient, then the preliminary analysis with a stethoscope and diagnostic checks on the patient is the data cleaning and exploration process, zeroing down on the ailing area and deciding which body part to operate on is data wrangling, and performing the surgery/operation is the modelling process.

Surgery/operation	Predictive modelling
Diagnostic checks/asking questions to fill missing pieces of information/discarding trivial information	Data exploration/Data cleaning
Zeroing down on specific body part/sourcing required pieces like blood, catheter	Data wrangling
Operating the area	Modelling the data

A surgeon can vouch for the fact that zeroing down on a specific body part is the most critical piece of the puzzle to crack down before one gets to the root of the ailment. The same is the case with data wrangling. The data is not always at one place or in one table, maybe the information you need for your model is scattered across different datasets. What does one do in such cases? One doesn't always need the entire data. Many a times, one needs only a column or a few rows or a combination of a few rows and columns. How to do all this jugglery? This is the crux of this chapter. Apart from this, the chapter tries to provide the reader with all the props needed in their tryst with predictive modelling.

At the end of the chapter, the reader should be comfortable with the following functions:

- **Sub-set a dataset**: Slicing and dicing data, selecting few rows and columns based on certain conditions that is similar to filtering in Excel

- **Generating random numbers**: Generating random numbers is an important tool while performing simulations and creating dummy data frames

- **Aggregating data**: A technique that helps to group the data by categories in the categorical variable

- **Sampling data**: This is very important before venturing into the actual modelling; dividing a dataset between training and testing data is essential

- **Merging/appending/concatenating datasets**: This is the solution of the problem that arises when the data required for the purpose of modelling is scattered over different datasets

We will be using a variety of public datasets in this chapter. Another good way of demonstrating these concepts is to use dummy datasets created using random numbers. In fact, random numbers are used heavily for this purpose. We will be using a mix of both public datasets and dummy datasets, created using random numbers.

Let us now kick-start the chapter by learning about subsetting a dataset. As it unfolds, one will realize how ubiquitous and indispensable this is.

Subsetting a dataset

As discussed in the introductory section, the task of subsetting a dataset can entail a lot of things. Let us look at them one by one. In order to demonstrate it, let us first import the Customer Churn Model dataset, which we used in the last chapter:

```
import pandas as pd
data=pd.read_csv('E:/Personal/Learning/Predictive Modeling Book/Book
Datasets/Customer Churn Model.txt')
```

Selecting columns

Very frequently, an analyst might come across situations wherein only a handful of columns among a vast number of columns are useful and are required in the model. It then becomes important, to select particular columns. Let us see how to do that.

If one wishes to select the `Account Length` variable of the data frame we just imported, one can simply write:

```
account_length=data['Account Length']
account_length.head()
```

The square bracket (`[ ]`) syntax is used to subset a column of a data frame. One just needs to type the appropriate column name in the square brackets. Selecting one column returns a `Series` object (an object similar to a data frame) consisting of the values of the selected column. The output of the preceding snippet is as follows:

```
0       128
1       107
2       137
3        84
4        75
Name: Account Length, dtype: int64
```

Fig. 3.1: First few entries of the Account Length column

The fact that this process returns a series can be confirmed by typing `type(account_length)`, this will return something similar to the following output, as a result:

```
pandas.core.series.Series
```

Selecting multiple columns can be accomplished in a similar fashion. One just needs to add an extra square bracket to indicate that it is a list of column names that they are selecting and not just one column.

If one wants to select `Account Length`, `VMail Message`, and `Day Calls`, one can write the code, as follows:

```
Subdata = data[['Account Length','VMail Message','Day Calls']]
subdata.head()
```

The output of the preceding snippet should be similar to the following screenshot:

	Account Length	VMail Message	Day Calls
0	128	25	110
1	107	26	123
2	137	0	114
3	84	0	71
4	75	0	113

Fig. 3.2: First few entries of the Account Length and VMail Message columns

Unlike in the case of selecting a single column, selecting multiple columns throws up a data frame, as the result:

```
type(subdata)
```

```
pandas.core.frame.DataFrame
```

One can also create a list of required columns and pass the list name as the parameter inside the square bracket to subset a data frame. The following code snippet will give the same result, as shown in *Fig. 3.3*, in the next section:

```
wanted_columns=['Account Length','VMail Message','Day Calls']
subdata=data[wanted]
subdata.head()
```

In some cases, one might want to delete or remove certain columns from the dataset before they proceed to modelling. The same approach, as taken in the preceding section, can be taken in such cases.

This approach of subsetting columns from data frames works fine when the list of columns is relatively small (3-5 columns). After this, the time consumed in typing column names warrants some more efficient methods to do this. The trick is to manually create a list to complement (a list not containing the elements that are present in the other set) the bigger list and create the bigger list using looping. The complement list of a big table will always be small; hence, we need to make the method a tad bit efficient.

Let us have a look at the following code snippet to observe how to implement this:

```
wanted=['Account Length','VMail Message','Day Calls']
column_list=data.columns.values.tolist()
sublist=[x for x in column_list if x not in wanted]
subdata=data[sublist]
subdata.head()
```

The `sublist` as expected contains all the column names except the ones listed in the `wanted` list, as shown in the following screenshot:

```
array(['State', 'Area Code', 'Phone', "Int'l Plan", 'VMail Plan',
       'Day Mins', 'Day Charge', 'Eve Mins', 'Eve Calls', 'Eve Charge',
       'Night Mins', 'Night Calls', 'Night Charge', 'Intl Mins',
       'Intl Calls', 'Intl Charge', 'CustServ Calls', 'Churn?'], dtype=object)
```

Fig. 3.3: Column names of the subdata data frame

In the third line of the preceding code snippet, a list comprehension has been used. It is a convenient method to run for loops over lists and get lists as output. Many of you, who have experience with Python, will know of this. For others, it is not rocket science; just a better way to run `for` loops.

Selecting rows

Selecting rows is similar to selecting columns, in the sense that the same square bracket is used, but instead of column names the row number or indices are used. Let us see some examples to know how to select a particular number of rows from a data frame:

- If one wants to select the first 50 rows of the data frame, one can just write:

  `data[1:50]`

- It is important to note that one needs to pass a range of numbers to subset a data frame over rows. To select 50 rows starting from 25th column, we will write:

  `data[25:75]`

- If the lower limit is not mentioned, it denotes that the upper limit is the starting row of the data, which is row 1 in most cases. Thus, `data[:50]` is similar to `data[1:50]`.

In the same way, if the upper limit is not mentioned, it is assumed to be the last row of the dataset. To select all the rows except the first 50 rows, we will write `data[51:]`.

A variety of permutations and combinations can be performed on these rules to fetch the row that one needs.

Another important way to subset a data frame by rows is conditional or Boolean subsetting. In this method, one filters the rows that satisfy certain conditions. The condition can be either an inequality or a comparison written inside the square bracket. Let us see a few examples of how one can go about implementing them:

- Suppose, one wants to filter the rows that have clocked Total Mins to be greater than 500. This can be done as follows:

```
data1=data[data['Total Mins']>500]
data1.shape
```

- The newly created data frame, after filtering, has 2720 rows compared to 3333 in the unfiltered data frame. Clearly, the balance rows have been filtered by the condition.

- Let us have a look at another example, where we provide equality as a condition. Let us filter the rows for which the state is VA:

```
data1=data[data['State']=='VA']
data1.shape
```

- This data frame contains only 77 rows, while the rest get filtered.

- One can combine multiple conditions, as well, using AND (&) and OR (|) operators. To filter all the rows in the state VA that have Total Mins greater than 500, we can write:

```
data1=data[(data['Total Mins']>500) & (data['State']=='VA')]
data1.shape
```

- This data frame contains only 64 rows; it's lesser than the previous data frame. It also has two conditions, both of which must be satisfied to get filtered. The AND operator has a subtractive effect.

- To filter all the rows that are either in state VA or have Total Mins greater than 500, we can write the following code:

```
data1=data[(data['Total Mins']>500) | (data['State']=='VA')]
data1.shape
```

- This data frame has 2733 rows, which is greater than 2720 rows obtained with just one filter of Total Mins being greater than 500. The OR operator has an additive affect.

Selecting a combination of rows and columns

This is the most used form of subsetting a dataset. Earlier in this chapter we selected three columns of this dataset and called the sub-setted data frame a `subdata`. What if we wish to look at specific rows of that sub-setted data frame? How can we do that? We just need another square bracket adjacent to the one already existing.

Let's say, we need to look at the first 50 rows of that sub-setted data frame. We can write a snippet, as shown:

```
subdata_first_50=data[['Account Length','VMail Message','Day Calls']]
[1:50]
subdata_first_50
```

We can use the already created `subdata` data frame and subset it for the first 50 rows by typing:

```
subdata[1:50] or subdata[:50]
```

Alternatively, one can subset the columns using the list name as explained earlier and then subset for rows.

Another effective (but a little unstable, as its behavior changes based on the version of Python installed) method to select both rows and columns together is the `.ix` method. Let's see how to use this method.

Basically, in the `.ix` method, we can provide row and column indices (in a lay man's term, row and column numbers) inside the square bracket. The syntax can be summarized, as follows:

- The data frame name is appended with `ix`
- Inside the square bracket, specify the row number (range) and column number (range) in that order

Now, let's have a look at a few examples:

- Selecting the first 100 rows of the first 5 columns:

```
data.ix[1:100,1:6]
```

The output looks similar to the following screenshot:

	Account Length	Area Code	Phone	Int'l Plan	VMail Plan
1	107	415	371-7191	no	yes
2	137	415	358-1921	no	no
3	84	408	375-9999	yes	no
4	75	415	330-6626	yes	no
5	118	510	391-8027	yes	no

Fig. 3.4: First 100 rows of the first 5 columns

- Selecting all rows from the first five columns:

  ```
  data.ix[:,1:6]
  ```

- Selecting first 100 rows from all the columns:

  ```
  data.ix[1:100,:]
  ```

The row and column numbers/name can be passed off as a list, as well. Let's have a look at how it can be done:

- Selecting the first 100 rows from the 2nd, 5th, and 7th columns:

  ```
  data.ix[1:100,[2,5,7]]
  ```

The output looks similar to the following screenshot:

	Area Code	VMail Plan	Day Mins
1	415	yes	161.6
2	415	no	243.4
3	408	no	299.4
4	415	no	166.7
5	510	no	223.4

Fig. 3.5: First 100 rows of the 2nd, 5th and 7th columns

- Selecting the 1st, 2nd and 5th rows from the 2nd, 5th and 7th columns:

  ```
  data.ix[[1,2,5],[2,5,7]]
  ```

The output looks similar to the following screenshot:

	Area Code	VMail Plan	Day Mins
1	415	yes	161.6
2	415	no	243.4
5	510	no	223.4

Fig. 3.6: 1st, 2nd and 5th rows of the 2nd, 5th and 7th columns

Instead of row and column indices or numbers, we can also write corresponding column names, as shown in the following example:

```
data.ix[[1,2,5],['Area Code','VMail Plan','Day Mins']]
```

Creating new columns

Many times during the analysis, we are required to create a new column based on some calculation or modification of the existing columns containing a constant value to be used in the modelling. Hence, the knowledge of creating new columns becomes an indispensable tool to learn. Let's see how to do that.

Suppose, in the `Customer Churn Model` dataset, we want to calculate the total minutes spent during the day, evening, and night. This requires summing up the 3 columns, which are `Day Mins`, `Eve Mins`, and `Night Mins`. It can be done, as shown in the following snippet:

```
data['Total Mins']=data['Day Mins']+data['Eve Mins']+data['Night Mins']
data['Total Mins'].head()
```

The output of the snippet is, as follows:

```
0    707.2
1    611.5
2    527.2
3    558.2
4    501.9
Name: Total Mins, dtype: float64
```

Fig. 3.7: First few entries of the new Total Mins column

Generating random numbers and their usage

Random numbers are just like any other number in their property except for the fact that they assume a different value every time the `call` statement to generate a random number is executed. Random number generating methods use certain algorithms to generate different numbers every time, which are beyond the scope of this book. However, after a finitely large period, they might start generating the already generated numbers. In that sense, these numbers are not truly random and are sometimes called pseudo-random numbers.

In spite of them actually being pseudo-random, these numbers can be assumed to be random for all practical purposes. These numbers are of critical importance to predictive analysts because of the following points:

- They allow analysts to perform simulations for probabilistic multicase scenarios
- They can be used to generate dummy data frames or columns of a data frame that are needed in the analysis
- They can be used for the random sampling of data

Various methods for generating random numbers

The method used to deal with random number is called `random` and is found in the `numpy` library. Let's have a look at the different methods of generating random numbers and their usage.

Let's start by generating a random integer between 1 and 100. This can be done, as follows:

```
import numpy as np
np.random.randint(1,100)
```

If you run the preceding snippet, it will generate a random number between 1 and 100. When I ran it, it gave me 43 as the result. It might give you something else.

To generate a random number between 0 and 1, we can write something similar to the following code:

```
import numpy as np
np.random.random()
```

These methods allow us to generate one random number at a time. What if we wanted to generate a list of numbers, all lying within a given interval and generated randomly. Let's define a function that can generate a list of n random numbers lying between a and b.

All one needs to do is define a function, wherein an empty list is created and the randomly generated numbers are appended to the list. The recipe to do that is shown in the following code snippet:

```
def randint_range(n,a,b):
    x=[]
    for i in range(n):
        x.append(np.random.randint(a,b))
    return x
```

After defining this function we can generate, let's say, 10 numbers lying between 2 and 1000, as shown:

```
rand_int_gen(10,2,1000)
```

On the first run, it gives something similar to the following output:

[229, 650, 318, 498, 746, 951, 649, 605, 131, 623]

Fig. 3.8: 10 random integers between 2 and 1000

The randrange method is an important method to generate random numbers and is in a way an extension to the randint method, as it provides a step argument in addition to the start and stop argument in the case of randint function.

To generate three random numbers between 0 and 100, which are all multiples of 5, we can write:

```
import random
for i in range(3):
    print random.randrange(0,100,5)
```

You should get something similar to the following screenshot, as a result (the actual numbers might change):

```
70
15
20
```

Another related useful method is `shuffle`, which shuffles a list or an array in random order. It doesn't generate a random number, per se, but nevertheless it is very useful. Lets see how it works. Lets generate a list of consecutive `100` integers and then shuffle the list:

```
a=range(100)
np.random.shuffle(a)
```

The list looks similar to the following screenshot before and after the shuffle:

```
[0,                                          [37,
 1,                                           19,
 2,                                           68,
 3,                                           78,
 4,                                           64,
 5,                                           85,
 6,                                           39,
 7,                                           87,
 8,
```

list a before shuffle   *list a after shuffle*

The `choice` method is another important technique that might come in very handy in various scenarios including creating simulations, depending upon selecting a random item from a list of items. The `choice` method is used to pick an item at random from a given list of items.

To see an example of how this method works, let's go back to the data frame that we have been using all along in this chapter. Let's import that data again and get the list of column names, using the following code snippet:

```
import pandas as pd
data=pd.read_csv('E:/Personal/Learning/Predictive Modeling Book/Book
Datasets/Customer Churn Model.txt')
column_list=data.columns.values.tolist()
```

To select one column name from the list, at random, we can write it similar to the following example:

```
np.random.choice(column_list)
```

This should result in one column name being chosen at random from the list of the column names. I got `Day Calls` for my run. Of course, one can loop over the choice method to get multiple items, as we did for the `randint` method.

Seeding a random number

At the onset of this section on random numbers, we discussed how random numbers change their values on every execution of their call statement. They repeat their values but only after a very large period. Sometimes, we need to generate a set of random numbers that retain their value. This can be achieved by seeding the generation of random numbers. Basically, the particular instance of generating a random number is given a seed (sort of a key), which when used can regenerate the same set of random numbers. Let's see this with an example:

```
np.random.seed(1)
for i in range(5):
    print np.random.random()
```

In the first line, we set the seed as `1` and then generated `5` random numbers. The output looks something similar to this:

```
0.417022004703
0.720324493442
0.000114374817345
0.302332572632
0.146755890817
```

Fig. 3.9: Five random numbers generated through random method with seed 1

If one removes the seed and then generates random numbers, one will get different random numbers. Let's have a look:

```
for i in range(5):
    print np.random.random()
```

By running the preceding code snippet, one indeed gets different random numbers, as shown in the following output screenshot:

```
0.0923385947688
0.186260211378
0.345560727043
0.396767474231
0.538816734003
```

Fig. 3.10: Five random number generated through random method without seed 1

However, if one brings back the seed used to generate random numbers, we can get back the same numbers. If we try running the following snippet, we will have to regenerate the numbers, as shown in the first case:

```
np.random.seed(1)
for i in range(5):
    print np.random.random()
```

Generating random numbers following probability distributions

If you have taken a probability class in your school or college, you might have heard of probability distributions. There are two concepts that you might want to refresh.

Probability density function

For a random variable, it is just the count of times that the random variable attains a particular value x or the number of times that the value of the random variable falls in a given range (bins). This gives the probability of attaining a particular value by the random variable. Histograms plot this number/probability on the y axis and it can be identified as the y axis value of a distribution plot/histogram:

```
PDF = Prob(X=x)
```

Cumulative density function

For a random variable, it is defined as the probability that the random variable is less than or equal to a given value x. It is the total probability that the random variable is less than or equal to a given value. For a given point on the x axis, it is calculated as the area enclosed by the frequency distribution curve between by values less than x.

Mathematically, it is defined as follows:

```
CDF(x) = Prob(X<=x)
```

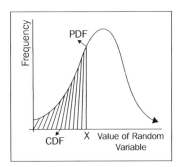

Fig. 3.11: CDF is the area enclosed by the curve till that value of random variable. PDF is the frequency/ probability of that particular value of random variable.

There are various kinds of probability distributions that frequently occur, including the normal (famously known as the **Bell Curve**), uniform, poisson, binomial, multinomial distributions, and so on.

Many of the analyses require generating random numbers that follow a particular probability distribution. One can generate random numbers in such a fashion using the same `random` method of the `numpy` library.

Let's see how one can generate two of the most commonly used distributions, which are normal and uniform distributions.

Uniform distribution

A uniform distribution is defined by its endpoints—the start and stop points. Each of the points lying in between these endpoints are supposed to occur with the same (uniform) probability and hence the name of the distribution.

If the start and stop points are **a** and **b**, each point between **a** and **b** would occur with a frequency of **1/(b-a)**:

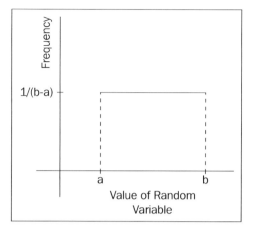

Fig. 3.12: In a uniform distribution, all the random variables occur with the same (uniform) frequency/probability

As the uniform distribution is defined by its start and stop points, it is essential to know these points while generating random numbers following a uniform distribution. Thus, these points are taken as input parameters for the uniform function that is used to generate a random number following a uniform distribution. The other parameter of this function is the number of random numbers that one wants to generate.

To generate 100 random numbers lying between 1 and 100, one can write the following:

```
import numpy as np
randnum=np.random.uniform(1,100,100)
```

To check whether it indeed follows the uniform distribution, let's plot a histogram of these numbers and see whether they occur with the same probability or not. This can be done using the following code snippet:

```
import numpy as np
import matplotlib.pyplot as plt
%matplotlib inline
a=np.random.uniform(1,100,100)
b=range(1,101)
plt.hist(a)
```

The output that we get is not what we expected. It doesn't have the same probability for all the numbers, as seen in the following output:

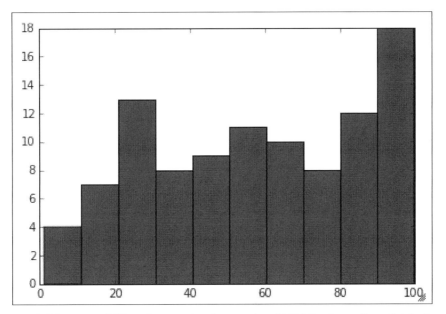

Fig. 3.13: Histogram of 100 random numbers between 1 and 100 following uniform distribution

The reason for this is that 100 is a very small number, given the range (1-100), to showcase the property of the uniform distribution. We should try generating more random numbers and then see the results. Try generating around a million (1,000,000) numbers by changing the parameter in the `uniform` function, and then see the results of the preceding code snippet.

It should look something like the following:

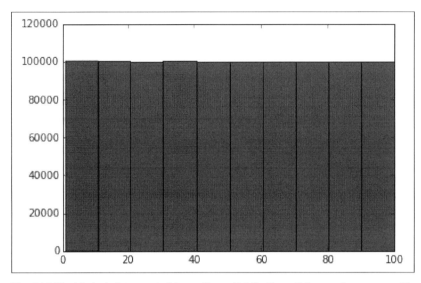

Fig. 3.14: The kind of plot expected for uniform distribution, all the numbers occur with the same frequency/probability

If you observe the preceding plot properly, each bin that contains 10 numbers occurs roughly with a frequency of 100,000 (and hence a probability of *100000/1000000=1/10*). This means that each number occurs with a probability of *1/10*1/10=1/100*, which is equal to the probability that we would have expected from a set of numbers following the uniform distribution between 1 and 100 *(1/(100-1)=1/99)*.

Normal distribution

Normal distribution is the most common form of probability distribution arising from everyday real-life situations. Thus, the exam score distribution of students in a class would roughly follow the normal distribution as would the heights of the students in the class. An interesting behavior of all the probability distributions is that they tend to follow/align to a normal distribution as the sample size of the numbers increase. In a sense, one can say that a normal distribution is the most ubiquitous and versatile probability distribution around.

The parameters that define a normal distribution are the mean and standard deviation. A normal distribution with a `0` mean and `1` standard deviation is called a standard normal distribution. The `randn` function of the `random` method is used to generate random numbers following a normal distribution. It returns random numbers following a standard normal distribution.

To generate `100` such numbers, one simply writes the following:

```
import numpy as np
a=np.random.randn(100)
```

To take a look at how random these values actually are, let's plot them against a list of integers:

```
import numpy as np
import matplotlib.pyplot as plt
%matplotlib inline
a=np.random.randn(100)
b=range(1,101)
plt.plot(b,a)
```

The output looks something like the following image. The numbers are visibly random.

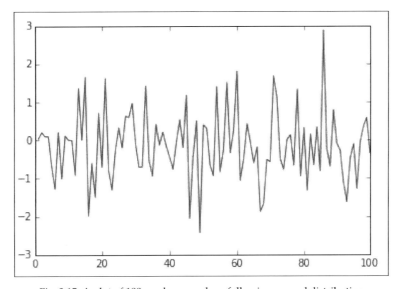

Fig. 3.15: A plot of 100 random numbers following normal distribution

One can pass a list defining the shape of the expected array. If one passes, let's say, `(2,4)` as the input, one would get a 2 x 4 array of numbers following a standard normal distribution:

```
import numpy as np
a=np.random.randn(2,4)
```

If no numbers are specified, it generates a single random number from the standard normal distribution.

To get numbers following normal distributions (with mean and standard deviation other than `0` and `1`, let's say, mean `1.5` and standard deviation `2.5`), one can write something like the following:

```
import numpy as np
a=2.5*np.random.randn(100)+1.5
```

The preceding calculation holds because the standard normal distribution S is created from a normal distribution X, with mean μ and standard deviation σ, using the following formula:

$$S = (X - \mu) / \sigma$$

Let's generate enough random numbers following a standard normal distribution and plot them to see whether they follow the shape of a standard normal distribution (a bell curve). This can be done using the following code snippet:

```
import numpy as np
import matplotlib.pyplot as plt
%matplotlib inline
a=np.random.randn(100000)
b=range(1,101)
plt.hist(a)
```

The output would look something like this, which roughly looks like a bell curve (if one joins the top points of all the bins to form a curvilinear line):

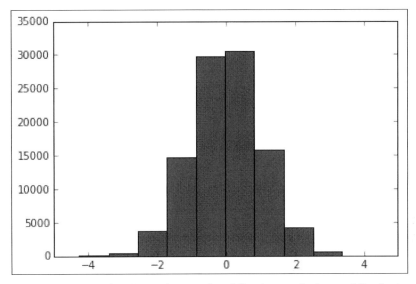

Fig. 3.16: Histogram of 100000 random numbers following standard normal distribution.

Using the Monte-Carlo simulation to find the value of pi

Till now, we have been learning about various ways to generate random numbers. Let's now see an application of random numbers. In this section, we will use random numbers to run something called Monte-Carlo simulations to calculate the value of pi. These simulations are based on repeated random sampling or the generation of numbers.

Geometry and mathematics behind the calculation of pi

Consider a circle of radius r unit circumscribed inside a square of side **2r** units such that the circle's diameter and the square's sides have the same dimensions:

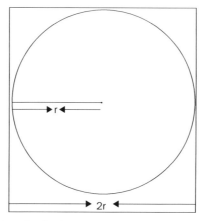

Fig. 3.17: A circle of radius r circumscribed in a square of side 2r

What is the probability that a point chosen at random would lie inside the circle? This probability would be given by the following formulae:

$$Prob\left(point\ lying\ inside\ the\ circle\right) = Area\ of\ circle\ /\ Area\ of\ square$$

$$p = pi*r*r\ /\left(2r*2r\right)$$

$$p = pi\ /\ 4$$

Thus, we find out that the probability of a point lying inside the circle is pi/4. The purpose of the simulation is to calculate this probability and use this to estimate the value of pi. The following are the steps to be implemented to run this simulation:

1. Generate points with both x and y coordinates lying between 0 and 1.

2. Calculate $x*x + y*y$. If it is less than 1, it lies inside the circle. If it is greater than 1, it lies outside the circle.

3. Calculate the total number of points that lie inside the circle. Divide it by the total number of points generated to get the probability of a point lying inside the circle.

4. Use this probability to calculate the value of pi.

5. Repeat the process for a sufficient number of times, say, 1,000 times and generate 1,000 different values of pi.

6. Take an average of all the 1,000 values of pi to arrive at the final value of pi.

Let's see how one can implement these steps in Python. The following code snippet would do just this:

```
pi_avg=0
pi_value_list=[]
for i in range(100):
    value=0
    x=np.random.uniform(0,1,1000).tolist()
    y=np.random.uniform(0,1,1000).tolist()
    for j in range(1000):
            z=np.sqrt(x[j]*x[j]+y[j]*y[j])
            if z<=1:
                value+=1
    float_value=float(value)
    pi_value=float_value*4/1000
    pi_value_list.append(pi_value)
    pi_avg+=pi_value

pi=pi_avg/100
print pi
ind=range(1,101)
fig=plt.plot(ind,pi_value_list)
fig
```

The preceding snippet generates 1,000 random points to calculate the probability of a point lying inside the circle and then repeats this process 100 times to get at the final averaged value of pi. These 100 values of pi have been plotted and they look as follows:

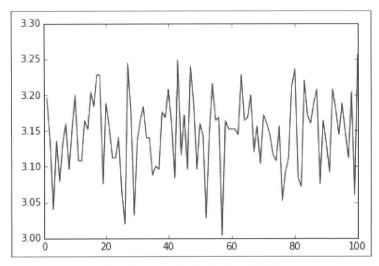

Fig. 3.18: Values of pi over 100 simulations of 1000 points each

The final averaged value of pi comes out to be 3.14584 in this run. As we increase the number of runs, the accuracy increases. One can easily wrap the preceding snippet in a function and pass the number of runs as an input for the easy comparison of pi values as an increasing number of runs are passed to this function. The following code snippet is a function to do just this:

```
def pi_run(nums,loops):
    pi_avg=0
    pi_value_list=[]
    for i in range(loops):
        value=0
        x=np.random.uniform(0,1,nums).tolist()
        y=np.random.uniform(0,1,nums).tolist()
        for j in range(nums):
            z=np.sqrt(x[j]*x[j]+y[j]*y[j])
            if z<=1:
```

```
            value+=1
        float_value=float(value)
        pi_value=float_value*4/nums
        pi_value_list.append(pi_value)
        pi_avg+=pi_value

    pi=pi_avg/loops
    ind=range(1,loops+1)
    fig=plt.plot(ind,pi_value_list)
    return (pi,fig)
```

To call this function, write `pi_run(1000,100)`, and it should give you a similar result as was given previously with the hardcoded numbers. This function would return both the averaged value of pi as well as the plot.

Generating a dummy data frame

One very important use of generating random numbers is to create a dummy data frame, which will be used extensively in this book to illustrate concepts and examples.

The basic concept of this is that the array/list of random numbers generated through the various methods described in the previous sections can be passed as the columns of a data frame. The column names and their descriptions are passed as the keys and values of a dictionary.

Let's see an example where a dummy data frame contains two columns, A and B, which have 10 random numbers following a standard normal distribution and normal distribution, respectively.

To create such a data frame, one can run the following code snippet:

```
import pandas as pd
d=pd.DataFrame({'A':np.random.randn(10),'B':2.5*np.random.
randn(10)+1.5})
d
```

The following screenshot is the output of the code:

	A	B
0	-0.676761	-1.792542
1	0.897748	1.248321
2	-1.076665	2.308246
3	-0.816676	1.837449
4	-0.588539	0.391636
5	1.150768	1.435749
6	-0.639738	-1.490854

Fig. 3.19: A dummy data frame containing 2 columns – one having numbers following standard normal distribution, the second having random numbers following normal distribution with mean 1.5 and standard deviation 2.5

Categorical/string variables can also be passed as a list to be part of a dummy data frame. Let's go back to our example of the Customer Churn Model data and use the column names as the list to be passed. This can be done as described in the following snippet:

```
import pandas as pd
data = pd.read_csv('E:/Personal/Learning/Datasets/Book/Customer Churn
Model.txt')
column_list=data.columns.values.tolist()
a=len(column_list)
d=pd.DataFrame({'Column_Name':column_list,'A':np.random.
randn(a),'B':2.5*np.random.randn(a)+1.5})
d
```

The output of the preceding snippet is as follows:

	A	B	Column_Name
0	2.275675	3.596925	State
1	-0.744064	2.921731	Account Length
2	0.849137	2.450933	Area Code
3	-1.675697	2.492734	Phone
4	0.294543	2.303737	Int'l Plan
5	1.467060	0.709965	VMail Plan
6	0.264161	-1.246690	VMail Message
7	-1.170487	1.662483	Day Mins

Fig. 3.20: Another dummy data frame. Similar to the one above but with one extra column which has column names of the data data frame

The index can also be passed as one of the parameters of this function. By default, it gives a range of numbers starting from 0 as the index. If we want something else as the index, we can specify it in the index parameter as shown in the following example:

```
import pandas as pd
d=pd.DataFrame({'A':np.random.randn(10),'B':2.5*np.random.randn(10)+1.
5},index=range(10,20))
d
```

The output of the preceding code looks like the following:

	A	B
10	-0.656314	2.804017
11	1.277171	3.731968
12	-0.732919	-1.720575
13	-0.322853	-1.426347
14	-0.750510	0.390120

Fig. 3.21: Passing indices to the dummy data frame

Grouping the data – aggregation, filtering, and transformation

In this section, you will learn how to aggregate data over categorical variables. This is a very common practice when the data consists of categorical variables. This analysis enables us to conduct a category-wise analysis and take further decisions regarding the modelling.

To illustrate the concepts of grouping and aggregating data better, let's create a simple dummy data frame that has a rich mix of both numerical and categorical variables. Let's use whatever we have explored till now about random numbers to create this data frame, as shown in the following snippet:

```python
import numpy as np
import pandas as pd
a=['Male','Female']
b=['Rich','Poor','Middle Class']
gender=[]
seb=[]
for i in range(1,101):
    gender.append(np.random.choice(a))
    seb.append(np.random.choice(b))
height=30*np.random.randn(100)+155
weight=20*np.random.randn(100)+60
age=10*np.random.randn(100)+35
income=1500*np.random.randn(100)+15000

df=pd.DataFrame({'Gender':gender,'Height':height,'Weight':weight,'Age'
:age,'Income':income,'Socio-Eco':seb})
df.head()
```

The output data frame `df` looks something as follows:

	Age	Gender	Height	Income	Socio-Eco	Weight
0	39.820636	Male	162.011462	13746.221296	Poor	53.338449
1	28.960216	Female	153.428709	14552.728892	Middle Class	31.417536
2	44.843498	Male	164.903480	15117.058618	Middle Class	83.850653
3	37.321991	Male	203.915330	15081.493024	Poor	29.184765
4	36.867675	Male	156.924006	15807.781879	Rich	93.718256

Fig. 3.22: The resulting dummy data frame df containing 6 columns

As we can see from the preceding code snippet, the shape of the data frame is 100x6.

Grouping can be done over a categorical variable using the groupby function. The column name of the categorical variable needs to be specified for this. Suppose that we wish to group the data frame based on the Gender variable. This can be done by writing the following:

```
df.groupby('Gender')
```

If you run the preceding snippet on your IDE, you will get the following output indicating that a groupby object has been created:

```
<pandas.core.groupby.DataFrameGroupBy object at 0x000000000B5F7080>
```

Fig. 3.23: Prompt showing that the groupby object has been created

The groupby function doesn't split the original data frame into several groups, instead it creates a groupby object that has two attributes, which are name and group.

These attributes can be accessed by following the name of the groupby object with '.', followed by the name of the attribute. For example, to access the group attribute, one can write the following:

```
grouped = df.groupby('Gender')
grouped.groups
```

The following is the output:

```
{'Female': [1L,                                      'Male': [0L,
  9L,                                                  2L,
  10L,                                                 3L,
  14L,                                                 4L,
  15L,                                                 5L,
  16L,                                                 6L,
  17L,                                                 7L,
  18L,                                                 8L,
  20L,                                                 11L,
  21L,                                                 12L,
  22L,                                                 13L,
  23L,

group with gender female                         group with gender male
```

Fig. 3.24: Two groups based on gender

The numbers indicate the row numbers that belong to that particular group.

One important feature of these attributes is that they are iterable, and the same operation can be applied to each group just by looping. This comes in very handy when the number of groups are large and one needs results of the operation separately for each group.

Let's perform a simple operation to illustrate this. Let's try to print the name and groups in the `groupby` object that we just created. This can be done as follows:

```
grouped=df.groupby('Gender')
for names,groups in grouped:
    print names
    print groups
```

This prints the name of the group followed by the entire data for this group. The output looks something like the following:

```
Female
        Age  Gender    Height        Income     Socio-Eco     Weight
1   28.960216  Female  153.428709  14552.728892  Middle Class  31.417536
9   44.977099  Female  177.259378  15061.304869         Rich  51.064310
10  33.132451  Female  137.280203  14227.923156         Rich  81.648666
14  34.574261  Female   85.299546  16472.994997  Middle Class  55.724113
15  33.177149  Female  189.658218  15400.537167         Rich  60.323522
16  47.908176  Female  204.362022  17236.310625  Middle Class  98.160555
```

Fig. 3.25.1: Name and the data in the group with gender female

Here is the second group as a part of the output:

```
Male
        Age Gender    Height        Income     Socio-Eco     Weight
0   39.820636  Male  162.011462  13746.221296         Poor  53.338449
2   44.843498  Male  164.903480  15117.058618  Middle Class  83.850653
3   37.321991  Male  203.915330  15081.493024         Poor  29.184765
4   36.867675  Male  156.924006  15807.781879         Rich  93.718256
5   32.530679  Male  165.675146  15287.499136         Poor  65.317624
6   46.448705  Male   98.141285  15211.196526  Middle Class  30.945197
7   24.516053  Male  127.405989  16747.849991         Rich  103.950859
```

Fig. 3.25.2: Name and the data in the group with gender male

A single group can be selected by writing the following:

```
grouped.get_group('Female')
```

This would generate only the first of the two groups, as shown in the preceding screenshot.

A data frame can be grouped over more than one categorical variable as well. As in this case, the data frame can be grouped over both `Gender` and `Soci-Eco` by writing something like the following:

```
grouped=df.groupby(['Gender','Socio-Eco'])
```

This should create six groups from a combination of two categories of `Gender` and three categories of the `Socio-Eco` variable. This can be checked by checking the length of the `groupby` object as follows:

```
len(grouped)
```

It indeed returns six. To look at how these groups look, let's run the same iteration on the group attributes as we did earlier:

```
grouped=df.groupby(['Gender','Socio-Eco'])
for names,groups in grouped:
    print names
    print groups
```

The code gives six groups' names and their entire data as the output. There would be six of such groups in total.

The first group looks like the following:

```
('Female', 'Middle Class')
        Age  Gender      Height        Income     Socio-Eco      Weight
1   28.960216  Female  153.428709  14552.728892  Middle Class  31.417536
14  34.574261  Female   85.299546  16472.994997  Middle Class  55.724113
16  47.908176  Female  204.362022  17236.310625  Middle Class  98.160555
17  29.328399  Female  127.990601  15133.343349  Middle Class  89.824323
```

Fig. 3.26.1: Name and the data in the group with gender female and Socio_Eco Middle Class

The second group looks like the following:

```
('Female', 'Poor')
        Age  Gender      Height        Income  Socio-Eco      Weight
20  27.611733  Female  159.454917  16586.398187       Poor   91.656941
28  48.122088  Female  182.919937  16791.223685       Poor  101.127316
36  37.005910  Female  145.988137  15765.753064       Poor   22.086710
48  19.256548  Female  176.075314  16445.605634       Poor   79.636263
61  56.134487  Female  108.394930  13417.761928       Poor   50.130305
```

Fig. 3.26.2: Name and the data in the group with gender female and Socio_Eco Middle Class

Aggregation

There are various aggregations that are possible on a data frame, such as sum, mean, describe, size, and so on. The aggregation basically means applying a function to all the groups all at once and getting a result from that particular group.

Let's see the sum function. We just need to write the following code snippet to see how it works:

```
grouped=df.groupby(['Gender','Socio-Eco'])
grouped.sum()
```

We gets the following table as the result:

Gender	Socio-Eco	Age	Height	Income	Weight
Female	Middle Class	632.068094	2872.983597	295519.026577	1195.181950
	Poor	563.320180	2519.788780	242720.410355	1013.542900
	Rich	659.706510	2831.036059	268344.809719	1212.579159
Male	Middle Class	694.153466	3177.694609	295826.059725	1292.375547
	Poor	547.555581	2446.000288	238920.452793	964.323454
	Rich	377.698185	1648.121064	165691.499527	696.885366

Fig. 3.27: Sum of each column for different groups

To get the number of rows in each group (or calculate the size of each group), we can write something similar to the following code snippet:

```
grouped=df.groupby(['Gender','Socio-Eco'])
grouped.size()
```

This results in a table, as shown in the following screenshot:

```
Gender   Socio-Eco
Female   Middle Class    19
         Poor            16
         Rich            18
Male     Middle Class    20
         Poor            16
         Rich            11
dtype: int64
```

Fig. 3.28: Size of each group

One can use the `describe` function to get the summary statistics for each group separately. The syntax is exactly the same as it is for the earlier two functions:

```
grouped=df.groupby(['Gender','Socio-Eco'])
grouped.describe()
```

This output looks similar to the following table:

Gender	Socio-Eco			Age	Height	Income	Weight
		count		19.000000	19.000000	19.000000	19.000000
		mean		33.266742	151.209663	15553.632978	62.904313
		std		10.611239	40.482077	1523.540184	17.510285
	Middle Class	min		10.064952	85.299546	13658.318482	31.097011
		25%		27.917383	126.356186	14236.461121	52.531948
		50%		34.574261	153.428709	15467.874570	62.702537
		75%		38.912742	181.389485	16638.950298	72.156058
		max		48.820587	213.687623	19048.888489	98.160555

Fig. 3.29: All the summary statistics of each column for different groups

The `groupby` objects behave similar to an individual data frame, in the sense that one can select columns from these `groupby` objects just as we do from the data frames:

```
grouped=df.groupby(['Gender','Socio-Eco'])
grouped_income=grouped['Income']
```

One can apply different functions to different columns. The `aggregate` method used to do this is shown in the following snippet. With the following snippet, one can calculate sum of `Income`, mean of `Age`, and standard deviation of `Height`, as shown:

```
grouped=df.groupby(['Gender','Socio-Eco'])
grouped.aggregate({'Income':np.sum,'Age':np.mean,'Height':np.std})
```

The output of the preceding snippet looks similar to the following table:

Gender	Socio-Eco	Age	Height	Income
Female	Middle Class	33.266742	40.482077	295519.026577
	Poor	35.207511	26.205776	242720.410355
	Rich	36.650362	27.800692	268344.809719
Male	Middle Class	34.707673	29.704421	295826.059725
	Poor	34.222224	27.558691	238920.452793
	Rich	34.336199	28.005210	165691.499527

Fig. 3.30: Selected summary statistics of selected columns for different groups

We can also define a function using the `lambda` method of defining a calculation in Python. Suppose you don't want the mean of age but the ratio of mean and standard deviation for height. You can define the formula for this ratio using the `lambda` method, illustrated as follows:

```
grouped=df.groupby(['Gender','Socio-Eco'])
grouped.aggregate({'Age':np.mean,'Height':lambda x:np.mean(x)/
np.std(x)})
```

Rather than applying different functions to different columns, one can apply several functions to all the columns at the same time, as shown:

```
grouped.aggregate([np.sum, np.mean, np.std])
```

The output of the code snippet contains the result of all the three functions applied on all the columns of the `groupby` object, as seen in the following screenshot:

		Age			Height		
		sum	mean	std	sum	mean	std
Gender	Socio-Eco						
Female	Middle Class	720.330688	37.912141	7.656700	2914.100064	153.373688	35.133537
	Poor	434.008870	31.000634	9.073765	2008.303702	143.450264	24.214356
	Rich	686.620647	36.137929	11.037672	2931.740987	154.302157	27.181854

Fig. 3.31: More than one selected summary statistics of selected columns for different groups

Filtering

One important operation that can be applied on the `groupby` objects is filter. We can filter elements based on the properties of groups. Suppose we want to choose elements from the `Age` column that are a part of the group wherein the sum of `Age` is greater than `700`. This filtering can be done by writing the following snippet:

```
grouped['Age'].filter(lambda x:x.sum()>700)
```

The output contains the row numbers that are part of the group where the sum of Age is greater than 700. The output is, as follows:

```
4      48.161761
10     21.047972
12     33.675666
16     42.284018
37     43.450477
40     34.965525
45     47.776592
49     29.703094
53     36.434912
56     44.251152
59     42.503696
60     42.420253
71     29.362086
78     43.254055
79     40.990966
82     44.369909
85     28.384383
92     39.166672
98     28.127499
Name: Age, dtype: float64
```

Fig. 3.32: The rows left after filtering it for elements, which are part of groups, where the sum of ages is greater than 700

Transformation

One can use the transform method to mathematically transform all the elements in a numerical column. Suppose, we wish to calculate the standard normal values for all the elements in the numerical columns of our data frame; this can be done in a manner as shown:

```
zscore = lambda x: (x - x.mean()) / x.std()
grouped.transform(zscore)
```

The output contains standard normal values for all the numerical columns in the data frame, as shown in the following screenshot:

	Age	Height	Income	Weight
0	1.782874	-0.249133	-1.685069	0.052094
1	-0.942944	0.243328	-0.748399	0.561731
2	-0.042892	0.350616	0.939274	0.331675
3	-0.187735	-1.285494	0.328040	-0.511561
4	1.338647	-1.982879	-0.118651	-0.435700
5	-0.351253	-1.465478	0.610867	1.946335

Fig. 3.33: Result of applying a lambda defined function on the columns of groups

The `transform` method comes in handy in a lot of situations. For example, it can be used to fill the missing values with the mean of the non-missing values, as shown:

```
f = lambda x: x.fillna(x.mean()
grouped.transform(f)
```

Miscellaneous operations

In many situations, one needs to select the *n*th row of each group of a `groupby` object, most often the first and the last row. This can be easily done once the `groupby` object is created. Let's see how:

- The first row of each group can be selected by writing the following code snippet:

```
grouped.head(1)
```

- While the last row of each group can be selected by writing the following code snippet:

```
grouped.tail(1)
```

The result of the former, is as shown:

	Age	Gender	Height	Income	Socio-Eco	Weight
0	49.603073	Male	138.392855	11777.221534	Poor	62.110718
1	25.730018	Female	160.916255	14144.568798	Rich	68.973639
2	38.146687	Male	168.017159	15990.565533	Middle Class	70.291151
4	48.161761	Female	83.708145	15242.128581	Middle Class	57.726991
6	48.050205	Female	128.830867	15728.126536	Poor	66.709733
19	41.454310	Male	141.051908	16115.552396	Rich	37.477869

Fig. 3.34: First few rows of the grouped element

In general, we can use the `nth` function to get the *n*th row from a group, as illustrated:

```
grouped=df.groupby('Gender')
grouped.nth(1)
```

This gives the following result:

Gender	Age	Height	Income	Socio-Eco	Weight
Female	48.161761	83.708145	15242.128581	Middle Class	57.726991
Male	38.146687	168.017159	15990.565533	Middle Class	70.291151

Fig. 3.35: First rows of each group

One can use any number (of course, less than the number of rows in each group) as the argument for the `nth` function.

It is always a good practice to sort the data frame for the relevant columns before creating the `groupby` object from the data frame. Suppose, you want to look at the youngest male and female members of this data frame.

This can be done by sorting the data frame, creating a `groupby` object, and then taking the first element of each group:

```
df1=df.sort(['Age','Income'])
grouped=df1.groupby('Gender')
grouped.head(1)
```

The output has two rows containing the details of the two youngest members from the two groups:

	Age	Gender	Height	Income	Socio-Eco	Weight
50	9.173014	Female	186.428968	14774.467196	Rich	58.500718
41	13.012938	Male	166.759783	13001.289219	Middle Class	95.971146

Fig. 3.36: Sorting by the age column before grouping by gender and then selecting the first row from each group can give you the oldest/youngest guy in the group

The oldest members can be identified in the same way by typing `grouped.tail(1)`.

Random sampling – splitting a dataset in training and testing datasets

Splitting the dataset in training and testing the datasets is one operation every predictive modeller has to perform before applying the model, irrespective of the kind of data in hand or the predictive model being applied. Generally, a dataset is split into training and testing datasets. The following is a description of the two types of datasets:

- The training dataset is the one on which the model is built. This is the one on which the calculations are performed and the model equations and parameters are created.
- The testing dataset is used to check the accuracy of the model. The model equations and parameters are used to calculate the output based on the inputs from the testing datasets. These outputs are used to compare the model efficiency in the light of the actuals present in the testing dataset.

This will become clearer from the following image:

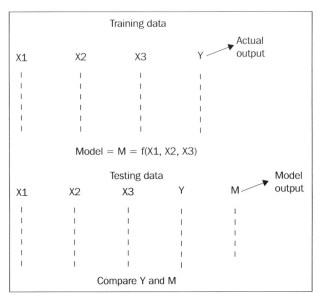

Fig. 3.37: Concept of sampling: Training and Testing data

Generally, the training and testing datasets are split in the ratio of 75:25 or 80:20. There are various ways to split the data into two halves. The crudest way that comes to mind is taking the first 75/80 percent rows as the training dataset and the rest as the testing dataset, or taking the first 25/20 percent rows as the testing and the rest as the training dataset. However, the problem with this approach is that it might bias the two datasets for a variety of reasons. The earlier rows might come from a different source or were observed during different scenarios. These situations might bias the model results from the two datasets. The rows should be chosen to avoid this bias. The most effective way to do that is to select the rows at random. Let us see a few methods to divide a dataset into training and testing datasets.

One way is to create as many standard normal random numbers, as there are rows in the dataset and then filter them for being smaller than a certain value. This filter condition is then used to partition the data in two parts. Let us see how it can be done.

Method 1 – using the Customer Churn Model

Let us use the same Customer Churn Model data that we have been using frequently. Let us go ahead and import it, as shown:

```
import pandas as pd
data = pd.read_csv('E:/Personal/Learning/Datasets/Book/Customer Churn
Model.txt')
len(data)
```

There are 3333 rows in the dataset. Next, we will generate random numbers and create a filter on which to partition the data:

```
a=np.random.randn(len(data))
check=a<0.8
training=data[check]
testing=data[~check]
```

The rows where the value of the random number is less than 0.8 becomes a part of the training variable, while the one with a value greater than 0.8 becomes a part of the testing dataset.

Let us check the lengths of the two datasets to see in what ratio the dataset has been divided. A 75:25 split between training and testing datasets would be ideal:

```
len(training)
len(testing)
```

The length of training dataset is 2635 while that of the testing dataset is 698; thus, resulting in a split very close to 75:25.

Method 2 – using sklearn

Very soon we will be introduced to a very powerful Python library used extensively for the purpose of modelling, scikit-learn or sklearn. This sklearn library has inbuilt methods to split a dataset in a training and testing dataset. Let's have a look at the procedure:

```
from sklearn.cross_validation import train_test_split
train, test = train_test_split(data, test_size = 0.2)
```

The test size specifies the size of the testing dataset: 0.2 means that 20 percent of the rows of the dataset should go to testing and the remaining 80 percent to training. If we check the length of these two (train and test), we can confirm that the split is indeed 80-20 percent.

Method 3 – using the shuffle function

Another method involves using the `shuffle` function in the `random` method. The data is read in line by line, which are shuffled randomly and then assigned to training and testing datasets in designated proportions, as shown:

```
import numpy as np
with open('E:/Personal/Learning/Datasets/Book/Customer Churn Model.
txt','rb') as f:
    data=f.read().split('\n')
np.random.shuffle(data)
train_data = data[:3*len(data)/4]
test_data = data[len(data)/4:]
```

In some cases, mostly during data science competitions like **Kaggle**, we would be provided with separate training and testing datasets to start with.

Concatenating and appending data

All the required information to build a model doesn't always come from a single table or data source. In many cases, two datasets need to be joined/merged to get more information (read new column/variable). Sometimes, small datasets need to be appended together to make a big dataset which contains the complete picture. Thus, merging and appending are important components of an analyst's armor.

Let's learn each of these methods one by one. For illustrating these methods, we will be using a lot of new interesting datasets. The one we are going to use first is a dataset about the mineral contents of wine; we will have separate datasets for red and white wine. Each sample represents a different sample of red or white wine.

Let us import this dataset and have a look at it. The delimiter for this dataset is `;` (a semi-colon), which needs to be taken care of:

```
import pandas as pd
data1=pd.read_csv('E:/Personal/Learning/Predictive Modeling Book/Book
Datasets/Merge and Join/winequality-red.csv',sep=';')
data1.head()
```

The output of this input snippet is similar to the following screenshot:

	fixed acidity	volatile acidity	citric acid	residual sugar	chlorides	free sulfur dioxide	total sulfur dioxide	density	pH	sulphates	alcohol	quality
0	7.4	0.70	0.00	1.9	0.076	11	34	0.9978	3.51	0.56	9.4	5
1	7.8	0.88	0.00	2.6	0.098	25	67	0.9968	3.20	0.68	9.8	5
2	7.8	0.76	0.04	2.3	0.092	15	54	0.9970	3.26	0.65	9.8	5
3	11.2	0.28	0.56	1.9	0.075	17	60	0.9980	3.16	0.58	9.8	6
4	7.4	0.70	0.00	1.9	0.076	11	34	0.9978	3.51	0.56	9.4	5

Fig. 3.38: First few entries of the wine quality-red dataset

The column names are as follows:

```
data1.columns.values
```

```
array(['fixed acidity', 'volatile acidity', 'citric acid',
       'residual sugar', 'chlorides', 'free sulfur dioxide',
       'total sulfur dioxide', 'density', 'pH', 'sulphates', 'alcohol',
       'quality'], dtype=object)
```

Fig. 3.39: Column names of the wine quality-red dataset

The size of the dataset is can be found out using the following snippet:

```
data1.shape
```

The output is 1599x12 implying that the dataset has 1599 rows.

Let us import the second dataset which is very similar to the preceding dataset except that the data points are collected for white wine:

```
import pandas as pd
data2=pd.read_csv('E:/Personal/Learning/Predictive Modeling Book/Book
Datasets/Merge and Join/winequality-white.csv',sep=';')
data2.head()
```

The output of this input snippet looks similar to the following screenshot:

	fixed acidity	volatile acidity	citric acid	residual sugar	chlorides	free sulfur dioxide	total sulfur dioxide	density	pH	sulphates	alcohol	quality
0	7.0	0.27	0.36	20.7	0.045	45	170	1.0010	3.00	0.45	8.8	6
1	6.3	0.30	0.34	1.6	0.049	14	132	0.9940	3.30	0.49	9.5	6
2	8.1	0.28	0.40	6.9	0.050	30	97	0.9951	3.26	0.44	10.1	6
3	7.2	0.23	0.32	8.5	0.058	47	186	0.9956	3.19	0.40	9.9	6
4	7.2	0.23	0.32	8.5	0.058	47	186	0.9956	3.19	0.40	9.9	6

Fig. 3.40: First few entries of the winequality-white dataset

As we can see, this dataset looks very similar to the preceding dataset. Let us confirm this by getting the column names for this dataset. They should be the same as the preceding array of column names:

```
array(['fixed acidity', 'volatile acidity', 'citric acid',
       'residual sugar', 'chlorides', 'free sulfur dioxide',
       'total sulfur dioxide', 'density', 'pH', 'sulphates', 'alcohol',
       'quality'], dtype=object)
```

Fig. 3.41: Column names of the winequality-white dataset

The size of the dataset is, as follows:

```
data2.shape
```

4898x12, this means that the dataset has 4898 rows.

So, we can see that the `data1` and `data2` are very similar (in terms of column names and column types) except the row numbers in the two datasets. These are ideal circumstances to append two datasets along the horizontal axis (`axis=0`).

In Python, the horizontal axis is denoted by `axis=0` and the vertical axis is denoted by `axis=1`.

Let us append these two datasets along `axis=0`. This can be done using the `concat` method of `pandas` library. After appending the datasets, the row numbers of the final dataset should be the same as the row numbers of both the datasets.

This can be accomplished as follows:

```
wine_total=pd.concat([data1,data2],axis=0)
```

Let us check the number of rows of the appended dataset `wine_total`:

```
wine_total.shape
```

The output is `6497x12`. It indicates that the final appended dataset has 6497 *(6497=1599+4898)* rows. One can see that the row numbers in the appended dataset is the sum of row numbers of the individual datasets.

Let us have a look at the final dataset just to ensure everything looks fine. While appending over `axis=0`, the two datasets are just stacked over one another. In this case, `data1` will be stacked over `data2` dataset. So, the first few rows of the final dataset `wine_total` will look similar to the first few rows of the first dataset `data1`. Let us check that:

```
wine_total.head()
```

The output looks similar to the following screenshot:

	fixed acidity	volatile acidity	citric acid	residual sugar	chlorides	free sulfur dioxide	total sulfur dioxide	density	pH	sulphates	alcohol	quality
0	7.4	0.70	0.00	1.9	0.076	11	34	0.9978	3.51	0.56	9.4	5
1	7.8	0.88	0.00	2.6	0.098	25	67	0.9968	3.20	0.68	9.8	5
2	7.8	0.76	0.04	2.3	0.092	15	54	0.9970	3.26	0.65	9.8	5
3	11.2	0.28	0.56	1.9	0.075	17	60	0.9980	3.16	0.58	9.8	6
4	7.4	0.70	0.00	1.9	0.076	11	34	0.9978	3.51	0.56	9.4	5

Fig. 3.42: First few entries of the final dataset obtained from appending data1 and data2

The preceding output is the same as the first few rows of the `data1`.

This `concat` method can be used to scramble data that is taken a few rows from here and there and stacking them over one another. The `concat` method takes more than two datasets also as an argument. The datasets are stacked over one another in order of appearance. If the datasets are `data1`, `data2`, and `data3`, in that order, then `data1` will be stacked over `data2` which will be stacked over `data3`.

Let us look at an example of such scrambling. We will use the `data1` dataset (coming from `winequality-red.csv`) and take 50 rows from head, middle, and tail to create three different data frames. These data frames will be then stacked over one another to create a final dataset:

```
data1_head=data1.head(50)
data1_middle=data1[500:550]
data1_tail=data.tail(50)
wine_scramble=pd.concat([data1_middle,data1_head,data1_tail],axis=0)
wine_scramble
```

The output dataset will contain 150 rows, as confirmed by the following snippet:

```
wine_scramble.shape
```

This returns 150x12 as the output.

The output dataset `wine_scramble` looks similar to the following screenshot:

	fixed acidity	volatile acidity	citric acid	residual sugar	chlorides	free sulfur dioxide	total sulfur dioxide	density	pH	sulphates	alcohol	quality
500	7.8	0.520	0.25	1.90	0.081	14	38	0.99840	3.43	0.65	9.0	6
501	10.4	0.440	0.73	6.55	0.074	38	76	0.99900	3.17	0.85	12.0	7
502	10.4	0.440	0.73	6.55	0.074	38	76	0.99900	3.17	0.85	12.0	7
503	10.5	0.260	0.47	1.90	0.078	6	24	0.99760	3.18	1.04	10.9	7
504	10.5	0.240	0.42	1.80	0.077	6	22	0.99760	3.21	1.05	10.8	7
505	10.2	0.490	0.63	2.90	0.072	10	26	0.99680	3.16	0.78	12.5	7

Fig. 3.43: First few rows of the scrambled data frame with rows from the data1_middle at the top

Since, the order of the appended dataset is `data1_middle`, `data1_head`, `data1_tail`, the rows contained in the `data1_middle` come at the top followed by the `data1_head` and `data1_tail` rows.

If you change the order of the stacking, the view of the appended dataset will change. Let's try that:

```
data1_head=data1.head(50)
data1_middle=data1[500:550]
data1_tail=data.tail(50)
wine_scramble=pd.concat([data1_head,data1_middle,data1_tail],axis=0)
wine_scramble
```

The output looks similar to the following screenshot, wherein, as expected the rows in the `data1_head` appear at the top:

	fixed acidity	volatile acidity	citric acid	residual sugar	chlorides	free sulfur dioxide	total sulfur dioxide	density	pH	sulphates	alcohol	quality
0	7.4	0.700	0.00	1.9	0.076	11	34	0.99780	3.51	0.56	9.4	5
1	7.8	0.880	0.00	2.6	0.098	25	67	0.99680	3.20	0.68	9.8	5
2	7.8	0.760	0.04	2.3	0.092	15	54	0.99700	3.26	0.65	9.8	5
3	11.2	0.280	0.56	1.9	0.075	17	60	0.99800	3.16	0.58	9.8	6
4	7.4	0.700	0.00	1.9	0.076	11	34	0.99780	3.51	0.56	9.4	5

Fig. 3.44: First few rows of the scrambled data frame with rows from the data1_head at the top

Let's see another scenario where the `concat` function comes as a savior. Suppose, you have to deal with the kind of data that comes in several files containing similar data. One example of such a scenario is the daily weather data of a city where the same metrics are tracked everyday but the data for each day is stored in a separate file. Many a time, when we do analysis of such files, we are required to append them into a single consolidated file before running any analyses or models.

I have curated some data that has these kind of properties to illustrate the method of consolidation into a single file. Navigate to the `Chapter 3` folder in the Google Drive and then to the `lotofdata` folder. You will see 332 CSV files, each named with its serial number. Each CSV file contains pollutant measure levels at different points of time in a single day. Each CSV file represents a day worth of pollutant measure data.

Let us go ahead and import the first file and have a look at it. Looking at one file will be enough, as the others will be very similar to this (exactly similar except the number of rows and the data points):

```
data=pd.read_csv('E:/Personal/Learning/Predictive Modeling Book/Book
Datasets/Merge and Join/lotofdata/001.csv')
data.head()
```

The one feature of this data is that it is very sparse and it contains a lot of missing values that would be visible once we look at the output of the preceding code snippet. The sparseness doesn't affect the analyses in this case because the dataset has sufficient rows with non-missing values. Even 100 rows with non-missing values should give us a good picture of the pollutant levels for a day. However, for the same reason, appending such a dataset becomes all the more important so that we have a significant amount of data with the non-missing values for our analyses.

Let us look at the first CSV file of the lot and the output of the preceding snippet:

	Date	sulfate	nitrate	ID
0	2003-01-01	NaN	NaN	1
1	2003-01-02	NaN	NaN	1
2	2003-01-03	NaN	NaN	1
3	2003-01-04	NaN	NaN	1
4	2003-01-05	NaN	NaN	1
5	2003-01-06	NaN	NaN	1
6	2003-01-07	NaN	NaN	1

Fig. 3.45: First few entries of the first file out of 332 CSV files

The size of the dataset is 1461x4 indicating that there are 1,461 rows and four columns. The name of the columns are **Date, sulfate, nitrate**, and **ID**. ID would be **1** for the first dataset, **2** for the 2nd, and so on. The number of rows in the other CSV files should be in the same range while the number of rows with non-missing values might vary.

Let us now move towards our goal of this discussion that is to demonstrate how to consolidate such small and similar files in a single file. To be able to do so, one needs to do the following in that sequence:

1. Import the first file.

2. Loop through all the files.

3. Import them one by one.

4. Append them to the first file.

5. Repeat the loop.

Let us now look at the code snippet, which will achieve this:

```
import pandas as pd
filepath='E:/Personal/Learning/Predictive Modeling Book/Book Datasets/
Merge and Join/lotofdata'
data_final=pd.read_csv('E:/Personal/Learning/Predictive Modeling Book/
Book Datasets/Merge and Join/lotofdata/001.csv')
for i in range(1,333):
    if i<10:
        filename='0'+'0'+str(i)+'.csv'
    if 10<=i<100:
        filename='0'+str(i)+'.csv'
    if i>=100:
        filename=str(i)+'.csv'

    file=filepath+'/'+filename
    data=pd.read_csv(file)

    data_final=pd.concat([data_final,data],axis=0)
```

In the code snippet, the `read_csv` is taking a file variable that consists of `filepath` and `filename` variables. The `if` condition takes care of the changing filenames (three conditions arise – first, when filename contains a single non-zero digit; second, when the filename contains two non-zero digits, and third, when the filename contains all the three non-zero digits).

The first file is imported and named as `data_final`. The subsequent files are imported and appended to `data_final`. The `for` loop runs over all the 332 files wherein the importing and appending of the files occur.

The size of the `data_final` data frame is 773548x4 rows, indicating that it has 7,73,548 rows because it contains the rows from all the 332 files.

If one looks at the last rows of the `data_final` data frame, one can confirm that all the files have been appended if the **ID** column contains 332 as value. This means that the last few rows come from the 332nd file.

Date	sulfate	nitrate	ID
2004-12-27	NaN	NaN	332
2004-12-28	NaN	NaN	332
2004-12-29	NaN	NaN	332
2004-12-30	NaN	NaN	332
2004-12-31	NaN	NaN	332

Fig. 3.46: Last few entries of the data_final data frame. They have ID as 332 indicating that they come from the 332nd CSV file.

The **ID** column indeed contains 332 observations, confirming that all the 332 files have been successfully appended.

Another way to confirm whether all the rows from all the files have been successfully appended or not, one can sum up the row numbers of each file and compare them to the row numbers of the final appended data frame. They should be equal if they have been appended successfully.

Let us check. We can use the same code as the preceding one, for this process with some minor tweaks. Let us see how:

```
import pandas as pd
filepath='E:/Personal/Learning/Predictive Modeling Book/Book Datasets/
Merge and Join/lotofdata'
data_final=pd.read_csv('E:/Personal/Learning/Predictive Modeling Book/
Book Datasets/Merge and Join/lotofdata/001.csv')
data_final_size=len(data_final)
for i in range(1,333):
    if i<10:
        filename='0'+'0'+str(i)+'.csv'
    if 10<=i<100:
        filename='0'+str(i)+'.csv'
    if i>=100:
        filename=str(i)+'.csv'

    file=filepath+'/'+filename
    data=pd.read_csv(file)
```

```
    data_final_size+=len(data)


    data_final=pd.concat([data_final,data],axis=0)
  print data_final_size
```

Here, we are summing-up the row numbers of all the files (in the line highlighted) and the summed-up number is printed in the last line. The output is 773,548; it confirms that the final data frame has the same number of rows as the sum of rows in all the files.

Merging/joining datasets

Merging or joining is a mission critical step for predictive modelling and, more often than not, while working on actual problems, an analyst will be required to do it. The readers who are familiar with relational databases know how there are multiple tables connected by a common key column across which the required columns are scattered. There can be instances where two tables are joined by more than one key column. The merges and joins in Python are very similar to a table merge/join in a relational database except that it doesn't happen in a database but rather on the local computer and that these are not tables, rather data frames in pandas. For people familiar with Excel, you can find similarity with the VLOOKUP function in the sense that both are used to get an extra column of information from a sheet/table joined by a key column.

There are various ways in which two tables/data frames can be merged/joined. The most commonly used ones are Inner Join, Left Join, Right Join, and so on. We will go in to detail and understand what each of these mean. But before that, let's go ahead and perform a simple merge to get a feel of how it is done.

We will be using a different dataset to illustrate the concept of merge and join. These datasets can be found in the Google Drive folder in Merge and the Join/ Medals folder. The main dataset Medals.csv contains details of medals won by individual players at different Olympic events. The two subsidiary datasets contain details of the nationality and sports of the individual player. What if we want to see the nationality or sport played by the player together with all the other medal information for each player? The answer is to merge both the datasets and to get the relevant columns. In data science parlance, merging, joining, and mapping are used synonymously; although, there are minor technical differences.

Let us import all of them and have a cursory look at them:

```
import pandas as pd
data_main=pd.read_csv('E:/Personal/Learning/Predictive Modeling Book/
Book Datasets/Merge and Join/Medals/Medals.csv')
data_main.head()
```

The `Medals.csv` looks similar to the following screenshot:

	Athlete	Age	Year	Closing Ceremony Date	Gold Medals	Silver Medals	Bronze Medals	Total Medals
0	Michael Phelps	23	2008	08/24/2008	8	0	0	8
1	Michael Phelps	19	2004	08/29/2004	6	0	2	8
2	Michael Phelps	27	2012	08/12/2012	4	2	0	6
3	Natalie Coughlin	25	2008	08/24/2008	1	2	3	6
4	Aleksey Nemov	24	2000	10/01/2000	2	1	3	6

Fig. 3.47: First few entries of the Medals dataset

As we can see, this is the information about the **Olympic Year** in which the medals were won, details of how many Gold, Silver, and Bronze medals were won and the **Age** of the player. There are 8,618 rows in the dataset. One more thing one might be interested to know about this dataset is how many unique athletes are there in the dataset, which will come in handy later when we learn and apply different kinds of joins:

```
a=data_main['Athlete'].unique().tolist()
len(a)
```

The output of this snippet is `6956`, which means that there are many athletes for whom we have records in the datasets. The other entries come because many athletes may have participated in more than one Olympics.

Let us now import the `Athelete Country Map.csv` and have a look at it:

```
country_map=pd.read_csv('E:/Personal/Learning/Predictive Modeling
Book/Book Datasets/Merge and Join/Medals/Athelete_Country_Map.csv')
country_map.head()
```

The output data frame looks similar to the following screenshot, with two columns: **Athlete** and **Country**:

	Athlete	Country
0	Michael Phelps	United States
1	Natalie Coughlin	United States
2	Aleksey Nemov	Russia
3	Alicia Coutts	Australia
4	Missy Franklin	United States

Fig. 3.48: First few entries of the Athelete_Country_Map dataset

There are 6,970 rows in this dataset. If you try to find out the unique number of athletes in this data frame, it will still be 6,956. The 14 extra rows come from the fact that some players have played for two countries in different Olympics and have won medals. Search for `Aleksandar Ciric` and you will find that he has played for both `Serbia` and `Serbia and Montenegro`.

 (**Disclaimer**: This might not be the actual case and this might be an issue with the mapping file, which can be taken care of by removing duplicate values, as we would show later in this chapter).

You can do this by using the following code snippet:

```
country_map[country_map['Athlete']=='Aleksandar Ciric']
```

	Athlete	Country
1029	Aleksandar Ciric	Serbia
1086	Aleksandar Ciric	Serbia and Montenegro

Fig. 3.49: Subsetting the country_map data frame for Aleksandar Ciric

Let us finally import the `Athelete Sports Map.csv` and have a look at it:

```
sports_map=pd.read_csv('E:/Personal/Learning/Predictive Modeling Book/
Book Datasets/Merge and Join/Medals/Athelete_Sports_Map.csv')
sports_map.head()
```

The `sports_map` data frame looks as shown in the following screenshot:

	Athlete	Sport
0	Michael Phelps	Swimming
1	Natalie Coughlin	Swimming
2	Aleksey Nemov	Gymnastics
3	Alicia Coutts	Swimming
4	Missy Franklin	Swimming

Fig. 3.50: First few entries of the Athelete_Sports_Map dataset

There are 6,975 rows in this dataset because, yes you guessed it right, there are very few athletes in this mapping data frame who have played more than one game and have won medals. Watch out for athletes, such as `Chen Jing`, `Richard Thompson` and `Matt Ryan` who have played more than one game.

This can be done by writing a code, such as the following snippet:

```
sports_map[(sports_map['Athlete']=='Chen Jing') | (sports_
map['Athlete']=='Richard Thompson') | (sports_map['Athlete']=='Matt
Ryan')]
```

The output looks similar to the following screenshot:

	Athlete	Sport
528	Richard Thompson	Athletics
1308	Chen Jing	Volleyball
1419	Chen Jing	Table Tennis
2727	Matt Ryan	Rowing
5003	Matt Ryan	Equestrian
5691	Richard Thompson	Baseball

Fig. 3.51: Subsetting the sports_map data frame for athletes Richard Thompson and Matt Ryan

Let's now merge the `data_main` and `country_map` data frames to get the country for all the athletes. There is a `merge` method in pandas, which facilitates this:

```
import pandas as pd
merged=pd.merge(left=data_main,right=country_map,left_
on='Athlete',right_on='Athlete')
merged.head()
```

The output looks, as follows. It has a country column as expected:

	Athlete	Age	Year	Closing Ceremony Date	Gold Medals	Silver Medals	Bronze Medals	Total Medals	Country
0	Michael Phelps	23	2008	08/24/2008	8	0	0	8	United States
1	Michael Phelps	19	2004	08/29/2004	6	0	2	8	United States
2	Michael Phelps	27	2012	08/12/2012	4	2	0	6	United States
3	Natalie Coughlin	25	2008	08/24/2008	1	2	3	6	United States
4	Natalie Coughlin	21	2004	08/29/2004	2	2	1	5	United States

Fig. 3.52: First few entries of the merged data frame. It has a country column.

The length of the merged data frame is 8,657, which is more than the total number of rows (8,618) in the `data_main` data frame. This is because when we join these two data frames without any specified conditions, an inner join is performed wherein the join happens based on the common key-values present in both the data frames. Also, we saw that some athletes have played for two countries and the entries for such athletes will be duplicated for such athletes. If you look at `Aleksandar Ciric` in the merged data frame, you will find something similar to this:

```
merged[merged['Athlete']=='Aleksandar Ciric']
```

	Athlete	Age	Year	Closing Ceremony Date	Gold Medals	Silver Medals	Bronze Medals	Total Medals	Country
1503	Aleksandar Ciric	30	2008	08/24/2008	0	0	1	1	Serbia
1504	Aleksandar Ciric	30	2008	08/24/2008	0	0	1	1	Serbia and Montenegro
1505	Aleksandar Ciric	26	2004	08/29/2004	0	1	0	1	Serbia
1506	Aleksandar Ciric	26	2004	08/29/2004	0	1	0	1	Serbia and Montenegro
1507	Aleksandar Ciric	22	2000	10/01/2000	0	0	1	1	Serbia
1508	Aleksandar Ciric	22	2000	10/01/2000	0	0	1	1	Serbia and Montenegro

Fig. 3.53 Subsetting the merged data frame for athlete Aleksandar Ciric

The problem is not with the type of join but with the kind of mapping file we have. This mapping file is one-many and hence the number increases because for each key multiple rows are created in such a case.

To rectify this issue, one can remove the duplicate entries from the `country_map` data frame and then perform the merge with `data_main`. Let's do that. This can be done using the `drop_duplicates` method, as shown:

```
country_map_dp=country_map.drop_duplicates(subset='Athlete')
```

The length of the `country_map_dp` is 6,956 rows, which is the same as the number of unique athletes. Let us now merge this with `data_main`.

```
merged_dp=pd.merge(left=data_main,right=country_map_dp,left_
on='Athlete',right_on='Athlete')
len(merged_dp)
```

The number of rows in the `merged_dp` is indeed 8,618, which is the actual number of rows in the `data_main`.

The next step is to merge `sports_map` with the `merged_dp` to get the country and sports along with other details in the same data frame.

We have seen similar issue of increase in the number of rows for `sports_map`, as was the case for `country_map` data frame. To take care of that, let's remove the duplicates from the `sports_map` before merging it with `merged_dp`:

```
sports_map_dp=sports_map.drop_duplicates(subset='Athlete')
len(sports_map_dp)
```

The length of the `sports_map_dp` is 6,956, which is the same as the number of rows in the `data_main` data frame, as expected.

The next step is to merge this with the `merge_pd` data frame to get the sports played by the athlete in the final merged table:

```
merged_final=pd.merge(left=merged_dp,right=sports_map_dp,left_
on='Athlete',right_on='Athlete')
merged_final.head()
```

	Athlete	Age	Year	Closing Ceremony Date	Gold Medals	Silver Medals	Bronze Medals	Total Medals	Country	Sport
0	Michael Phelps	23	2008	08/24/2008	8	0	0	8	United States	Swimming
1	Michael Phelps	19	2004	08/29/2004	6	0	2	8	United States	Swimming
2	Michael Phelps	27	2012	08/12/2012	4	2	0	6	United States	Swimming
3	Natalie Coughlin	25	2008	08/24/2008	1	2	3	6	United States	Swimming
4	Natalie Coughlin	21	2004	08/29/2004	2	2	1	5	United States	Swimming

Fig. 3.54: First few entries of the merged_final dataset. The duplicates from country_map were deleted before the merge

As we can see, the **Sport** column is present in the `merged_final` data frame after the merge. The `merged_final` data frame has 8,618 rows as expected.

Let us now look at various kinds of merge/joins that we can apply to two data frames. Although you would come across many kinds of joins in different texts, it is sufficient to know the concept behind the three of them — Inner Join, Left Join, and Right Join. If you consider the two tables/data frames as sets, then these joins can be well represented by **Venn Diagrams**.

Inner Join

The characteristics of the Inner Join are as follows:

- Returns a data frame containing rows, which have a matching value in both the original data frames being merged.

- The number of rows will be equal to the minimum of the row numbers of the two data frames. If data frame *A* containing 100 rows is being merged with data frame *B* having 80 rows, the merged data frame will have 80 rows.

- The Inner Join can be thought of as an intersection of two sets, as illustrated in the following figure:

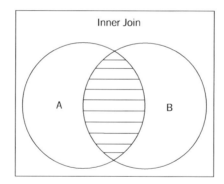

Fig. 3.55: Inner Join illustrated via a Venn diagram

Left Join

The characteristics of the Left Join are, as follows:

- Returns a data frame containing rows, which contains all the rows from the left data frame irrespective of whether it has a match in the right data frame or not.

- In the final data frame, the rows with no matches in the right data frame will return NAs in the columns coming from right data frame.

- The number of rows will be equal to the number of rows in the left data frame. If data frame *A* containing 100 rows is being merged with data frame *B* having 80 rows, the merged data frame would have 100 rows.

- The Left Join can be thought of as the set containing the entire left data frame, as illustrated in the following figure:

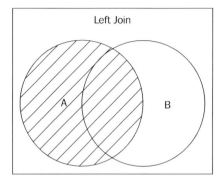

Fig. 3.56: Left Join illustrated via a Venn Diagram

Right Join

The characteristics of the Right Join are as follows:

- Returns a data frame containing rows, which contains all the rows from the right data frame irrespective of whether it has a match in the left data frame or not.

- In the final data frame, the rows with no matches in the left data frame will return NAs in the columns coming from left data frame.

- The number of rows will be equal to the number of rows in the left data frame. If data frame *A* containing 100 rows is being merged with data frame *B* having 80 rows, the merged data frame will have 80 rows

- The Right Join can be thought of as the set containing the entire right data frame, as illustrated in the following figure:

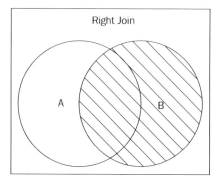

Fig. 3.57: Right Join illustrated via a Venn diagram

The comparison between join type and set operation is summarized in the following table:

Join type	Set operation
Inner Join	Intersection
Left Join	Set **A** (left data frame)
Right Join	Set **B** (right data frame)
Outer Join	Union

Let us see some examples of how different kinds of mappings actually work. For that, a little data preparation is needed. Currently, both our mapping files contain matching entries for all the rows in the actual data frame `data_main`. So, we can't see the effects of different kind of merges. Let's create a country and sports mapping file which doesn't have the information for some of the athletes and let's see how it reflects in the merged table. This can be done by creating a new data frame that doesn't have country/sports information for some of the athletes, as shown in the following code:

```
country_map_dlt=country_map_dp[(country_map_dp['Athlete']<>'Michael
Phelps') & (country_map_dp['Athlete']<>'Natalie Coughlin') & (country_
map_dp['Athlete']<>'Chen Jing')
                & (country_map_dp['Athlete']<>'Richard Thompson')
& (country_map_dp['Athlete']<>'Matt Ryan')]
len(country_map_dlt)
```

Using this snippet, we have created a `country_map_dlt` data frame that doesn't have country mapping for five athletes, that is `Michael Phelps`, `Natalie Coughlin`, `Chen Jing`, `Richard Thompson`, and `Matt Ryan`. The length of this data frame is 6,951; it is five less than the actual mapping file, indicating that the information for five athletes has been removed.

Let's do the same for `sports_map` as well as the `data_main` data frame using the following snippets:

```
sports_map_dlt=sports_map_dp[(sports_map_dp['Athlete']<>'Michael
Phelps') & (sports_map_dp['Athlete']<>'Natalie Coughlin') & (sports_
map_dp['Athlete']<>'Chen Jing')
                        & (sports_map_dp['Athlete']<>'Richard Thompson') &
(sports_map_dp['Athlete']<>'Matt Ryan')]
len(sports_map_dlt)
```

```
data_main_dlt=data_main[(data_main['Athlete']<>'Michael
Phelps') & (data_main['Athlete']<>'Natalie Coughlin') & (data_
main['Athlete']<>'Chen Jing')
                        & (data_main['Athlete']<>'Richard Thompson') &
(data_main['Athlete']<>'Matt Ryan')]
len(data_main_dlt)
```

The length of `data_main_dlt` becomes 8,605 because the `data_main` contains multiple rows for an athlete.

An example of the Inner Join

One example of Inner join would be to merge `data_main` data frame with `country_map_dlt`. This can be done using the following snippet:

```
merged_inner=pd.merge(left=data_main,right=country_map_
dlt,how='inner',left_on='Athlete',right_on='Athlete')
len(merged_inner)
```

This merge should give us information for the athletes who are present in both the data frames. As the `country_map_dlt` doesn't contain information about five athletes present in `data_main`, these five athletes wouldn't be a part of the merged table.

The length of the `merged_inner` comes out to be 8,605 (similar to `data_main_dlt`) indicating that it doesn't contain information about those five athletes.

An example of the Left Join

One example of Left Join would be to merge `data_main` data frame with `country_map_dlt`. This can be done using the following snippet:

```
merged_left=pd.merge(left=data_main,right=country_map_
dlt,how='left',left_on='Athlete',right_on='Athlete')
len(merged_left)
```

This merge should give us the information about all the athletes that are present in the left data frame (`data_main`) even if they aren't present in the right data frame (`country_map_dlt`). So, the `merged_left` data frame should contain 8,618 rows (similar to the `data_main`) even if the `country_map_dlt` doesn't contain information about five athletes present in `data_main`. These five athletes will have a **NaN** value in the **Country** column.

The length of `merged_left` indeed comes out to be 8,618. Let's check the `merged_left` for an athlete whose information is not present in the `country_map_dlt`. It should contain **NaN** for the **Country** column:

```
merged_left_slt=merged_left[merged_left['Athlete']=='Michael Phelps']
merged_left_slt
```

The output is similar to the following screenshot. It indeed contains **NaN** for **Michael Phelps**' **Country** because it doesn't have a mapping in `country_map_dlt`:

	Athlete	Age	Year	Closing Ceremony Date	Gold Medals	Silver Medals	Bronze Medals	Total Medals	Country
0	Michael Phelps	23	2008	08/24/2008	8	0	0	8	NaN
1	Michael Phelps	19	2004	08/29/2004	6	0	2	8	NaN
2	Michael Phelps	27	2012	08/12/2012	4	2	0	6	NaN

Fig. 3.58: Merged_left data frame sub-setted for Michael Phelps contains NaN values, as expected

An example of the Right Join

One example of Right Join will be to merge data frame `data_main` with `country_map_dlt`. This can be done using the following snippet:

```
merged_right=pd.merge(left=data_main_dlt,right=country_map_
dp,how='right',left_on='Athlete',right_on='Athlete')
len(merged_right)
```

This should contain the **NaN** values for the columns coming from `data_main_dlt`, in the rows where there is no athlete information in `data_main_dlt`.

As shown in the following table:

	Athlete	Age	Year	Closing Ceremony Date	Gold Medals	Silver Medals	Bronze Medals	Total Medals	Country
8605	Michael Phelps	NaN	NaN	NaN	NaN	NaN	NaN	NaN	United States

Fig. 3.59: merged_right data frame sub-setted for Michael Phelps contains NaN values, as expected

There will be one row created for each athlete who is not there in the `data_main_dlt` but is present in the `country_map_dp`. Hence, there will be five extra rows, one for each deleted athlete. The number of rows in the `merged_right` is thus equal to 8,610.

There are other joins like Outer Joins, which can be illustrated as the Union of two data frames. The Outer join would contain rows from both the data frames, even if they are not present in the other. It will contain `NaN` for the columns which it can't get values for. It can be easily performed setting the `how` parameter of the `merge` method to `outer`.

Summary of Joins in terms of their length

The effect of these joins can be more effectively explained if we summarize the number of samples present in the data frames that were used for merging and in the resultant data frames.

The first table provides the number of samples present in the data frames that were used for merging. All these data frames have been defined earlier in this section of the chapter:

Data frame	Length (# rows)
`data_main`	8618
`data_main_dlt`	8605
`country_map_dp`	6956
`country_map_dlt`	6951

This table provides the number of samples present in the merged data frames:

Merged data frame	Components	Length
merged_inner	data_main with country_map_dlt	8605
merged_left	data_main with country_map_dlt	8618
merged_right	data_main_dlt with country_ma_dp	8610

Summary

Quite a long chapter! Isn't it? But, this chapter will form the core of anything you learn and implement in data-science. Let us wrap-up the chapter by summarizing the key takeaways from the chapter:

- Data can be sub-setted in a variety of ways: by selecting a column, selecting few rows, selecting a combination of rows and columns; using `.ix` method and `[ ]` method, and creating new columns.

- Random numbers can be generated in a number of ways. There are many methods like `randint()`, `raandarrange()` in the `random` library of `numpy`. There are also methods like `shuffle` and `choice` to randomly select an element out of a list. `Randn()` and `uniform()` are used to generate random numbers following normal and uniform probability distributions. Random numbers can be used to run simulations and generate dummy data frames.

- The `groupby()` method creates a `groupby` element on which `aggregate`, `transform`, and `filter` operations can be applied. This is a good method to summarize data for each categorical variable at once.

- A data must be split between training and testing datasets before a modelling is performed. The training dataset is the one on which the model equations are developed. The testing dataset is used to test the performance of the model comparing the actual result (present in testing dataset) to the model output. There are various ways to perform this split. One can use `choice` and `shuffle`. Scikit-learn has a readymade method for this.

- Two datasets can be merged just like two tables in a relational database. There are various kind of joins—Inner, Left, Right, Outer, and so on. These joins can be understood better if the datasets are assumed analogous to sets. Inner Join is then Intersection, Outer Join is Union, and Left and Right joins are entire left and right data frame.

Wrangling data and bringing it in the form you desire is a big challenge before one proceeds to modelling. But, once done, it opens up a plethora of insights and information to be discovered using predictive models. As Bob Marley said, "If it is easy, it won't be amazing; if it is amazing, it won't be easy."

4
Statistical Concepts for Predictive Modelling

There are a few statistical concepts, such as hypothesis testing, p-values, normal distribution, correlation, and so on without which grasping the concepts and interpreting the results of predictive models becomes very difficult. Thus, it is very critical to understand these concepts, before we delve into the realm of predictive modelling.

In this chapter, we will be going through and learning these statistical concepts so that we can use them in the upcoming chapters. This chapter will cover the following topics:

- **Random sampling and central limit theorem**: Understanding the concept of random sampling through an example and illustrating the central limit theorem's application through an example. These two concepts form the backbone of hypothesis testing.

- **Hypothesis testing**: Understanding the meaning of the terms, such as null hypothesis, alternate hypothesis, confidence intervals, p-value, significance level, and so on. A step-by-step guide to implement a hypothesis test, followed by an example.

- **Chi-square testing**: Calculation of chi-square statistic. A description of usage of chi-square tests with a couple of examples.

- **Correlation**: The meaning and significance of correlations between two variables, the meaning and significance of correlation coefficients and calculating and visualizing the correlation between variables of a dataset.

Random sampling and the central limit theorem

Let's try to understand these two important statistical concepts using an example. Suppose one wants to find the average age of one state of India, lets say Tamil Nadu. Now, the safest and brute-force way of doing this will be to gather age information from each citizen of Tamil Nadu and calculate the average for all these ages. But, going to each citizen and asking their age or asking them to tell their age by some method will take a lot of infrastructure and time. It is such a humongous task that census, which attempts to do just that, happens once a decade and what will happen if you decided to do so in a non-census year?

The statisticians face such issues all the time. The answer lies in random sampling. Random sampling means that you take a group of 1000 individuals (or 10000, depending on your capacity, obviously the more the merrier) and calculate the average for this group. You call this *A1*. Getting to this is easier as 1000 or 10000 is within your reach. Then you select a second group of 1000 or 10000 people and calculate their average. You call this *A2*. You do this 100 times or 1000 times and call them *A3, A4,..., A100* or *A3, A4,..., A1000*.

Then according to the most fundamental theorem in statistics called the central limit theorem:

- The average of *A1, A2,..., A100* will be a good estimator of the average age of the residents of Tamil Nadu. If *Am* is the estimated average age of the residents of Tamil Nadu, then it is given by:

$$Am = A1 + A2 + \ldots\ldots + A100 / 100$$

- If the number of such samples is sufficiently large, then the distribution of these averages will roughly follow a normal distribution. In other words, *A1, A2,..., A100* will be normally distributed.

Now, the thing is that we are no more interested in finding the exact value of the average age, but we are settling for an estimator of the same. In such a case, we will have to make do with defining a range of values in which the actual value might lie. Since we have assumed a normal distribution for the average age values of these groups, we can apply all the properties of a normal distribution to quantify the chances of this average age being greater or lesser than a certain number.

Hypothesis testing

The concept we just discussed in the preceding section is used for a very important technique in statistics, called hypothesis testing. In hypothesis testing, we assume a hypothesis (generally related to the value of the estimator) called null hypothesis and try to see whether it holds true or not by applying the rules of a normal distribution. We have another hypothesis called alternate hypothesis.

Null versus alternate hypothesis

There is a catch in deciding what will be the null hypothesis and what will be the alternate hypothesis. The null hypothesis is the initial premise or something that we assume to be true as yet. The alternate hypothesis is something we aren't sure about and are proposing as an alternate premise (almost often contradictory to the null hypothesis) which might or might not be true.

So, when someone is doing a quantitative research to calibrate the value of an estimator, the known value of the parameter is taken as the null hypothesis while the new found value (from the research) is taken as the alternate hypothesis. In our case of finding the mean age of Tamil Nadu, we can say that based on the rich demographic dividend of India, a researcher can claim that the mean age should be less than 35. This can serve as the null hypothesis. If a new agency claims otherwise (that it is greater than 35), then it can be termed as the alternate hypothesis.

Z-statistic and t-statistic

Assume that the value of the parameter assumed in the null hypothesis is A_o. Take a random sample of 100 or 1000 people or occurrences of the event and calculate the mean of the parameter, such as mean age, mean delivery time for pizza, mean income, and so on. We can call it A_m. According to the central limit theorem, the distribution of population means that random samples will follow a normal distribution.

The Z-statistic is calculated to convert a normally distributed variable (the distribution of population mean of age) to a standard normal distribution. This is because the probability values for a variable following the standard normal distribution can be obtained from a precalculated table. The Z-statistic is given by the following formula:

$$Z = (Am - Ao) / (\sigma / \sqrt{n})$$

In the preceding formula, the σ stands for the standard deviation of the population/occurrences of events and n is the number of people in the sample.

Now, there can be two cases that can arise:

- **Z- test (normal distribution)**: The researcher knows the standard deviation for the parameter from his/her past experience. A good example of this is the case of pizza delivery time; you will know the standard deviation from past experiences:

$$Z = (Am - Ao)/(\sigma/\sqrt{n})$$

  A_o (from the null hypothesis) and n are known. A_m is calculated from the random sample. This kind of test is done when the standard deviation is known and is called the **z-test** because the distribution follows the normal distribution and the standard-normal value obtained from the preceding formula is called the **Z-value**.

- **t-test (Student-t distribution)**: The researcher doesn't know the standard deviation of the population. This might happen because there is no such data present from the historical experience or the number of people/event is very small to assume a normal distribution; hence, the estimation of mean and standard deviation by the formula described earlier. An example of such a case is a student's marks in an exam, age of a population, and so on. In this case, the mean and standard deviation become unknown and the expression assumes a distribution other than normal distribution and is called a **Student-t** distribution. The standard value in this case is called **t-value** and the test is called **t-test**.

  Standard distribution can also be estimated once the mean is estimated, if the number of samples is large enough. Let us call the estimated standard distribution S; then the S is estimated as follows:

$$S = \Sigma(Ai - Ao)^2 / (n-1)$$

  The t-statistic is calculated as follows:

$$t = (Am - Ao)/(S/\sqrt{n})$$

The difference between the two cases, as you can see, is the distribution they follow. The first one follows a normal distribution and calculates a Z-value. The second one follows a Student-t distribution and calculates a t-value. These statistics that is Z-statistics and t-statistics are the parameters that help us test our hypothesis.

Confidence intervals, significance levels, and p-values

Let us go back a little in the last chapter and remind ourselves about the cumulative probability distribution.

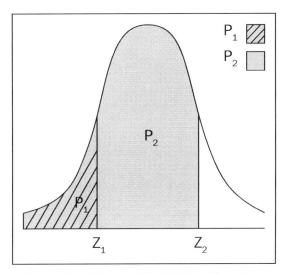

Fig. 4.1: A typical normal distribution with p-values

Let us have a look to the preceding figure, it shows a standard normal distribution. Suppose, Z1 and Z2 are two Z-statistics corresponding to two values of random variable and *p1* and *p2* are areas enclosed by the distribution curve to the right of those values. In other words, *p1* is the probability that the random variable will take a value lesser than or equal to Z1 and *p2* is the probability that the random variable will take a value greater than Z2.

If we represent the random variable by X, then we can write:

$$P(X < Z1) = p1$$
$$P(X < Z2) = p2$$

Also, since the sum of all the exclusive probabilities is always *1*, we can write:

$$P(X > Z1) = 1 - p1$$
$$P(X > Z2) = 1 - p2$$

For well-defined distributions, such as the normal distribution, one can define an interval in which the value of the random variable will lie with a confidence level (read probability). This interval is called the confidence interval. For example, for a normal distribution with mean μ and standard deviation σ, the value of the random variable will lie in the interval $[\mu\text{-}3\sigma, \mu\text{+}3\sigma]$ with 99% probability. For any estimator (essentially a random variable) that follows a normal distribution, one can define a confidence interval if we decide on the confidence (or probability) level. One can think of confidence intervals as thresholds of the accepted values to hold a null hypothesis as true. If the value of the estimator (random variable) lies in this range, it will be statistically correct to say that the null hypothesis is correct.

To define a confidence interval, one needs to define a confidence (or probability level). This probability needs to be defined by the researcher depending on the context. Lets call this *p*. Instead of defining this probability *p*, one generally defines (*1-p*) that is called level of significance. Let us represent it by *ß*. This represents the probability that the null hypothesis won't be true. This is defined by the user for each test and is usually of the order of 0.01-0.1.

An important concept to learn here is the probability value or just a p-value of a statistic. It is the probability that the random variable assumes, it's a value greater than the Z-value or t-value:

$$p - value = P(X > Z)$$

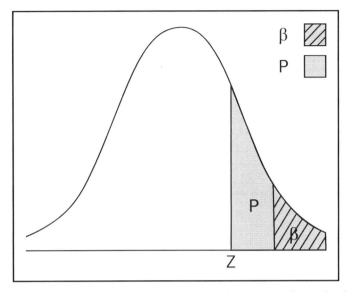

Fig. 4.2: A typical normal distribution with p-values and significance level

Now, this Z-value and the p-value has been obtained assuming that the null hypothesis is true. So, for the null hypothesis to be accepted, the Z-value has to lie outside the area enclosed by β. In other words, for the null hypothesis to be true, the p-value has to be greater than the significance level, as shown in the preceding figure.

To summarize:

- Accept the null hypothesis and reject the alternate hypothesis if *p-value>ß*
- Accept the alternate hypothesis and reject the null hypothesis if *p-value<ß*

Different kinds of hypothesis test

Due to the symmetry and nature of the normal distribution, there are three kinds of possible hypothesis tests:

- Left-tailed
- Right-tailed
- Two-tailed

Left-tailed: This is the case when the alternate hypothesis is a "less-than" type. The hypothesis testing is done on the left tail of the distribution and hence the name. In this case, for:

- Accepting a null hypothesis and rejecting an alternate hypothesis the *p-value>ß* or $Z > Z_\beta$

- Accepting an alternate hypothesis and rejecting a null hypothesis the *p-value<ß* or $Z < Z_\beta$

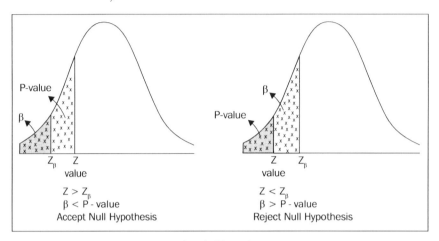

Fig. 4.3: Left-tailed hypothesis testing

Right-tailed: This is the case when the alternate hypothesis is of greater than type. The hypothesis testing is done on the right tail of the distribution, hence the name. In this case, for:

- Accepting a null hypothesis and rejecting an alternate hypothesis the *p-value>ß* or $Z < Z_\beta$

- Accepting an alternate hypothesis and rejecting a null hypothesis the *p-value<ß* or $Z > Z_\beta$

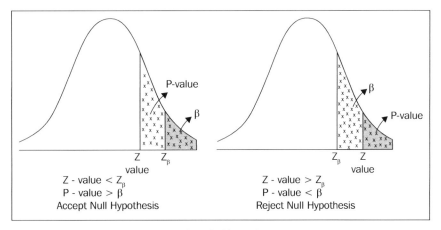

Fig. 4.4: Right-tailed hypothesis testing

Two-tailed: This is the case when the alternate hypothesis has an inequality—less than or more than is not mentioned. It is just an OR operation over both kind of tests. If either of the left- or right-tailed tests reject the null hypothesis, then it is rejected. The hypothesis testing is done on both the tails of the distribution; hence, the name.

A step-by-step guide to do a hypothesis test

So how does one accept one hypothesis and reject the other? There has to be a logical way to do this. Let us summarize and put to use whatever we have learned till now in this section, to make a step-by-step plan to do a hypothesis test. Here is a step-by-step guide to do a hypothesis test:

1. Define your null and alternate hypotheses. The null hypothesis is something that is already stated and is assumed to be true, call it H_o. Also, assume that the value of the parameter in the null hypothesis is A_o.

2. Take a random sample of 100 or 1000 people/occurrences of events and calculate the value of estimator (for example, mean of the parameter that is mean age, mean delivery time for pizza, mean income, and so on). You can call it *Am*.

3. Calculate the standard normal value or Z-value as it is called using this formula:

$$Z = (Am - Ao)/(\sigma / \sqrt{n})$$

In the preceding formula, σ is the standard deviation of the population or occurrences of events and n is the number of people in the sample.

The probability associated with the Z-value calculated in step 3 is compared with the significance level of the test to determine whether null hypothesis will be accepted or rejected.

An example of a hypothesis test

Let us see an example of hypothesis testing now. A famous pizza place claims that their mean delivery time is 20 minutes with a standard deviation of 3 minutes. An independent market researcher claims that they are deflating the numbers for market gains and the mean delivery time is actually more. For this, he selected a random sample of 64 deliveries over a week and found that the mean is 21.2 minutes. Is his claim justified or the pizza place is correct in their claim? Assume a significance level of 5%.

First things first, let us define a null and alternate hypothesis:

$$Ho : Do = 20 (\textit{What the pizza guy claims})$$
$$Ha : Do > 20 (\textit{what researcher claims})$$
$$\sigma = 3, n = 64 \, and \, Dm = 24, \beta = 0.05$$

Let us calculate the Z-value:

$$Z = (21.2 - 20)/\left(3/\sqrt{64}\right) = 3.2$$

When we see the standard normal table for this Z-value, we find out that this value has an area of .9993 to the left of it; hence, the area to the right is **1-.99931**, which is less than **0.05**.

Hence, *p-value<ß*. Thus, the null hypothesis is rejected. This can be summarized in the following figure:

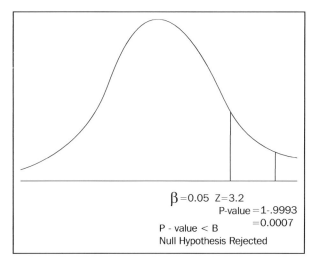

Fig. 4.5: Null Hypothesis is rejected because p-value<significance level

Hence, the researcher's claim that the mean delivery time is more than 20 minutes is statistically correct.

Chi-square tests

The chi-square test is a statistical test commonly used to compare observed data with the expected data assuming that the data follows a certain hypothesis. In a sense, this is also a hypothesis test. You assume one hypothesis, which your data will follow and calculate the expected data according to that hypothesis. You already have the observed data. You calculate the deviation between the observed and expected data using the statistics defined in the following formula:

$$chi - square\,value(g) = \Sigma(O - E)^2 \,/\, E$$

Where O is the observed value and E is the expected value while the summation is over all the data points.

The chi-square test can be used to do the following things:

- Show a causal relationship or independence between one input and output variable. We assume that they are independent and calculate the expected values. Then we calculate the chi-square value. If the null hypothesis is rejected, it suggests a relationship between the two variables. The relationship is not just by chance but statistically proven.

- Check whether the observed data is coming from a fair/unbiased source. If the observed data is more skewed towards one extreme, compared to the expected data, then it is not coming from a fair source. But, if it is very close to the expected value then it is.

- Check whether a data is too good to be true. As, it is a random experiment and we don't expect the values to toe the assumed hypothesis. If they do toe the assumed hypothesis, then the data has probably been tampered to make it look good and is too good to be true.

Let us create a hypothetical experiment where a coin is tossed 10 times. How many times do you expect it to turn heads or tails? Five, right? Now, what if we do this experiment 1000 times and record the scores (number of heads and tails). Suppose we observed heads 553 times and a tails in the rest of the trials:

$$Ho : The\ proportion\ of\ head\ and\ tail\ is\ 0.5$$

$$Ha : The\ proportion\ is\ not\ 0.5$$

	Head	Tail
Observed	553	447
Expected	1000*0.5=500	1000*0.5=500

Let us calculate the chi-square value:

$$g = \left[(553 - 500)^2 + (447 - 500)^2 \right] / 500 = 11.236$$

This chi-square value is compared to the value on a chi-square distribution for a given degree of freedom and a given significance level. The degrees of freedom is the number of categories -1. In this case, it is *2-1=1*. Let us assume a significance level of 0.05.

The chi-square distribution looks a little different than the normal distribution. It also has a peak but has a much longer tail than the normal distribution and is only on one side. As the degree of freedom increases, they start looking similar to a normal distribution:

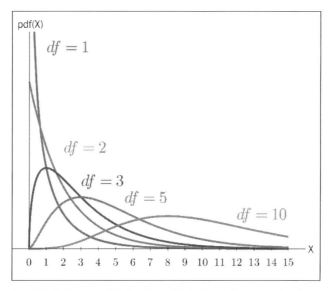

Fig. 4.6: Chi-square distribution with different degrees of freedom

When we look at the chi-square distribution table for a degree of freedom 1 and a significance level of 0.05, we get a value of 3.841. At a significance level of 0.01, we get 6.635. In both the cases, the chi-square statistic is greater than the value from the chi-square distribution, meaning that the chi-square statistic lies on the right of the value from the distribution table.

Hence, the null hypothesis is rejected. That means that the coin is not fair.

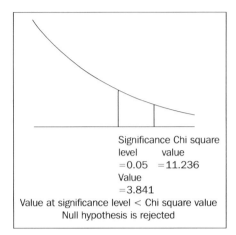

Fig. 4.7: Null hypothesis is rejected because the value of the chi-square statistic at the significance level is less than the value of the chi-square statistic

Let us look at another example where we want to prove that the gender of a student and the subjects they choose are independent.

Suppose, in a group of students, the following table represents the number of boys and girls who have taken Maths, Arts, and Commerce, as their main subjects.

The observed number of boys and girls in each subject is as shown in the following table:

	Maths	Arts	Commerce	Total
Boys	68	52	90	200
Girls	28	37	35	100
Total	96	89	125	300

If the choice of the subjects is irrespective of the gender, then the expected number of boys and girls taking different subjects is, as follows:

	Maths	Arts	Commerce	Total
Boys	(200/300)*96=64	(200/300)*89=59.3	(200/300)*125=83.3	200
Girls	(100/300)*96=32	(100/300)*89=29.7	(100/300)*125=41.7	100
Total	96	89	125	300

The deviation element is calculated for each cell using the $(O-E)^2/E$ formula:

	Maths	Arts	Commerce
Boys	$(68-64)^2/64$	$(52-59.3)^2/59.3$	$(90-83.3)^2/83.3$
Girls	$(28-32)^2/32$	$(37-29.7)^2/29.7$	$(35-41.7)^2/41.7$

On calculating and summing up all the values, the chi-square value comes out to be 5.05. The degree of freedom is the number of categories-1, which amounts to *[(3x2)-1=5]*. Let us assume a significance level of 0.05.

Looking at the chi-square distribution, one can find out that for a 5-degree freedom chi-square distribution, the value of the chi-square statistic at a significance level of 0.05 is 11.07.

The calculated chi-square statistic < chi-square statistic (at significance level=0.05).

Since, the chi-square statistic lies on the left of the value at the significance level, the null hypothesis can't be rejected. Hence, the choice of subjects is independent of the gender.

Correlation

Another statistical idea which is very basic and important while finding a relation between two variables is called correlation. In a way, one can say that the concept of correlation is the premise of predictive modelling, in the sense that the correlation is the factor relying on which we say that we can predict outcomes.

A good correlation between two variables suggests that there is a sort of dependence between them. If one is changed, the change will be reflected in the other as well. One can say that a good correlation certifies a mathematical relation between two variables and due to this mathematical relationship, we might be able to predict outcomes. This mathematical relation can be anything. If x and y are two variables, which are correlated, then one can write:

$$Y = f(x)$$

If f is a linear function, then a and b are linearly correlated. If f is an exponential function, then a and b are exponentially correlated:

$$Linear\ correlation: y = ax + b$$

$$Exponential\ correlation: y = \exp(a) + b$$

The degree of correlation between the two variables x and y is quantified by the following equation:

$$correlation\ coefficient(h) = \frac{\Sigma((x - xm) * (y - ym))}{\sqrt{\Sigma(x - xm)^{2*}\ \Sigma(y - ym)^2}}$$

Where xm and ym are mean values of x and y

A few points to note about the correlation coefficient are as follows:

- The value of the correlation coefficient can range from -1 to 1, that is -1<h<1.

- A positive correlation coefficient means that there is a direct relationship between the two variables; if one variable increases, the other variable will also increase and if one decreases the other will decrease as well.

- A positive correlation coefficient means that there is an inverse relationship between the two variables; if one variable increases, the other variable will decrease and if one decreases the other will increase.

- The more the value of the correlation coefficient, the stronger the relation between the two variables.

Although, a strong correlation suggests that there is some kind of a relationship that can be leveraged to predict one based on the other; it doesn't imply that its relation with the other variable is the only factor explaining this, there can be several others. Hence, the most often used quote related to correlation is, *"Correlation doesn't imply causation."*

Let us try to understand this concept better by looking at a dataset and trying to find the correlation between the variables. The dataset that we will be looking at is a very popular dataset about various costs incurred on advertising by different mediums and the sales for a particular product. We will be using it later to explore the concepts of linear regression. Let us import the dataset and calculate the correlation coefficients:

```
import pandas as pd
advert=pd.read_csv('E:/Personal/Learning/Predictive Modeling Book/Book
Datasets/Linear Regression/Advertising.csv')
advert.head()
```

	TV	Radio	Newspaper	Sales
0	230.1	37.8	69.2	22.1
1	44.5	39.3	45.1	10.4
2	17.2	45.9	69.3	9.3
3	151.5	41.3	58.5	18.5
4	180.8	10.8	58.4	12.9

Fig. 4.8: Dummy dataset

Let us try to find out the correlation between the advertisement costs on TV and the resultant sales. The following code will do the job:

```
import numpy as np
advert['corrn']=(advert['TV']-np.mean(advert['TV']))*(advert['Sales']-
np.mean(advert['Sales']))
advert['corrd1']=(advert['TV']-np.mean(advert['TV']))**2
advert['corrd2']=(advert['Sales']-np.mean(advert['Sales']))**2
corrcoeffn=advert.sum()['corrn']
corrcoeffd1=advert.sum()['corrd1']
corrcoeffd2=advert.sum()['corrd2']
corrcoeffd=np.sqrt(corrcoeffd1*corrcoeffd2)
corrcoeff=corrcoeffn/corrcoeffd
corrcoeff
```

In this code snippet, the formula written above has been converted to code. The value of the correlation coefficient comes out to be 0.78 indicating that there is a descent in positive correlation between TV-advertisement costs and sales; it implies that if the TV-advertisement cost is increased, as a result sales will increase.

Let us convert the preceding calculation to a function, so that we can calculate all the pairs of correlation coefficients very fast just by replacing the variable names. One can do that using the following snippet wherein a function is defined to parameterize the name of the data frame and the column names for which the correlation coefficient is to be calculated:

```
def corrcoeff(df,var1,var2):
    df['corrn']=(df[var1]-np.mean(df[var1]))*(df[var2]-np.
mean(df[var2]))
    df['corrd1']=(df[var1]-np.mean(df[var1]))**2
    df['corrd2']=(df[var2]-np.mean(df[var2]))**2
    corrcoeffn=df.sum()['corrn']
    corrcoeffd1=df.sum()['corrd1']
    corrcoeffd2=df.sum()['corrd2']
    corrcoeffd=np.sqrt(corrcoeffd1*corrcoeffd2)
    corrcoeff=corrcoeffn/corrcoeffd
    return corrcoeff
```

This function can be used to calculate correlation coefficient for any two variables of any data frame.

For example, to calculate the correlation between *TV* and *Sales* columns of the `advert` data frame, we can write it as follows:

$$TV\ \&\ Sales \qquad corrcoeff\,(advert, 'TV', 'Sales')\quad 0.78$$
$$Radio\ \&\ Sales \qquad corrcoeff\,(advert, 'Radio', 'Sales')\quad 0.57$$

We can summarize the pair-wise correlation coefficients between the variables in the following table:

	TV	**Radio**	**Newspaper**	**Sales**
TV	1	0.05	0.06	0.78
Radio	0.05	1	0.35	0.57
Newspaper	0.06	0.35	1	0.23
Sales	0.78	0.57	0.23	1

This table is called **Correlation Matrix**. As you can see, it is a symmetric matrix because the correlation between **TV** and **Sales** will be the same as that between **Sales** and **TV**. Along the diagonal, all the entries are **1** because, by definition, the correlation of a variable with itself will always be **1**. As can be seen, the strongest correlation can be found between TV advertisement cost and sales.

Let us see the nature of this correlation by plotting `TV` and `Sales` variables of the advert data frame. We can do this using the following code snippet:

```
import matplotlib.pyplot as plt
%matplotlib inline
plt.plot(advert['TV'],advert['Sales'],'ro')
plt.title('TV vs Sales')
```

The result is similar to the following plot:

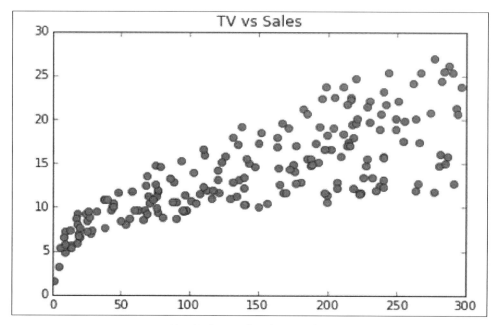

Fig. 4.9: Scatter plot of TV vs Sales

Looking at this plot, we can see that the points are more or less compact and not scattered far away and as the TV advertisement cost increases, the sales also increase. This is the characteristic of two variables that are positively correlated. This is supported by a strong correlation coefficient of 0.78.

Let us plot the variables and see how they are distributed to corroborate their correlation coefficient. For `Radio` and `Sales`, this can be plotted as follows:

```
import matplotlib.pyplot as plt
%matplotlib inline
plt.plot(advert['Radio '],advert['Sales'],'ro')
plt.title('Radio vs Sales')
```

The plot we get is as shown in the following figure:

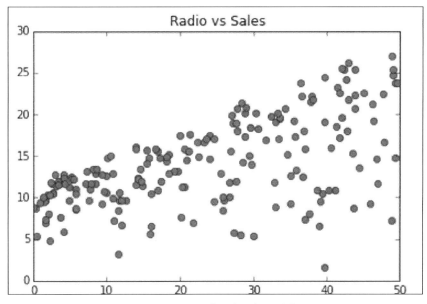

Fig. 4.10: Scatter plot of Radio vs Sales

For Radio and Sales, the points are a little more scattered than TV versus Sales and this is corroborated by the fact that the correlation coefficient for this pair (0.57) is less than that for TV and Sales (0.78).

For plotting `Newspaper vs Sales` data, we can write something similar to the following code:

```
import matplotlib.pyplot as plt
%matplotlib inline
plt.plot(advert['Newspaper'],advert['Sales'],'ro')
plt.title('Newspaper vs Sales')
```

The output plot looks similar to the following figure:

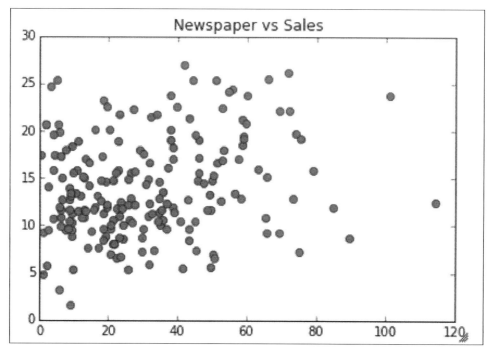

Fig. 4.11: Scatter plot of Newspaper vs Sales

For Newspaper and Sales, the points are way more scattered than in the case of TV and Sales and Radio and Sales. This is further strengthened by a small correlation coefficient of 0.23 between Newspaper and Sales, compared to 0.78 between TV and Sales, and 0.57 between Radio and Sales.

Summary

In this chapter, we skimmed through the basic concepts of statistics. Here is a brief summary of the concepts we learned:

- Hypothesis testing is used to test the statistical significance of a hypothesis. The one which already exists or is assumed to be true is a null hypothesis, the one which someone is not sure about or is being proposed as an alternate premise is an alternate hypothesis.

- One needs to calculate a statistic and the associated p-value to conduct the test.

- Hypothesis testing (p-values) is used to test the significance of the estimates of the coefficients calculated by the model.

- The chi-square test is used to test the causal relationship between a predictor and an input variable. It can also be used to check whether the data is fair or fake.

- The correlation coefficient can range from -1 to 1. The closer it is to the extremes, the stronger is the relationship between the two variables.

Linear regression is part of the family of algorithms called supervised algorithms as the dataset on which they are built has an output variable. In a sense, one can say that this output variable governs or supervises the development of the model and hence the name. More on this is covered in the next chapter.

5

Linear Regression
with Python

If you have mastered the content of the last two chapters, implementing predictive models will be a cake walk. Remember the 80-20% split between the data cleaning + wrangling and modelling? Then what is the need of dedicating a full chapter to illustrate the model? The reason is not about running a predictive model; it is about understanding the mathematics (algorithms) that goes behind the ready-made methods which we will be using to implement these algorithms. It is about interpreting the swathe of results these models spew after the model implementation and making sense of them in the context. Thus, it is of utmost importance to understand the mathematics behind the algorithms and the result parameters of these models.

With this chapter onwards, we will deal with one predictive modelling algorithm in each chapter. In this chapter, we will discuss a technique called **linear regression**. It is the most basic and generic technique to create a predictive model out of a historical dataset with an output variable.

The agenda of this chapter is to thoroughly understand the mathematics behind linear regression and the results generated by it by illustrating its implementation on various datasets. The broad agenda of this chapter is, as follows:

- **The maths behind the linear regression**: How does the model work? How is the equation of the model created based on the dataset? What are the assumptions for this calculation?

- **Implementing linear regression with Python**: There are a couple of ready-made methods to implement linear regression in Python. Instead of using these ready-made methods, one can write one's own Python code snippet for the entire calculation with custom inputs. However, as linear regression is a regularly used algorithm, the use of ready-made methods is quite common. Its implementation from scratch is generally used to illustrate the maths behind the algorithm.

- **Making sense of result parameters**: There will be tons of result parameters, such as slope, co-efficient, p-values, and so on. It is very important to understand what each parameter means and the range their values lie in, for the model to be an efficient model.

- **Model validation**: Any predictive model needs to be validated. One common method of validating is splitting the available dataset into training and testing datasets, as discussed in the previous chapter. The training dataset is used to develop the model while the testing is used to compare the result predicted by the model to the actual values.

- **Handling issues related to linear regression**: Issues, such as multi-collinearity, handling categorical variables, non-linear relationships, and so on come up while implementing a linear regression; these need to be taken care of to ensure an efficient model.

Before we kick-start the chapter, let's discuss what a model means and entails. A mathematical/statistical/predictive model is nothing but a mathematical equation consisting of input variables yielding an output when values of the input variables are provided. For example, let us, for a moment, assume that the price (P) of a house is linearly dependent upon its size (S), amenities (A), and availability of transport (T). The equation will look like this:

$$P = a_1 * S + a_2 * A + a_3 * T$$

This is called the **model** and the variables α_1, α_2, and α_3 are called the variable coefficients. The variable P is the predicted output while the S, A, and T are input variables. Here, S, A, and T are known but α_1, α_2, and α_3 are not. These parameters are estimated using the historical input and output data. Once, the value of these parameters is found, the equation (model) becomes ready for testing. Now, S, A, and T can be numerical, binary, categorical, and so on; while P can also be numerical, binary, or categorical and it is this need to tackle various types of variables that gives rise to a large number of models.

Understanding the maths behind linear regression

Let us assume that we have a hypothetical dataset containing information about the costs of several houses and their sizes (in square feet):

Size (square feet) X	Cost (lakh INR) Y
1500	45
1200	38
1700	48
800	27

There are two kinds of variables in a model:

- The input or predictor variable, the one which helps predict the value of output variable
- The output variable, the one which is predicted

In this case, cost is the output variable and the size is the input variable. The output and the input variables are generally referred as Y and X respectively.

In the case of linear regression, we assume that Y (*Cost*) is a linear function of X (*Size*) and to estimate Y, we write:

$$Y_e = \alpha + \beta * X \text{ or } Cost = \alpha + \beta * Size$$

Where Y_e is the estimated or predicted value of Y based on our linear equation.

The purpose of linear regression is to find statistically significant values of a and β, which minimize the difference between Y and Y_e. If we are able to determine the values of these two parameters satisfying these conditions, then we will have an equation which we can predict the values of Y, given the value of X.

So, to summarize, linear regression (like any other supervised algorithm) requires historical data with one output variable and one or more than one input variables to make a model/equation, using which output variables can be calculated/predicted if the input variable is present. In the preceding case, if we find the value of $\alpha=2$ and $\beta=.3$, then the equation will be:

$$Y_e = 2 + .03X$$

Using this equation, we can find the cost of a home of any size. For a 900 square feet house, the cost will be:

$$Y_e = 2 + 900 * .03 = 29 units$$

The next question that we can ask is how do we estimate a and β. We use a method called least square sum of the difference between Y and Y_e. The difference between the Y and Y_e can be represented as e:

$$e = (Y - Y_e)$$

Thus, the objective is to minimize $\sum(Y - Ye)^2 = \sum(Y - (\alpha + \beta * X))^2$; the summation is over all the data points.

We can also minimize: $\sum e^2 = e_1^2 + e_2^2 + \ldots\ldots en^2$, where n is the number of data points.

Using calculus, we can show that the values of the unknown parameters are as follows:

$$\beta = \sum(Xi - Xm)(Yi - Ym) / \sum(Xi - Xm)^2$$
$$\alpha = Ym - \beta * Xm$$

where Xm – mean of X values and Ym-mean of Y values

If you are interested to know how these formulae come up, you can go through the following information box, which describes the derivation. The steps for this derivation can be summarized, as follows:

- Take partial derivatives of e^2 with respect to all the variable coefficients and equate them to 0 (at maxima or minima, the derivative of a function is 0). This will give us as many equations, as there are variables:

$$\frac{\partial S(\hat{\alpha}, \hat{\beta})}{\partial \hat{\alpha}} = -2\sum_{i=1}^{n}\left(y_i - \hat{\alpha} - \hat{\beta} * x_i\right) = 0$$

$$\frac{\partial S(\hat{\alpha}, \hat{\beta})}{\partial \hat{\beta}} = -2\sum_{i=1}^{n}\left(y_i - \hat{\alpha} - \hat{\beta} * x_i\right)x_i = 0$$

where S= (Y-Y$_e$), Y-actual value of Y, Y$_e$-estimated/predicted value of Y= a+ ß*X

- Solve these equations to get the values of the variable coefficients:

$$\Pi : \sum_{i=1}^{n} \left(yi - \hat{\alpha} - \hat{\beta} * x_i \right) x_i = 0$$

$$\Rightarrow \sum_{i=1}^{n} y_i x_i - \hat{\alpha} x_i - \hat{\beta} x_i^2 = 0$$

$$\Rightarrow \sum_{i=1}^{n} y_i x_i - \left(\overline{y} - \hat{\beta} \overline{x} \right) x_i - \hat{\beta} x_i^2 = 0$$

$$\Rightarrow \sum_{i=1}^{n} y_i x_i - \overline{y} x_i + \hat{\beta} \overline{x} x_i - \hat{\beta} x_i^2 = 0 \Rightarrow \sum_{i=1}^{n} \left(y_i - \overline{y} + \hat{\beta} \overline{x} - \hat{\beta} x_i \right) x_i = 0$$

$$\sum_{i=1}^{n} y_i - \overline{y} + \hat{\beta} \left(\overline{x} - x_i \right) = 0 \Rightarrow \sum_{i-1}^{n} \left(y_i - \overline{y} \right) = -\hat{\beta} \sum_{i=1}^{n} \left(\overline{x} - x_i \right)$$

$$\Rightarrow \hat{\beta} = \frac{\sum_{i=1}^{n} \left(y_i - \overline{y} \right)}{\sum_{i=1}^{n} \left(x_i - \overline{x} \right)}$$

$$\Rightarrow \hat{\beta} = \frac{\sum_{i=1}^{n} \left(y_i - \overline{y} \right)\left(x_i - \overline{x} \right)}{\sum_{i=1}^{n} \left(x_i - \overline{x} \right)^2} = \frac{Cov(x, y)}{Var(x)} = X'X^{-1}X'y$$

Almost all the statistical tools have ready-made programs to calculate the coefficients α and β. However, it is still very important to understand how they are calculated behind the curtain.

Linear regression using simulated data

For the purpose of linear regression, we write that $Y_e = \alpha + \beta * X$; whereas Y will rarely be perfectly linear and would have an error component or residual and we write $Y = \alpha + \beta * X + K$.

In the above example, K is the error component or residual. It is a random variable and is assumed to be normally distributed.

Fitting a linear regression model and checking its efficacy

Let us simulate the data for the X and Y variables and try to look at how the predicted values (Y_e) differ from the actual value (Y).

For X, we generate 100 normally distributed random numbers with mean 1.5 and standard deviation 2.5 (you can take any other number of your choice and try). For predicted value(Y_e),we assume an intercept of 2 and a slope of .3 and we write $Y_e =2+.3*x$. Later, we will calculate the values of α and β using the preceding data and see how that changes the efficacy of the model. For the actual value, we add a residual term (res) that is nothing but a random variable distributed normally with mean 0 and a standard deviation of .5.

The following is the code snippet to generate these numbers and convert these three columns in a data frame:

```
import pandas as pd
import numpy as np
x=2.5*np.random.randn(100)+1.5
res=.5*np.random.randn(100)+0
ypred=2+.3*x
yact=2+.3*x+res
xlist=x.tolist()
ypredlist=ypred.tolist()
yactlist=yact.tolist()
df=pd.DataFrame({'Input_Variable(X)':xlist,'Predicted_Output(ypred)':y
predlist,'Actual_Output(yact)':yactlist})
df.head()
```

The resultant data frame *df* output looks similar to the following table:

	Actual_Output(yact)	Input_Variable(X)	Predicted_Output(ypred)
0	2.139327	0.111424	2.033427
1	2.720764	3.099065	2.929720
2	3.236767	3.990388	3.197117
3	4.030849	3.711527	3.113458
4	3.612762	2.876211	2.862863

Fig. 5.1: Dummy dataset

Let us now plot both, the actual output (`yact`) and predicted output (`ypred`) against the input variable (*x*) for the sake of comparing `yact` and `ypred` and see what the difference between them is. This ultimately answers the bigger question, as to how accurately the proposed equation has been able to predict the value of the output:

```
import numpy as np
import matplotlib.pyplot as plt
import pandas as pd
%matplotlib inline
x=2.5*np.random.randn(100)+1.5
res=.5*np.random.randn(100)+0
ypred=2+.3*x
yact=2+.3*x+res
plt.plot(x,ypred)
plt.plot(x,yerr,'ro')

plt.title('Actual vs Predicted')
```

The output of the snippet looks similar to the following screenshot. The red dots are the actual values (`yact`) while the blue line is the predicted value (`ypred`):

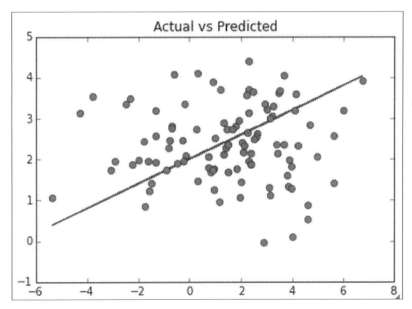

Fig. 5.2: Plot of Actual vs Predicted values from the dummy dataset

Let us add a line representing the mean of the actual values for a better perspective of the comparison. The line in green represents the mean of the actual values:

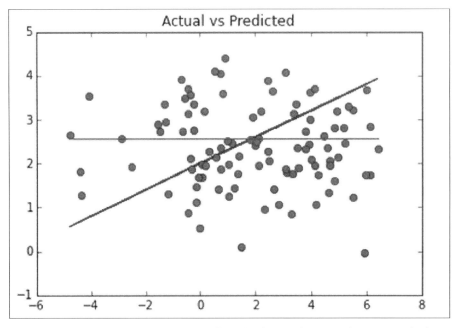

Fig. 5.3: Plot of Actual vs. Predicted values from the dummy dataset with mean actual value

This could be achieved by the following code snippet that is obtained by a little tweaking of the preceding code snippet:

```
import numpy as np
import matplotlib.pyplot as plt
import pandas as pd
%matplotlib inline
x=2.5*np.random.randn(100)+1.5
res=.5*np.random.randn(100)+0
ypred=2+.3*x
yact=2+.3*x+res
ymean=np.mean(yact)
yavg=[ymean for i in range(1,len(xlist)+1)]
plt.plot(x,ypred)
plt.plot(x,yact,'ro')
plt.plot(x,yavg)
plt.title('Actual vs Predicted')
```

Now, the question to be asked is why we chose to plot the mean value of the `yact`. This is because in the case when we don't have any predictor model, our best bet is to go with the mean value of the observed value and say that this will be the predicted value.

Another point to think about is how to judge the efficacy of our model. If you pass any data containing two variables — one input and one output, the statistical program will generate some values of alpha and beta. But, how do we understand that these values are giving us a good model?

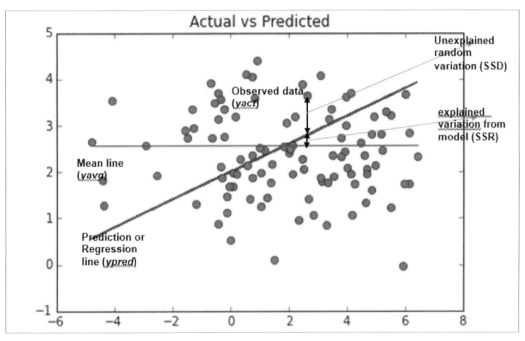

Fig. 5.4: Actual vs. Predicted vs. Fitted (Regressed) line from the dummy dataset (a picture to always keep in mind whenever you think of R^2)

In case, there is no model and the total variability is explained as the Total Sum of Squares or SST:

$$SST = \sum (yact - yavg)^2$$

Now, this total error is composed of two terms — one which is the difference between the regression value and the mean value, this is the difference which the model seeks to explain and is called Regression Sum of Squares or SSR:

$$SSR = \sum (ypred - yavg)^2$$

The unexplained random term, let us call it, Difference Sum of Squares or SSD is:

$$SSD = \sum(yact - ypred)^2$$

As you can see, in the preceding figure or you can guess intuitively that:

$$SST = SSR + SSD$$

Where, SSR is the difference explained by the model; SSD is the difference not explained by the model and is random; SST is the total error.

The more the share of SSR in SST, the better the model is. This share is quantified by something called R^2 or R-squared or coefficient of determination

$$R^2 = SSR / SST$$

Since $SST > SSR$, the value of R^2 can range from 0 to 1. The closer it is to 1, the better the model. A model with $R^2=0.9$ will be compared to a model with $R^2=0.6$, all the other factors remaining the same. That being said, a good R^2 alone doesn't mean that the model is a very efficient one. There are many other factors that we need to analyze before we come to that conclusion. But, R^2 is a pretty good indicator that a linear regression model will be effective.

Let us see what the value of R^2 is for the dataset that we created in the preceding section. When we perform a linear regression, the R^2 value will be calculated automatically. Nevertheless, it is great to have an understanding of how it is calculated.

In the following code snippet, SSR and SST have been calculated according to the formulae described in the preceding section and have been divided to calculate R^2:

```
df['SSR']=(df['Predicted_Output(ypred)']-ymean)**2
df['SST']=(df['Actual_Output(yact)']-ymean)**2
SSR=df.sum()['SSR']
SST=df.sum()['SST']
SSR/SST
```

The value of R^2 comes out to be 0.57, suggesting that `ypred` provides a decent prediction of the `yact`. In this case, we have randomly assumed some values for α and β. $\alpha=2$, $\beta=.3$. This might or might not be the best values of α, β. We have seen earlier that a least sum of square methods is used to find an optimum value for α, β. Let us use these formulae to calculate $\alpha+\beta*X$ and see if there is an improvement in R^2 or not. Hopefully, there will be.

Finding the optimum value of variable coefficients

Let us go back to the data frame *df* that we created a few pages back. The `Input_Variable(X)` column is the predictor variable using which the (α, ß) model will be derived. The `Actual_Output(yact)` variable, as the name suggests, is the actual output variable. Using these two variables, we will calculate the values of α and ß, according to the formulae described previously.

One thing to be cautious about while working with random numbers is that they might not produce the same result, most of the times. It is very likely that you will get a number different than what is mentioned in this text and it is alright as long as you grasp the underlying concept.

To calculate the coefficients, we will create a few more columns in the *df* data frame that is already defined, as we did while calculating the value of R^2. Just to reiterate, here are the formulas again:

$$\beta = \sum \left(Xi - Xm \right)\left(Yi - Ym \right) / \sum \left(Xi - Xm \right)^2$$
$$\alpha = Ym - \beta * Xm$$

We write the following code snippet to calculate these values:

```
xmean=np.mean(df['Input_Variable(X)'])
ymean=np.mean(df['Actual_Output(yact)'])
df['beta']=(df['Input_Variable(X)']-xmean)*(df['Actual_Output(yact)']-ymean)
df['xvar']=(df['Input_Variable(X)']-xmean)**2
betan=df.sum()['beta']
betad=df.sum()['xvar']
beta=betan/betad

alpha=ymean-(betan/betad)*xmean
beta,alpha
```

If you go through the code carefully, you will find out that `betan` and `betad` are the numerators and denominators of the formula to calculate beta. Once, beta is calculated, getting alpha is a cakewalk. The snippet outputs the value of alpha and beta. For my run, I got the following values:

$$\alpha = 1.982, \beta = 0.318$$

As we can see, the values are a little different from what we had assumed earlier, that is α=2 and β=.3. Let us see how the value of R^2 changes if we use the values predicted by the model consisting of these parameters. The equation for the model can be written as:

$$y \bmod el = 1.98 + 0.31 * x$$

Let us create a new column in our *df* data frame to accommodate the values generated by this equation and call this `ymodel`. To do that we write the following code snippet:

```
df['ymodel']=beta*df['Input_Variable(X)']+alpha
```

Let us calculate the value of R^2 based on this column and see whether it has improved or not. To calculate that, we can reuse the code snippet we wrote earlier by replacing the `Predicted_Output(ypred)` variable with `ymodel` variable:

```
df['SSR']=(df['ymodel']-ymean)**2
df['SST']=(df['Actual_Output(yact)']-ymean)**2
SSR=df.sum()['SSR']
SST=df.sum()['SST']
SSR/SST
```

The value of new R^2 comes out to be 0.667, a decent improvement from the value of 0.57 when we assumed the values for α and β.

Let us also plot this new result derived from the model equation against the actual and our earlier assumed model, just to get a better visual understanding. We will introduce one more line to represent the model equation we just created:

```
%matplotlib inline
plt.plot(x,ypred)
plt.plot(x,df['ymodel'])
plt.plot(x,yact,'ro')
plt.plot(x,yavg)
plt.title('Actual vs Predicted vs Model')
```

The graph looks similar to the following figure. As we can see, the `ymodel` and `ypred` are more or less overlapping, as the values of α and β are not very different.

Legend: Blue line –ypred, green line – ymodel, red line – ymean, red dots -x

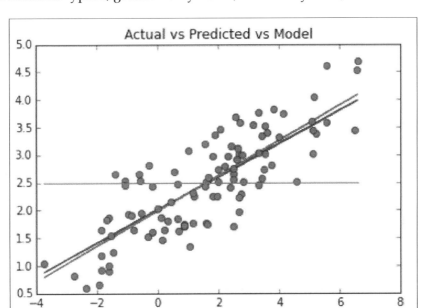

Fig. 5.5: Actual vs Predicted vs Fitted line from the dummy dataset where model coefficients have been calculated rather than assumed

Making sense of result parameters

Apart from the R^2 statistic, there are other statistics and parameters that one needs to look at in order to do the following:

1. Select some variables and discard others for the model.

2. Assess the relationship between the predictor and output variable and check whether a predictor variable is significant in the model or not.

3. Calculate the error in the values predicted by the selected model.

Let us now see some of the statistics which helps to address the issues discussed earlier.

p-values

One thing to realize here is that the calculation of α and β are estimates and not the exact calculations. Whether their values are significant or not need to be tested using a hypothesis test.

The hypothesis tests whether the value of β is non-zero or not; in other words whether there is a sufficient correlation between X and `yact`. If there is, the β will be non-zero.

In the equation, $y=\alpha+\beta*x$, if we put $\beta=0$, there will be no relation between y and x. Hence the hypothesis test is defined, as shown in the following:

$$Null\ hypothesis - Ho : \beta = 0$$
$$Alternate\ Hypothesis - Ha : \beta \lozenge 0$$

So, whenever a regression task is performed and β is calculated, there will be an accompanying t-statistic and a p-value corresponding to this hypothesis test, calculated automatically by the program. Our task is to assume a significance level of our choice and compare this with the p-value. It will be a two-tailed test and if the p-value is less than the chosen significance level, then the null hypothesis that $\beta=0$ is rejected.

If p-value for the t-statistic is less than the significance level, then the null-hypothesis is rejected and β is taken to be significant and non-zero. The values of p-value larger than the significance level demonstrate that β is not very significant in explaining the relationship between the two variables. As we see in the case of multiple regression (multiple input variables/predictors), this fact can be used to weed out unwanted columns from the model. The higher the p-value, the less significant they are to the model and the less significant ones can be weeded out first.

F-statistics

When one moves from a simple linear regression to a multiple regression, there will be multiple βs and each of them will be an estimate. In such a case, apart from testing the significance of the individual variables in the model by checking the p-values associated with their estimation, it is also required to check whether, as a group all the predictors are significant or not. This can be done using the following hypothesis:

$$Null\ hypothesis - Ho : \beta_1 = \beta_2 = \beta_3 = \ldots\ldots = \beta_n = 0$$
$$Alternate\ Hypothesis - Ha : One\ of\ the\ \beta_i\ is\ not\ equal\ to\ 0$$

The statistic that is used to test this hypothesis is called the **F-statistic** and is defined as follows:

$$F - statistic = \frac{(SST - SSD)/p}{SSD/(n-p-1)}$$

Where SST and SSD have been defined earlier as:

$$SST = \sum (yact - yavg)2 \qquad SSD = \sum (yact - ypred)2$$

where n=number of rows in the dataset; p- number of predictor variables in the model

The F-statistics follows the F-distribution. There will be a p-value that is associated with this F-statistic. If this p-value is small enough (smaller than the significance level chosen), the null hypothesis can be rejected.

The significance of F-statistic is as follows:

- p-values are about individual relationships between one predictor and one outcome variable. In case of more than one predictor variable, one predictor's relationship with the output might get changed due to the presence of other variables. The F-statistics provides us with a way to look at the partial change in the associated p-value because of the addition of a new variable.

- When the number of predictors in the model is very large and all the β_i are very close to 0, the individual p-values associated with the predictors might give very small values. In such a case, if we rely solely on individual p-values, we might incorrectly conclude that there is a relationship between the predictors and the outcome, when it is not there actually. In such cases, we should look at the p-value associated with the F-statistic.

Residual Standard Error

Another concept to learn is the concept of **Residual Standard Error (RSE)**. It is defined as:

$$RSE = \sqrt{\frac{1}{n-2} * \sum_{i=1}^{n} (yact - y\,mod\,el)^2} \quad \text{and} \quad SSD = \sum_{i=1}^{n} (yact - y\,mod\,el)^2$$

So, RSE can be written as $RSE = \sqrt{\frac{1}{n-2} * SSD}$ for a simple linear regression model.

Where *n=number* of data points. In general, $RSE = \sqrt{\frac{1}{n-p-1} * SSD}$ where *p=number* of predictor variables in the model.

The RSE is an estimate of the standard deviation of the error term (*res*). This is the error that is inevitable even if the model coefficients are known correctly. This may be the case because the model lacks something else, or may be another variable in the model (we have just looked at one variable regression till now, but in most of the practical scenarios we have to deal with multiple regression, where there would be more than one input variable. In multiple regressions, values of the RSE generally go down, as we add more variables that are more significant predictors of the output variable).

The RSE for a model can be calculated using the following code snippet. Here, we are calculating the RSE for the data frame we have used for the model, df:

```
df['RSE']=(df['Actual_Output(yact)']-df['ymodel'])**2
RSEd=df.sum()['RSE']
RSE=np.sqrt(RSEd)/98
RSE
```

The value of the RSE comes out to be 0.46 in this case. As you might have guessed, the smaller the RSE, the better the model is. Again, the benchmark to compare this error is the mean of the actual values, yact. As we have seen earlier, this value is *ymean=2.53*. So, we will observe an error of 0.46 over 2.53 that amounts to around an 18% error.

Implementing linear regression with Python

Let's now go ahead and try to make a simple linear regression model and see what are the issues that we face and how can they be resolved to make the model more robust. We will use the advertising data that we used earlier for illustrating the correlation.

The following two methods implement linear regression in Python:

- The ols method and the statsmodel.formula.api library
- The scikit-learn package

Let's implement a simple linear regression using the first method and then build upon a multiple-linear regression model. We will then also look at how the second method is used to do the same.

Linear regression using the statsmodel library

Let's first import the `Advertising` data, as shown:

```
import pandas as pd
advert=pd.read_csv('E:/Personal/Learning/Predictive Modeling Book/Book
Datasets/Linear Regression/Advertising.csv')
advert.head()
```

To reiterate, this dataset contains data about the advertising budget spent on TV, Radio, and Newspapers, for a particular product and the resulting sales. We will expect a positive correlation between such advertising costs and sales. We have already seen that there is a good correlation between TV advertising costs and sales. Let's see whether it is present or not. If yes, how does the relationship look like and to do that we write the following code:

```
import statsmodels.formula.api as smf
model1=smf.ols(formula='Sales~TV',data=advert).fit()
model1.params
```

In this code snippet, we have assumed a linear relationship between advertising costs on TV and sales. We have also created a best fit using the least sum of square method. This snippet will output the values for model parameters that is α and β. The following is the output:

```
Intercept      7.032594
TV             0.047537
dtype: float64
```

In the notation that we have been using, α is the intercept and β is the slope. Thus:

$$a = 7.03 \, and \, \beta = 0.047$$

The equation for the model will be:

$$Sales = 7.032 + 0.047 * TV$$

The equation implies that an increase of 100 units in advertising costs will increase the sale by four units.

If you remember, we learnt that the values of these parameters are estimates and there will be a p-value associated to these. If the p-values are very small, then it can be accepted that these parameters have a non-zero value and are statistically significant in the model. Let's have a look at the p-values for these parameters:

```
model1.pvalues
```

```
Intercept      1.406300e-35
TV             1.467390e-42
dtype: float64
```

As it can be seen, the p-values are very small; hence, the parameters are significant.

Let's also check another important indicator of the model efficacy and that is R^2. As we saw earlier, there is a ready-made method for doing this. This can be done by typing the following code line:

```
model1.rsquared
```

The value comes out to be 0.61.

If we want the entire important model parameters at one go, we can take a look at the model summary by writing this snippet:

```
model1.summary()
```

The result is as follows:

OLS Regression Results			
Dep. Variable:	Sales	R-squared:	0.612
Model:	OLS	Adj. R-squared:	0.610
Method:	Least Squares	F-statistic:	312.1
Date:	Mon, 07 Sep 2015	Prob (F-statistic):	1.47e-42
Time:	01:30:20	Log-Likelihood:	-519.05
No. Observations:	200	AIC:	1042.
Df Residuals:	198	BIC:	1049.
Df Model:	1		

	coef	std err	t	P>|t|	[95.0% Conf. Int.]
Intercept	7.0326	0.458	15.360	0.000	6.130 7.935
TV	0.0475	0.003	17.668	0.000	0.042 0.053

Fig. 5.6: Model 1 Summary

As we can see, the F-statistic for this model is very high and the associated p-value is negligible, suggesting that the parameter estimates for this model were all significant and non-zero.

Let's now predict the values of sales based on the equation we just derived. This can be done using the following snippet:

```
sales_pred=model1.predict(pd.DataFrame(advert['TV']))
sales_pred
```

This equation basically calculates the predicted sales value for each row based on the model equation using TV costs. One can plot `sales_pred` against the TV advertising costs to find the line of best fit. Let's do that:

```
import matplotlib.pyplot as plt
%matplotlib inline
advert.plot(kind='scatter', x='TV', y='Sales')
plt.plot(pd.DataFrame(advert['TV']),sales_pred,c='red',linewidth=2)
```

We get the following plot as the output. The red line is the line of best fit (obtained from the model). The blue dots represent the actual data present:

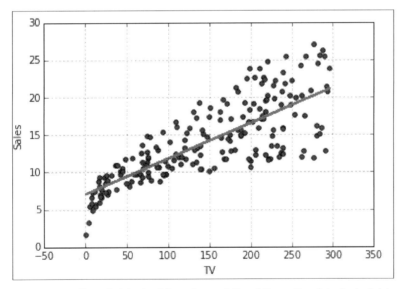

Fig. 5.7: Line of best fit (obtained from the model) and the scatter plot of actual data

Now, let's calculate the RSE term for our prediction using the following code snippet:

```
advert['sales_pred']=0.047537*advert['TV']+7.03
advert['RSE']=(advert['Sales']-advert['sales_pred'])**2
RSEd=advert.sum()['RSE']
RSE=np.sqrt(RSEd/198)
salesmean=np.mean(advert['Sales'])
error=RSE/salesmean
RSE,salesmean,error
```

The output consists of three numbers, first of which is *RSE=3.25*, second is `salesmean` (mean of actual sales) = 14.02 and error is their ratio, which is equal to 0.23. Thus, on an average this model will have 23%, even if the coefficients are correctly predicted. This is a significant amount of errors and we would like to bring it down by some means. Also, the R^2 value of 0.61 can be improved upon. One thing we can try is to add more columns in the model, as predictors and see whether it improves the result or not.

Multiple linear regression

When linear regression involves more than one predictor variable, then it is called multiple linear regression. The nature of the model remains the same (linear), except that there might be separate slope (β) coefficients associated with each of the predictor variables. The model will be represented, as follows:

$$y \bmod el = \alpha + \beta_1 X_1 + \beta_2 X_2 + \beta_3 X_3 \ldots\ldots + \beta_n X_n$$

Each β_i will be estimated using the same least sum of squares method; hence, would have a p-value associated with the estimation. The smaller the p-value associated with a variable, the more the significance of that variable to the model. The variables with large p-values should be eliminated from the model as they aren't good predictors of the output variable.

While the multiple regression gives us with the possibility of using more variables as predictors; hence, it increases the efficiency of the model. It also increases the complexity of the process of model building, as the selection of the variables to be kept and discarded in the model becomes tedious.

With this simple dataset of three predictor variables, there can be seven possible models. They are as follows:

- Model 1: Sales~TV
- Model 2: Sales~Newspaper
- Model 3: Sales~Radio

- Model 4: Sales~TV+Radio
- Model 5: Sales~TV+Newspaper
- Model 6: Sales~Newspaper+Radio
- Model 7: Sales~TV+Radio+Newspaper

For a model with p possible predictor variables, there can be 2^p-1 possible models; hence, as the number of predictors increases, the selection becomes tedious.

It would have been a tedious task to choose from so many possible models. Thankfully, there are a few guidelines to filter some of these and then navigate towards the most efficient one. The following are the guidelines:

- Keep the variables with low p-values and eliminate the ones with high p-values
- Inclusion of a variable to the model should ideally increase the value of R^2 (although it is not a very reliable indicator of the same and looking at the adjusted R^2 is preferred. The concept of adjusted R^2 and why it is a better indicator than R^2 will be explained later in this chapter).

Based on these guidelines, there are two kinds of approaches to select the predictor variables to go in the final model:

- **Forward selection**: In this approach, we start with a null model without any predictor and then start adding predictor variables one by one. The variable whose addition results into a model with the lowest residual sum of squares will be added first to the model. If the p-value for the variable is small enough and the value of the adjusted R^2 goes up; the predictor variable is included in the model. Otherwise, it is not included in the model.
- **Backward selection**: In this approach, one starts with a model that has all the possible predictor variables in the model and discards some of them. If the p-value of a predictor variable is large and the value of the adjusted R^2 goes up, the predictor variable is discarded from the model. Otherwise, it remains a part of the model.

Many of the statistical programs, including the Python, give us an option to select from the two preceding approaches while implementing a linear regression. The statistical program then implements the linear regression using the selected approach.

For now, let us manually add a few variables and see how it changes the model parameters and efficacy, so that we can get a better glimpse of what goes on behind the curtain when these approaches are implemented by the statistical program.

We have already seen one model assuming a linear relationship between sales and TV advertising costs. We can ignore the other models consisting of single variables (that is newspaper and radio, as they have a small correlation compared to TV). Let us now try to add more variables to the model we already have and see how the parameters and efficacy change.

Let us try adding the newspaper variable to the model using the following code snippet:

```
import statsmodels.formula.api as smf
model2=smf.ols(formula='Sales~TV+Newspaper',data=advert).fit()
model2.params
```

The following are the results:

```
Intercept    5.774948        Intercept    3.145860e-22
TV           0.046901        TV           5.507584e-44
Newspaper    0.044219        Newspaper    2.217084e-05
dtype: float64                dtype: float64
```

Fig. 5.8: Model 2 coefficients and p-values

The p-values for the coefficients are very small, suggesting that all the estimates are significant. The equation for this model will be:

$$Sales = 5.77 + 0.046 * TV + 0.04 * Newspaper$$

The values of R^2 and adjusted R^2 are 0.646 and 0.642, which is just a minor improvement from the value obtained in the earlier model.

The values can be predicted using the following snippet:

```
sales_pred=model2.predict(advert[['TV','Newspaper']])
sales_pred
```

To calculate the RSE, we modify the snippet a little:

```
import numpy as np
advert['sales_pred']=5.77 + 0.046*advert['TV'] +
0.04*advert['Newspaper']
advert['RSE']=(advert['Sales']-advert['sales_pred'])**2
RSEd=advert.sum()['RSE']
RSE=np.sqrt(RSEd/197)
salesmean=np.mean(advert['Sales'])
error=RSE/salesmean
RSE,salesmean,error
```

The value of RSE comes out to be 3.12 (22%), not very different from the model with only TV. The number 197 comes from the (n-p-1) term in the formula for RSE, where $n=200$, $p=2$ for the current model. The following table is the model summary:

OLS Regression Results			
Dep. Variable:	Sales	R-squared:	0.646
Model:	OLS	Adj. R-squared:	0.642
Method:	Least Squares	F-statistic:	179.6
Date:	Wed, 09 Sep 2015	Prob (F-statistic):	3.95e-45
Time:	19:11:41	Log-Likelihood:	-509.89
No. Observations:	200	AIC:	1026.
Df Residuals:	197	BIC:	1036.
Df Model:	2		

Fig. 5.9: Model 2 Summary

Although as the F-statistic decreases, the associated p-value also decreases. But, it is just a marginal improvement to the model, as we can see in the adj. R^2 value. So, adding newspaper didn't improve the model significantly.

Let's try adding radio to the model instead of the newspaper. Radio had the second best correlation with the `Sales` variable in the correlation matrix we created earlier in the chapter. Thus, one expects some significant improvement in the model upon its addition to the model. Let's see if that happens or not:

```
import statsmodels.formula.api as smf
model3=smf.ols(formula='Sales~TV+Radio',data=advert).fit()
model3.params
```

The output parameters and the associated p-values of this model are, as follows:

```
Intercept     2.921100     Intercept     4.565557e-19
TV            0.045755     TV            5.436980e-82
Radio         0.187994     Radio         9.776972e-59
dtype: float64            dtype: float64
```

Fig. 5.10: Model 2 coefficients and p-values

The model can be represented as the following:

$$Sales = 2.92 + 0.045 * TV + 0.18 * Radio$$

The values can be predicted based on the preceding model using the following snippet:

```
sales_pred=model3.predict(advert[['TV','Radio']])
sales_pred
```

The model summary looks something similar to the following screenshot:

OLS Regression Results			
Dep. Variable:	Sales	R-squared:	0.897
Model:	OLS	Adj. R-squared:	0.896
Method:	Least Squares	F-statistic:	859.6
Date:	Tue, 08 Sep 2015	Prob (F-statistic):	4.83e-98
Time:	00:15:23	Log-Likelihood:	-386.20
No. Observations:	200	AIC:	778.4
Df Residuals:	197	BIC:	788.3
Df Model:	2		

Fig. 5.11: Model 3 summary

One thing to observe here is that the R^2 value has improved considerably due to the addition of radio to the model. Also, the F-statistic has increased significantly from the last model indicating a very efficient model.

The RSE can be calculated using the same method described previously. The value for this model comes out to be 1.71 (around 12%),which is much better than the 23% and 22% in the previous model.

Thus, we can conclude that radio is a great addition to the model and TV and radio advertising costs have been able to describe the sales very well and this model itself is a very efficient model. But, can we improve it a bit further by combining all three predictor variables?

The last thing that we should try is, all the predictor variables together by using the following code:

```
import statsmodels.formula.api as smf
model4=smf.ols(formula='Sales~TV+Radio+Newspaper',data=advert).fit()
model4.params
```

The estimates of the coefficients and the associated p-values for this model will be as follows:

```
Intercept    2.938889          Intercept    1.267295e-17
TV           0.045765          TV           1.509960e-81
Radio        0.188530          Radio        1.505339e-54
Newspaper   -0.001037          Newspaper    8.599151e-01
dtype: float64                 dtype: float64
```

Fig. 5.12: Model 4 coefficients and p-values

The p-values for the coefficients are very small, suggesting that all the estimates are significant. The equation for this model will be:

$$Sales = 2.93 + 0.045 * TV + 0.18 * Radio - 0.01 * Newspaper$$

The values of sales can be predicted using the following snippet:

```
sales_pred=model4.predict(advert[['TV','Radio','Newspaper']])
sales_pred
```

The summary of the model is shown in the following table:

OLS Regression Results			
Dep. Variable:	Sales	**R-squared:**	0.897
Model:	OLS	**Adj. R-squared:**	0.896
Method:	Least Squares	**F-statistic:**	570.3
Date:	Thu, 10 Sep 2015	**Prob (F-statistic):**	1.58e-96
Time:	22:05:18	**Log-Likelihood:**	-386.18
No. Observations:	200	**AIC:**	780.4
Df Residuals:	196	**BIC:**	793.6
Df Model:	3		

Fig. 5.13: Model 4 summary

The most striking feature of this model is that the estimate of the coefficients is very similar to that in the previous model. The intercept, coefficient for TV, and the coefficient for Radio are more or less the same. The values of R^2 and *adj-R²* are also similar to the previous model.

The value of RSE can be calculated in a similar way, as before. The value comes out to 2.57 (18%), which is more than the previous model.

Other things to note about this model are the following:

- There is a small negative coefficient for the newspaper. When we considered only TV and newspaper in the model, the coefficient of the newspaper was significantly positive. Something affected the coefficient of the newspaper when it became a part of the model in presence of TV and radio.

- For this model, the F-statistic has decreased considerably to 570.3 from 859.6 in the previous model. This suggests that the partial benefit of adding newspaper to the model containing TV and radio is negative.

- The value of RSE increases on addition of newspaper to the model.

All these point in the direction that the model actually became a little less efficient on addition of newspaper to the previous model. What is the reason?

Multi-collinearity

Multi-collinearity is the reason for the sub-optimal performance of the model when newspaper was added to the final model. Multi-collinearity alludes to the correlation between the predictor variables of the model.

These are some of the signs of a common problem encountered during a regression called multi-collinearity. Go back a few pages to the correlation matrix that we created for this dataset and you will find that there is a significant correlation of 0.35 between radio and newspaper. This means that the expense on Newspaper is related to that on the Radio. This relationship between the predictor variable increases the variability of the co-efficient estimates of the related predictor variables.

The t-statistic for these coefficients is calculated by dividing the mean value by the variability (or error). As this error goes up, the value of t-statistic goes down and the value of p-value increases. Thus, the chances that the null hypothesis for the hypothesis test associated with the F-statistic will be accepted are increased. This decreases the significance of the variable in the model.

$$t - statistic = \left(\beta_m - 0 \right) / SE \left(\beta_m \right)$$

Where β_m=mean of estimates of β, $SE(\beta_m)$=variability in the estimate of β.

Thus collinearity is an issue that needs to be taken care of. For highly correlated predicted variables, we need to do a deep-dive with these variables and see whose inclusion in the model makes the model more efficient.

It is a good practice to identify the pair of predictor variables with high correlation, using the correlation matrix and check the pairs of multi-collinearity effect on the model. The culprit variables should be removed from the model. The VIF is a method to tackle this issue.

Variance Inflation Factor

A fool-proof way to detect this menace called multi-collinearity is a statistic called **Variance Inflation Factor (VIF)**. It is a method to quantify the rise in the variability of the coefficient estimate of a particular variable because of high correlation between two or more than two predictor variables. The VIF needs to be calculated for each of the variables and if the value is very high for a particular variable, then that predictor needs to be eliminated from the model. Some statistical processes calculate VIF when fed with the option to do so. The following process goes under the hood for calculation of VIF:

1. Write X_i as a linear function of other predictor variables:

$$X_i = a_1 X_1 + a_2 X_2 + \ldots\ldots + a_{i-1} X_{i-1} + \ldots\ldots + a_{i+1} X_{i+1} + \ldots\ldots a_n X_n$$

2. Calculate the coefficient of determination for this model and call it R_i^2. The VIF for Xi is given by:

$$VIF = \frac{1}{1 - Ri^2}$$

3. If the *VIF=1*, then the variables are not correlated. If *1<VIF<5*, then the variables are moderately correlated with other predictor variables and can still be part of the model. If *VIF>5*, then variables are highly correlated and need to be eliminated from the model.

Let us write a short snippet to calculate the VIF to understand the calculation better:

```
model=smf.ols(formula='Newspaper~TV+Radio',data=advert).fit()
rsquared=model.rsquared
VIF=1/(1-rsquared)
VIF
```

This will give a VIF for the Newspaper. By changing the formula in the snippet, we can calculate the VIF for the other variables. The following are the values:

Newspaper	Radio	TV
1.14	1.14	1.04

The newspaper and TV have almost the same VIF, indicating that they are correlated to just one another and not the TV.

In this case, radio and newspaper are correlated. However, the model with TV and radio, as predictor variables, are far superior to the model with TV and newspaper as the predictor variables. The model with the all the three variables as predictors doesn't improve the model much. In fact, it increases the variability and the F-statistic. It will be a decent choice to drop the newspaper variable from the model and pick model 3 as the best candidate for the final model:

$$Model3: Sales = 2.92 + 0.045 * TV + 0.18 * Radio$$

Model validation

Any predictive model needs to be validated to see how it is performing on different sets of data, whether the accuracy of the model is constant over all the sources of similar data or not. This checks the problem of over-fitting, wherein the model fits very well on one set of data but doesn't fit that well on another dataset. One common method is to validate a model train-test split of the dataset. Another method is k-fold cross validation, about which we will learn more in the later chapter.

Training and testing data split

Ideally, this step should be done right at the onset of the modelling process so that there are no sampling biases in the model; in other words, the model should perform well even for a dataset that has the same predictor variables, but their means and variances are very different from what the model has been built upon. This can happen because the dataset on which the model is built (training) and the one on which it is applied (testing) can come from different sources. A more robust way to do this is a process called the k-fold cross validation, about which we will read in detail in a little while.

Let's see how we can split the available dataset in the training and testing dataset and apply the model to the testing dataset to get other results:

```
import numpy as np
a=np.random.randn(len(advert))
check=a<0.8
training=advert[check]
testing=advert[~check]
```

The ratio of split between training and testing datasets is 80:20; in other words, 160 rows of the advert dataset will be in training and 40 rows in testing.

Let's create a model on training the data and test the model performance on the testing data. Let us create the only model that works best (we have found it already), the one with TV and radio variables, as predictor variables:

```
import statsmodels.formula.api as smf
model5=smf.ols(formula='Sales~TV+Radio',data=training).fit()
model5.summary()
```

OLS Regression Results			
Dep. Variable:	Sales	**R-squared:**	0.878
Model:	OLS	**Adj. R-squared:**	0.876
Method:	Least Squares	**F-statistic:**	529.7
Date:	Sat, 12 Sep 2015	**Prob (F-statistic):**	6.44e-68
Time:	12:21:12	**Log-Likelihood:**	-293.70
No. Observations:	150	**AIC:**	593.4
Df Residuals:	147	**BIC:**	602.4
Df Model:	2		

	coef	std err	t	P>|t|	[95.0% Conf. Int.]
Intercept	2.8606	0.361	7.917	0.000	2.147 3.575
TV	0.0468	0.002	27.901	0.000	0.043 0.050
Radio	0.1793	0.010	18.437	0.000	0.160 0.199

Fig. 5.14: Model 5 coefficients and p-values

Most of the model parameters, such as intercept, coefficient estimates, and R^2 are very similar. The difference in F-statistics can be attributed to a smaller dataset. The smaller the dataset, the larger the value of SSD and the smaller the value of the (n-p-1) term in F-statistic formula; both contribute towards the decrease in the F-statistic value.

The model can be written, as follows:

$$Sales \sim 2.86 + 0.04 * TV + 0.17 * Radio$$

Let us now predict the sales values for the testing dataset:

```
sales_pred=model5.predict(training[['TV','Radio']])
sales_pred
```

The value of RSE for this prediction on the testing dataset can be calculated using the following snippet:

```
import numpy as np
testing['sales_pred']=2.86 + 0.04*testing['TV'] +
0.17*testing['Radio']
testing['RSE']=(testing['Sales']-testing['sales_pred'])**2
RSEd=testing.sum()['RSE']
RSE=np.sqrt(RSEd/51)
salesmean=np.mean(testing['Sales'])
error=RSE/salesmean
RSE,salesmean,error
```

The value of RSE comes out to be 2.54 over a sales mean (in the testing data) of 14.80 amounting to an error of 17%.

We can see that the model doesn't generalize very well on the testing dataset, as the RSE for the same model is different in the two cases. It implies some degree of over fitting when we tried to build the model based on the entire dataset. The RSE with the training-testing split, albeit a bit more, is more reliable and replicable.

Summary of models

We have tried four models previously. Let us summarize the major results from each of the models, at one place:

Name	Definition	R2/Adj-R2	F-statistic	F-statistic (p-value)	RSE
Model 1	Sales ~ TV	0.612/0.610	312.1	$1.47e^{-42}$	3.25 (23%)
Model 2	Sales ~ TV+Newspaper	0.646/0.642	179.6	$3.95e^{-45}$	3.12(22%)
Model 3	Sales ~ TV+Radio	0.897/0.896	859.6	$4.83e^{-98}$	1.71(12%)
Model 4	Sales ~ TV+Radio+Newspaper	0.897/0.896	570.3	$1.58e^{-96}$	1.80(13%)

Guide for selection of variables

To summarize, for a good linear model, the predictor variables should be chosen based on the following criteria:

- **R²**: R^2 will always increase when you add a new predictor variable to the model. However, it is not a very reliable check of the increased efficiency of the model. Rather, for an efficient model, we should check the adjusted-R^2. This should increase on adding a new predictor variable.

- **p-values**: The lower the p-value for the estimate of the predictor variable, the better it is to add the predictor variable to the model.

- **F-statistic**: The value of the F-statistic for the model should increase after the addition of a new predictor variable for a predictor variable to be an efficient addition to the model. The increase in the F-statistic is a proxy to the improvement in the model brought upon solely by the addition of that particular variable. Alternatively, the p-value associated with the F-statistic should decrease on the addition of a new predictor variable.

- **RSE**: The value of RSE for the new model should decrease on the addition of the new predictor variable.

- **VIF**: To take care of the issues arising due to multi-collinearity one needs to eliminate the variables with large values of VIF.

Linear regression with scikit-learn

Let's now re-implement the linear regression model using the `scikit-learn` package. This method is more elegant as it has more in-built methods to perform the regular processes associated with regression. For example, you might remember from the last chapter that there is a separate method for splitting the dataset into training and testing datasets:

```
from sklearn.linear_model import LinearRegression
from sklearn.cross_validation import train_test_split
feature_cols = ['TV', 'Radio']
X = advert[feature_cols]
Y = advert['Sales']
trainX,testX,trainY,testY = train_test_split(X,Y, test_size = 0.2)
lm = LinearRegression()
lm.fit(trainX, trainY)
```

We split the advert dataset into train and test dataset and built the model on TV and radio variables from the test dataset. The following are the parameters of the model:

```
print lm.intercept_
print lm.coef_
```

The result is as follows: Intercept – 2.918, TV coefficient – 0.04, Radio coefficient – 0.186

A better way to look at the coefficients is to use the `zip` method to write the variable name and coefficient together. The required snippet and the output are mentioned in the following code:

```
zip(feature_cols, lm.coef_)
[('TV', 0.045706061219705982), ('Radio', 0.18667738715568111)]
```

The value of R^2 is calculated by typing the following code:

```
lm.score(trainX, trainY)
```

The value comes out to be around 0.89, very close to the value obtained by the method used earlier.

The model can be used to predict the value of sales using TV and radio variables from the test dataset, as follows:

```
lm.predict(testX)
```

Feature selection with scikit-learn

As stated before, many of the statistical tools and packages have in-built methods to conduct a variable selection process (forward selection and backward selection). If it is done manually, it will consume a lot of time and selecting the most important variables will be a tedious task compromising the efficiency of the model.

One advantage of using the `scikit-learn` package for regression in Python is that it has this particular method for feature selection. This works more or less like backward selection (not exactly) and is called **Recursive Feature Elimination** (**RFE**). One can specify the number of variables they want in the final model.

The model is first run with all the variables and certain weights are assigned to all the variables. In the subsequent iterations, the variables with the smallest weights are pruned from the list of variables till the desired number of variables is left.

Let us see how one can do a feature selection in `scikit-learn`:

```
from sklearn.feature_selection import RFE
from sklearn.svm import SVR
feature_cols = ['TV', 'Radio','Newspaper']
X = advert[feature_cols]
Y = advert['Sales']
```

```
estimator = SVR(kernel="linear")
selector = RFE(estimator,2,step=1)
selector = selector.fit(X, Y)
```

We use the methods named RFE and SVR in-built in `scikit-learn`. We indicate that we want to estimate a linear model and the number of desired variables in the model to be two.

To get the list of selected variables, one can write the following code snippet:

```
selector.support_
```

It results in an array mentioning whether the variables in X have been selected for the model or not. **True** means that the variable has been selected, while **False** means otherwise. In this case, the result is as follows:

```
array([ True,   True, False], dtype=bool)
```

Fig. 5.15: Result of feature selection process

In our case, X consists of three variables: TV, radio, and newspaper. The preceding array suggests that TV and radio have been selected for the model, while the newspaper hasn't been selected. This concurs with the variable selection we had done manually.

This method also returns a ranking, as described in the following example:

```
selector.ranking_
```

```
array([1, 1, 2])
```

Fig. 5.16: Result of feature selection process

All the selected variables will have a ranking of **1** while the subsequent ones will be ranked in descending order of their significance. A variable with rank **2** will be more significant to the model than the one with a rank of **3** and so on.

Handling other issues in linear regression

So far in this chapter, we have learnt:

- How to implement a linear regression model using two methods
- How to measure the efficiency of the model using model parameters

However, there are other issues that need to be taken care of while dealing with data sources of different types. Let's go through them one by one. We will be using a different (simulated) dataset to illustrate these issues. Let's import it and have a look at it:

```
import pandas as pd
df=pd.read_csv('E:/Personal/Learning/Predictive Modeling Book/Book
Datasets/Linear Regression/Ecom Expense.csv')
df.head()
```

We should get the following output:

	Transaction ID	Age	Items	Monthly Income	Transaction Time	Record	Gender	City Tier	Total Spend
0	TXN001	42	10	7313	627.668127	5	Female	Tier 1	4198.385084
1	TXN002	24	8	17747	126.904567	3	Female	Tier 2	4134.976648
2	TXN003	47	11	22845	873.469701	2	Male	Tier 2	5166.614455
3	TXN004	50	11	18552	380.219428	7	Female	Tier 1	7784.447676
4	TXN005	60	2	14439	403.374223	2	Female	Tier 2	3254.160485

Fig. 5.17: Ecom Expense dataset

The preceding screenshot is a simulated dataset from any-commerce website. It captures the information about several transactions done on the website. A brief description of the column names of the dataset is, as follows:

- **Transaction ID**: Transaction ID for the transaction
- **Age**: Age of the customer
- **Items**: Number of items in the shopping cart (purchased)
- **Monthly Income**: Monthly disposable income of the customer
- **Transaction Time**: Total time spent on the website during the transaction
- **Record**: How many times the customer has shopped with the website in the past
- **Gender**: Gender of the customer
- **City Tier**: Tier of the city
- **Total Spend**: Total amount spent in the transaction

The output variable is the `Total Spend` variable. The others are potential predictor variables and we suspect that the `Total Spend` is linearly related to all these predictor variables.

Handling categorical variables

Until now, we have assumed that the predictor variables can only be quantitative or numerical, but we know from real-life experiences that most of the times the dataset contains a categorical or qualitative variable and many of the times these variables will have a significant impact on the value of the output. However, the question is how to process these variables, so as to use them in the model?

We can't assign them values, such as 0, 1, 2, and so on, and then use them in the model, as it will give undue weightage to the categories because of the numbers assigned to them. Most of the time it might give a wrong result and will change, as the number assigned to a particular category changes.

In the data frame we just imported, **Gender** and **City Tier** are the categorical variables. In *Chapter 2, Data Cleaning*, we learnt how to create dummy variables from a categorical variable. That was exactly for this purpose. Let's see how it works and why it is required.

A linear regression is of the form:

$$y \bmod el = \alpha + \beta_1 X_1 + \beta_2 X_2 + \beta_3 X_3 \ldots \ldots + \beta_n X_n + d$$

Where one or more of the *Xi*'s can be categorical. Let's say X_m is that variable. For such a variable, we can define another dummy variable (if it has only two categories as in the case of Gender), such that:

$$Xg = 1, if\ customer\ is\ male$$
$$= 0, if\ customer\ is\ female$$

The model then becomes:

$$y \bmod el = \alpha + \beta 1 X 1 + \beta 2 X 2 + \beta 3 X 3 \ldots \ldots + \beta g \ldots \ldots + \beta n X n + d, if\ customer\ is\ male$$
$$y \bmod el = \alpha + \beta_1 X_1 + \beta_2 X_2 + \beta_3 X_3 \ldots \ldots + \beta_n X_n + d, if\ customer\ is\ female$$

If there are three levels in the categorical variable, then one needs to define two variables as compared to 1 when there were two levels in the categorical variable. For example, **City Tier** variable has three levels in our dataset.

For this, we can define two variables, such that:

$$X_{t1} = 1, if\ City\ is\ Tier\ 1 \qquad X_{t2} = 2, if\ City\ is\ Tier\ 2$$
$$0, if\ City\ is\ not\ Tier\ 1 \qquad = 0, if\ City\ is\ not\ Tier\ 2$$

The model then becomes:

$$y \bmod el = \alpha + \beta_1 X_1 + \beta_2 X_2 + \beta_3 X_3 + \ldots + \beta_{t1} X_{t1} \ldots + \beta_n X_n + d, \text{if customer is from tier 1 city}$$
$$y \bmod el = \alpha + \beta_1 X_1 + \beta_2 X_2 + \beta_3 X_3 + \ldots + \beta_{t2} X_{t2} \ldots + \beta_n X_n + d, \text{if customer is from tier 2 city}$$
$$y \bmod el = \alpha + \beta_1 X_1 + \beta_2 X_2 + \beta_3 X_3 + \ldots + \beta_n X_n + d, \text{if customer is from tier 3 city}$$

> Note that one doesn't have to create the third variable. This is because of the nature in which these variables are defined. If a customer doesn't belong to tier 1 or tier 2 city, then he will certainly belong to a tier 3 city. Hence, no one variable is required for one of the levels. In general, for categorical variables having n levels, one should create (n-1) dummy variables.

The process of creating dummy variables has been already enumerated in *Chapter 2, Data Cleaning*. Let's now create the dummy variables for both our categorical variables and then add them to our data frame, as shown:

```
dummy_gender=pd.get_dummies(df['Gender'],prefix='Sex')
dummy_city_tier=pd.get_dummies(df['City Tier'],prefix='City')
```

Let's see how they look and whether they satisfy the conditions we have defined earlier or not. This is how the dummy_city_tier looks:

	City_Tier 1	City_Tier 2	City_Tier 3
0	1	0	0
1	0	1	0
2	0	1	0
3	1	0	0
4	0	1	0
5	0	1	0
6	1	0	0

Fig. 5.18: City Tier dummy variables

The `dummy_gender` looks similar to the following table:

	Sex_Female	Sex_Male
0	1	0
1	1	0
2	0	1
3	1	0
4	1	0
5	0	1

Fig. 5.19: Gender dummy variables

Now, we have these dummy variables created but they are not a part of the main data frame yet. Let's attach these new variables to the main data frame so that they can be used in the model:

```
column_name=df.columns.values.tolist()
df1=df[column_name].join(dummy_gender)
column_name1=df1.columns.values.tolist()
df2=df1[column_name1].join(dummy_city_tier)
df2
```

	Transaction ID	Age	Items	Monthly Income	Transaction Time	Record	Gender	City Tier	Total Spend	Sex_Female	Sex_Male	City_Tier 1	City_Tier 2	City_Tier 3
0	TXN001	42	10	7313	627.668127	5	Female	Tier 1	4198.385084	1	0	1	0	0
1	TXN002	24	8	17747	126.904567	3	Female	Tier 2	4134.976648	1	0	0	1	0
2	TXN003	47	11	22845	873.469701	2	Male	Tier 2	5166.614455	0	1	0	1	0
3	TXN004	50	11	18552	380.219428	7	Female	Tier 1	7784.447676	1	0	1	0	0
4	TXN005	60	2	14439	403.374223	2	Female	Tier 2	3254.160485	1	0	0	1	0
5	TXN006	49	6	6282	48.974268	2	Male	Tier 2	2375.036467	0	1	0	1	0

Fig. 5.20: Ecom Expense dataset with dummy variables

There are five new columns in the data frame, two from the **Gender** dummy variables and three from the **City Tier** dummy variables.

If you compare it with the entire dataset, the **City_Tier_1** has value **1** if the **City_Tier** has value **Tier 1**, the **City_Tier_2** has value **1** if the **City_Tier** has value **Tier 2** and the **City_Tier_3** has value **1** if the **City_Tier** has value **Tier 3**. All the other dummy variables in that particular row will have values **0**. This is what we wanted.

Let's see how to include these dummy variables in the model and how to assess their coefficients.

For the preceding dataset, let's assume a linear relationship between the output variable `Total Spend` and the predictor variables: `Monthly Income` and `Transaction Time`, and both set of dummy variables:

```
from sklearn.linear_model import LinearRegression
feature_cols = ['Monthly Income','Transaction Time','City_Tier
1','City_Tier 2','City_Tier 3','Sex_Female','Sex_Male']
X = df2[feature_cols]
Y = df2['Total Spend']
lm = LinearRegression()
lm.fit(X,Y)
```

The model parameters can be found out, as follows:

```
print lm.intercept_
print lm.coef_
zip(feature_cols, lm.coef_)
```

The following is the output we get:

```
3655.72940769
[   0.15297825    0.12372609   119.6632516    -16.67901801 -102.9842336
  -94.15779883   94.15779883]
[('Monthly Income', 0.15297824609320518),
 ('Transaction Time', 0.12372608642620025),
 ('City_Tier 1', 119.66325160390109),
 ('City_Tier 2', -16.6790180079990315),
 ('City_Tier 3', -102.98423359591065),
 ('Sex_Female', -94.157798830320175),
 ('Sex_Male', 94.157798830320189)]
```

Fig. 5.21: Coefficients of the model

The R^2 for this model can be found out by writing the following:

```
lm.score(X,Y)
```

The value comes out to be `0.19`, which might be because we haven't used the other variables and the output might be related to them as well. We need to fine-tune the model by suitably transforming some of the variables and adding them to the model. For example, if you add `Record` variable to the model, the R^2 jumps to 0.91 (try that on your own). It is a good dataset to play with.

The model can be written, as follows:

Total_Spend=3655.72 + 0.12*Transaction Time + 0.15*Monthly Income + 119*City_Tier 1-16*City_Tier 2 - 102*City_Tier 3-94*Sex_Female+94*Sex_Male

The RSE can be calculated, as follows:

```
import numpy as np
df2['total_spend_pred']=3720.72940769 + 0.12*df2['Transaction
Time']+0.15*df2['Monthly Income']+119*df2['City_Tier 1']-16*df2['City_
Tier 2']
-102*df2['City_Tier 3']-94*df2['Sex_Female']+94*df2['Sex_Male']
df2['RSE']=(df2['Total Spend']-df2['total_spend_pred'])**2
RSEd=df2.sum()['RSE']
RSE=np.sqrt(RSEd/2354)
salesmean=np.mean(df2['Total Spend'])
error=RSE/salesmean
RSE,salesmean,error
```

The RSE comes out to be `2519` over a `Total Spend` mean of 6163, amounting to an error of around 40%, suggesting that there is a scope for improvement in the model.

However, the purpose of this section is to illustrate how the dummy variables are used in building a model and assessed in the final model.

As we can see, there are different coefficients for different dummy variables. For **City Tier**, **City_Tier_1** has 119, **City_Tier_2** has -16 and **City_Tier_3** has -102. This means that on an average, everything else being same, a customer from a **Tier 1** city will spend more than someone from **Tier 2** and **Tier 3** city. Someone from a **Tier 2** city will spend less than someone from **Tier 3**. If we take **City_Tier_1** as the baseline, the **Total Spend** is lesser by 135 units for a customer from **Tier 2** city, while it is lesser by 222 units for a customer from **Tier 3** city.

For different **Gender** and **City Tier**, the model will be reduced to following for different cases:

Gender	City Tier	Model
Male	1	Total_Spend=3655.72 + 0.12*Transaction Time + 0.15*Monthly Income + 119*City_Tier 1 +94*Sex_Male
Male	2	Total_Spend=3655.72 + 0.12*Transaction Time + 0.15*Monthly Income -16*City_Tier 2 +94*Sex_Male
Male	3	Total_Spend=3655.72 + 0.12*Transaction Time + 0.15*Monthly Income - 102*City_Tier 3 +94*Sex_Male
Female	1	Total_Spend=3655.72 + 0.12*Transaction Time + 0.15*Monthly Income + 119*City_Tier 1 - 94*Sex_Female
Female	2	Total_Spend=3655.72 + 0.12*Transaction Time + 0.15*Monthly Income -16*City_Tier 2 - 94*Sex_Female

One of the three dummy variables can be converted to baseline by masking it. Remember, we said earlier that only (n-1) dummy variables are needed for a categorical variable with n levels. However, here you are seeing three dummy variable for **City Tier** (three levels) and two dummy variables for *Gender* (two levels). This is just because it is easier to understand this way. There is only n-1 variables required for n-level categorical variables.

We can use (n-1) variables by masking one of the variables from the list of dummy variables going into the model. This masked variable will then become the baseline for the coefficients associated with these dummy variables.

Let's do that and see how the coefficients change:

```
dummy_gender=pd.get_dummies(df['Gender'],prefix='Sex').iloc[:, 1:]
dummy_city_tier=pd.get_dummies(df['City Tier'],prefix='City').iloc[:,
1:]
column_name=df.columns.values.tolist()
df3=df[column_name].join(dummy_gender)
column_name1=df3.columns.values.tolist()
df4=df3[column_name1].join(dummy_city_tier)
df4
```

It is the same process of converting categorical variables to dummy variables, but we are masking the first variable from the resulting list using the `iloc` method of subsetting.

The resulting data frame has one dummy variable for **Gender** and two for **City Tier** and is similar to the following screenshot:

	Transaction ID	Age	Items	Monthly Income	Transaction Time	Record	Gender	City Tier	Total Spend	Sex_Male	City_Tier 2	City_Tier 3
0	TXN001	42	10	7313	627.668127	5	Female	Tier 1	4198.385084	0	0	0
1	TXN002	24	8	17747	126.904567	3	Female	Tier 2	4134.976648	0	1	0

Fig. 5.22: Ecom expense dataset with only (n-1) dummy variables

Let's now use these variables into the model and see how the coefficients change:

```
from sklearn.linear_model import LinearRegression
feature_cols = ['Monthly Income','Transaction Time','City_Tier
2','City_Tier 3','Sex_Male']
X = df2[feature_cols]
Y = df2['Total Spend']
lm = LinearRegression()
lm.fit(X,Y)
```

The variables and their coefficients can be obtained in the same way as earlier. They are as follows:

```
print lm.intercept_
print lm.coef_
zip(feature_cols, lm.coef_)
```

```
3681.23486046
[  1.52978246e-01   1.23726086e-01  -1.36342270e+02  -2.22647485e+02
    1.88315598e+02]

[('Monthly Income', 0.15297824609320476),
 ('Transaction Time', 0.12372608642590303),
 ('City_Tier 2', -136.34226961189151),
 ('City_Tier 3', -222.64748519981214),
 ('Sex_Male', 188.31559766064041)]
```

Fig. 5.23: Coefficients of the model

As one might observe, the coefficients of **City_Tier_2** and **City_Tier_3** variables along with that of the **Sex_Male** variables have changed while that of all the others remain the same. The change in the coefficient doesn't change the model as such, but just the account for the absence of the baseline dummy variable. The new coefficient for **City_Tier_2** is -136, which can be thought of as its coefficient when the **City_Tier_1** has a coefficient of 0 (we saw earlier it has a coefficient of 119):

Variable	Coefficient earlier	Coefficient later
City_Tier_1	120	0
City_Tier_2	-16	-136 (-16-120)
City_Tier_3	-102	-222(-102-120)
Sex_Male	94	188 (94-(-94))
Sex_Female	-94	0

Transforming a variable to fit non-linear relations

Sometimes the output variable doesn't have a direct linear relationship with the predictor variable. They have a non-linear relationship. These relationships could be simple functions like quadratic, exponential, logarithm, or complex ones such as polynomials. In such cases, transforming the variable comes in very handy.

The following is a rough guideline about how to go about it:

- Plot a scatter plot of the output variable with each of the predictor variables. This can be thought of as a scatter plot matrix similar to the correlation matrix.

- If the scatter plot assumes more or less a linear shape for a predictor variable then it is linearly related to the output variable.

- If the scatter plot assumes a characteristic shape of any of the non-linear shapes for a predictor variable then transform that particular variable by applying that function.

Let's illustrate this with one example. We will use the `Auto.csv` dataset for this. This dataset contains information about **miles per gallon (mpg)** and horsepower for a number of car models and much more. The mpg is the predictor variable and is considered to be highly dependent on the horsepower of a car model.

Let's import the dataset and have a look at it before proceeding further:

```
import pandas as pd
data = pd.read_csv('E:/Personal/Learning/Predictive Modeling Book/Book
Datasets/Linear Regression/Auto.csv')
data.head()
```

This is how the dataset looks:

	mpg	cylinders	displacement	horsepower	weight	acceleration	model year	origin	car name
0	18	8	307	130	3504	12.0	70	1	chevrolet chevelle malibu
1	15	8	350	165	3693	11.5	70	1	buick skylark 320
2	18	8	318	150	3436	11.0	70	1	plymouth satellite
3	16	8	304	150	3433	12.0	70	1	amc rebel sst
4	17	8	302	140	3449	10.5	70	1	ford torino

Fig. 5.24: Auto dataset

It has 406 rows and 9 columns. Some of the variables have NA values and it makes sense to drop the NA values before using them.

Now, let's plot a scatter plot between the horsepower and the mpg variables to see whether they exhibit a linear shape or some non-linear shape:

```
import matplotlib.pyplot as plt
%matplotlib inline
data['mpg']=data['mpg'].dropna()
```

```
data['horsepower']=data['horsepower'].dropna()
plt.plot(data['horsepower'],data['mpg'],'ro')
plt.xlabel('Horsepower')
plt.ylabel('MPG (Miles Per Gallon)')
```

As can be seen in the output, the relationship doesn't seem to have a linear shape but rather assumes a non-linear shape; it is most probably an exponential or quadratic kind of relationship.

However, for the sake of comparison, let's try and fit a linear model for the relationship between mpg and horsepower first and then compare it with the scatter plot.

We are assuming that the model is:

$$mpg = c_0 + a_1.horsepower$$

While it looks like that the model is something similar to:

$$mpg = c_0 + a_1.horsepower^2$$

$$mpg = c_0 + a_1.horsepower + a_2.horsepower^2$$

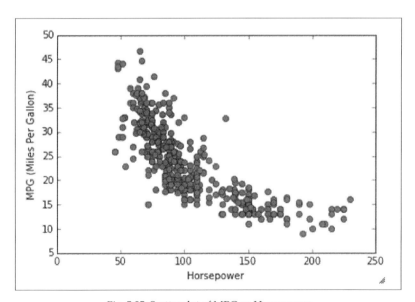

Fig. 5.25: Scatterplot of MPG vs Horsepower

The following code snippet will fit a linear model between `horsepower` and `mpg` variables. The NA values need to be dropped from the variables before they can be used in the model. Also simultaneously, let us create a model assuming a linear relationship between mpg and square of horsepower:

```
import numpy as np
from sklearn.linear_model import LinearRegression
X=data['horsepower'].fillna(data['horsepower'].mean())
Y=data['mpg'].fillna(data['mpg'].mean())
lm=LinearRegression()
lm.fit(X[:,np.newaxis],Y)
```

The linear regression method by default requires that X be an array of two dimensions. Using `np.newaxis`, we are creating a new dimension for it to function properly.

The line of best fit can be plotted by the following snippet:

```
import matplotlib.pyplot as plt
%matplotlib inline
plt.plot(data['horsepower'],data['mpg'],'ro')
plt.plot(X,lm.predict(X[:,np.newaxis]),color='blue')
```

The plot looks similar to the following graph. The blue line is the line of the best fit:

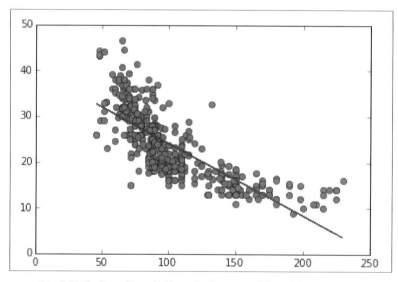

Fig. 5.26:The line of best fit (from the linear model) and the scatterplot

The R^2 for this model can be obtained using the following snippet:

```
lm1.score(X[:,np.newaxis],Y)
```

The value comes out to be 0.605.

Let's now calculate the RSE for this model in a different manner:

```
RSEd=(Y-lm.predict(X[:,np.newaxis]))**2
RSE=np.sqrt(np.sum(RSEd)/389)
ymean=np.mean(Y)
error=RSE/ymean
RSE,error
```

Here, we are using the predict method to calculate the predicted value from the model instead of writing them explicitly.

The value of RSE for this model comes out to be 5.14, which over a mean value of 23.51 gives an error of 21%.

If the model is of the form $mpg = c_0 + a_1.horsepower^2$, then it can be fitted after transforming the horsepower variable, as shown in the following snippet:

```
import numpy as np
from sklearn.linear_model import LinearRegression
X=data['horsepower'].fillna(data['horsepower'].
mean())*data['horsepower'].fillna(data['horsepower'].mean())
Y=data['mpg'].fillna(data['mpg'].mean())
lm=LinearRegression()
lm.fit(X[:,np.newaxis],Y)
```

The R^2 value for this model comes out to be around 0.51 and there is a scope of improvement in this model. The RSE can be calculated in the same manner, as shown in the preceding section using the following code snippet:

```
type(lm.predict(X[:,np.newaxis]))
RSEd=(Y-lm.predict(X[:,np.newaxis]))**2
RSE=np.sqrt(np.sum(RSEd)/390)
ymean=np.mean(Y)
error=RSE/ymean
RSE,error,ymean
```

The value of RSE for this model comes out to be 10.51, which over a mean value of 23.51 gives an error of 45%. The RSE increased when we transformed the variable exponentially.

Thus, we need to look at some other method to fit this seemingly non-linear data. What about polynomial fits that are, as follows:

$$Model: \ mpg = c_0 + a_1.horsepower + a_2.horsepower^2$$

This can be fitted using the `PolynomialFeatures` method in the `scikit-learn` library. In this model, we are assuming a polynomial relationship between mpg and horsepower:

```
from sklearn.preprocessing import PolynomialFeatures
from sklearn import linear_model
X=data['horsepower'].fillna(data['horsepower'].mean())
Y=data['mpg'].fillna(data['mpg'].mean())
poly = PolynomialFeatures(degree=2)
X_ = poly.fit_transform(X[:,np.newaxis])
clf = linear_model.LinearRegression()
clf.fit(X_, Y)
```

The `PolynomialFeatures` method used in this method automatically generates the powers (up to the specified degree) of the `X` variable using its `transform` feature. In this case, the R^2 value comes out to be 0.688. The R^2 value increased considerably when we introduced the polynomial regression.

The coefficients for this model come out to be, as follows:

```
print clf.intercept_
print clf.coef_
```

```
55.0261924471
[ 0.          -0.43404318   0.00112615]
```

Fig. 5.27: Model coefficients

The model can be written as:

$$mpg = 55.02 - 0.43 * horsepower + 0.001 * horsepower^2$$

Let us increase the degree and see whether it increases the R^2 further or not. One just needs to change the degree from 2 to 5.

```
from sklearn.preprocessing import PolynomialFeatures
from sklearn import linear_model
X=data['horsepower'].fillna(data['horsepower'].mean())
Y=data['mpg'].fillna(data['mpg'].mean())
poly = PolynomialFeatures(degree=5)
X_ = poly.fit_transform(X[:,np.newaxis])
clf = linear_model.LinearRegression()
clf.fit(X_, Y)
```

The model in this case will be:

$$mpg = c_0 + a_1.horsepower + a_2.horsepower^2 + a_3.horsepower^3 + a_4.horsepower^4 + a_5.horsepower^5$$

The R^2 for this model comes out to be 0.70. After that degree, an increase in degree doesn't improve the value of R^2.

The model coefficients can be found, as follows:

```
print clf.intercept_
print clf.coef_
```

```
-40.6938754274
[  0.00000000e+00    4.00021432e+00    -7.54801920e-02    6.19621369e-04
  -2.36220932e-06    3.41983087e-09]
```

Fig. 5.28: Model coefficients

$$mpg = -40.69 + 4*.horsepower + 7.54*horsepower^2 - 6.19*horsepower^3 - 2.32*horsepower^4 + 3.14horsepower^5$$

The reader can try the models of higher degrees as well and see how the coefficients change and whether it improves the model further (minimizing the error). The reader can also try to plot the results after the polynomial fit to see how it has improved the results.

Handling outliers

Outliers are the points in the dataset that are way out of the league of the other points. If a scatterplot of the concerned variable is drawn, the outliers can be easily identified, as they lay significantly away from the other data points.

The outliers need to be removed or properly treated before using the dataset for modelling. The outliers can distort the model and reduce its efficacy even if they are less in number, compared to the size of the dataset. As low as 1% outlier data is also capable enough to distort the model. It is actually not the number of outlier points but the degree to which it is different from an average point that determines the degree of distortion.

Let us look at a scatterplot of a dataset that has outliers:

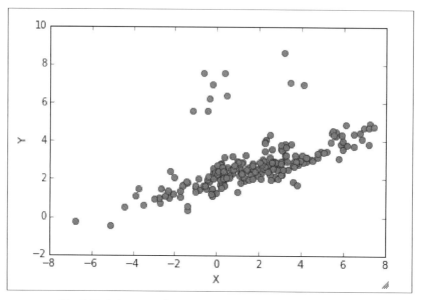

Fig. 5.29: A dataset with outliers. Outliers in the encircled region

As we can see, the points in the encircled region lie away from where the majority of the points lie. These points lying in the encircled regions are outliers.

Let's now see how it affects the modelling process. To illustrate that, let's look at the result of a linear regression model built upon the dataset with outliers. We will then compare this result to the results of a linear regression model derived from the dataset from which the outliers have been removed.

The best fit line for the model developed from the dataset with outliers looks similar to the following screenshot:

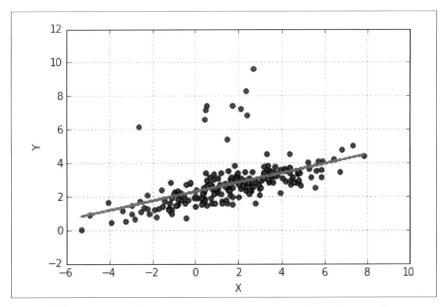

Fig. 5.30: Best fit line for the linear regression model developed over dataset with outliers

The model summary for this model is, as follows:

OLS Regression Results			
Dep. Variable:	Y	**R-squared:**	0.253
Model:	OLS	**Adj. R-squared:**	0.250
Method:	Least Squares	**F-statistic:**	70.61
Date:	Tue, 15 Sep 2015	**Prob (F-statistic):**	6.82e-15
Time:	22:45:01	**Log-Likelihood:**	-328.84
No. Observations:	210	**AIC:**	661.7
Df Residuals:	208	**BIC:**	668.4
Df Model:	1		

	coef	std err	t	P>|t|	[95.0% Conf. Int.]
Intercept	2.2896	0.098	23.456	0.000	2.097 2.482
X	0.2790	0.033	8.403	0.000	0.214 0.344

Fig. 5.31: Summary of the linear regression model developed over dataset with outliers

Let's now remove the outliers from the data and run the same linear regression model to check whether there is an improvement in the model or not.

The data without the outliers looks similar to the following screenshot:

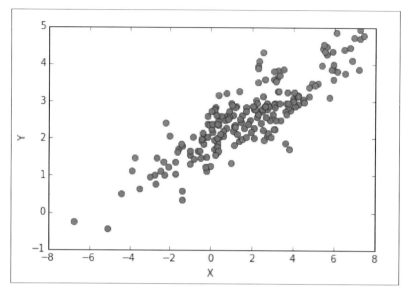

Fig. 5.32: The dataset after removing outliers

The best fit line for the model developed from the dataset without outliers looks as follows:

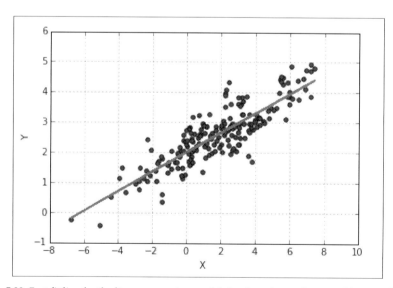

Fig. 5.33: Best fit line for the linear regression model developed over dataset without outliers

The model summary for this model is as follows:

OLS Regression Results			
Dep. Variable:	Y	**R-squared:**	0.739
Model:	OLS	**Adj. R-squared:**	0.738
Method:	Least Squares	**F-statistic:**	560.7
Date:	Tue, 15 Sep 2015	**Prob (F-statistic):**	1.16e-59
Time:	23:25:09	**Log-Likelihood:**	-145.84
No. Observations:	200	**AIC:**	295.7
Df Residuals:	198	**BIC:**	302.3
Df Model:	1		

	coef	std err	t	P>|t|	[95.0% Conf. Int.]
Intercept	2.0044	0.043	46.522	0.000	1.919 2.089
X	0.3241	0.014	23.678	0.000	0.297 0.351

Fig. 5.34: Summary of the linear regression model developed over the dataset without outliers

As we can see, the model has improved significantly especially in the terms of R^2 and F-statistic and the associated p-values. The model coefficients have also changed.

The following table is a comparison between the two models in terms of the parameters:

Parameter	Model w/o outliers	Model with outlier
R2	0.739	0.253
F-statistic	560.7	70.61
Coefficient	2.004	2.289
Intercept	0.3241	0.279
RSE	19.5%	41.4%

As it can be seen in the preceding comparison table, the model without outliers is better than the model with outliers in all the aspects. Thus, it is essentials to check for outliers in variables of the dataset and remove them from the dataset before using it for modelling.

The following are the ways in which one can identify outliers in the dataset:

- Plotting a scatter plot of the concerned variable.
- Boxplots are potent tools to spot outliers in a distribution. Any value *1.5*IQR* below the 1st quartile and *1.5*IQR* above the 1st quartile can be classified as an outlier. The difference in the 1st and 3rd quartile values is called the **Inter Quartile Range (IQR)**.
- Another method is to calculate the error (the difference between the actual value and the value predicted from the model) and set a cut-off for the error. Anything outside this cut-off will be an outlier.

Other considerations and assumptions for linear regression

There are certain assumptions and considerations that need to be taken into account before finalizing on the model. Here are some of these.

Residual plots: The residual is the difference between the actual value and the predicted value of the output variable. A plot of the residuals plotted against the predictor variable should be randomly (normally with mean zero and constant variance) distributed and shouldn't have an identifiable shape. If the residual follows a characteristic curve, then it means that these errors can be predicted, which means something is wrong with the model and there is a scope for improvement. The error term for a fair estimate should be random and that's why if the residual plot shows a characteristic pattern there is a reason to improvise upon the model.

Ideally, the points in a residual plot should be:

- Symmetrically distributed or tending to cluster towards the middle of the plot
- There are no clear patterns in the plot

The non-ideal residual plots having characteristic shapes are observed because of one of the following reasons:

- Non-linear relationship
- Presence of outliers
- Very large *Y*-axis datapoint

This can be taken care of by transforming the variable or removing the outlier:

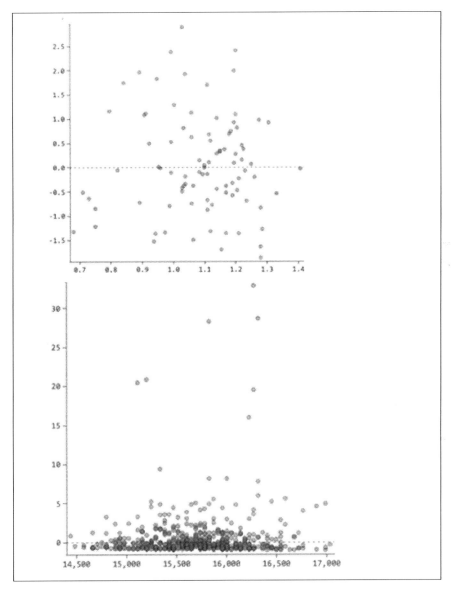

Fig. 5.35: What residual plot should look like vs. what residual plot shouldn't look like

Non-constant variance of error terms: The error term associated with the model is assumed to have a constant variance and several calculations, standard errors, and confidence intervals. Hypothesis tests rely upon this assumption.

This problem is called **heteroscedasticity** and can be identified by a funnel shaped pattern in the residual plot. Transforming the output variable using a concave function, such as *sqrt(Y)* or *log(Y)* generally solves the problem.

High leverage points: In contrast to outliers, which have high values for the output variables, the high leverage points have a very high value of predictor variables. Such a value can distort the model. For a model with single predictor, it is easy to identify this issue. It can be done in the same way, as in the case of outliers.

It is difficult to do so in case of multiple regressions, where there are more than one predictor variable. In this case, a variable can have a value which brings a considerable change in the output variable compared to the same change in another variable; such points are called high leverage points. These need to be removed and sometimes, their removal increases the efficiency of the model more than the removal of the outlier.

To identify high leverage points in such cases, one calculates something called leverage statistics, which is defined as:

$$Leverage = \frac{1}{n} + \frac{\left(xi - xm\right)^2}{\Sigma\left(x'i - xm\right)^2}$$

Where:

- *xi*: This is the value of the ith row of predictor variable *x*
- *xm*: This is the mean of the predictor variable *x*

The denominator is summed over all the variables for that particular row.

The rows with high values of leverage statistics are ruled out of the dataset before kicking off the modelling process.

Summary

This chapter marks the beginning of the introduction to the algorithms, which are the backbone of predictive modelling. These algorithms are converted into mathematical equations based on the historical data. These equations are the predictive models.

In this chapter, we discussed the simplest and the most widely used predictive modelling technique called linear regression.

Here is a list of things that we learned in this chapter:

- Linear regression assumes a linear relationship between an output variable and one or more predictor variables. The one with a single predictor variable is called a simple linear regression while the one with multiple variables is called multiple linear regression.

- The coefficients of the linear relationship (model) are estimated using the least sum of squares method.

- In Python, `statsmodel.api` and `scikit-learn` are the two methods to implement Python.

- The coefficient of determination, R^2, is a good way to gauge the efficiency of the model in explaining the error between the predicted value and the actual value. The more the value of R^2, the lesser the error and the better the model.

- The model parameters, such as p-values associated with the estimates of the co-efficients, F-statistic, and RSE should be analyzed to further assess the efficiency of the model.

- Multi-collinearity is an issue that arises when two of the input variables in a multiple regression model are highly correlated. This increases the variability of the coefficient estimates of the correlated variables. Variance Inflation Factor or VIF statistic can be used to select variables getting affected due to multi-collinearity. Variables with a very high VIF should be removed from the model.

- A dataset can be broken into training and testing data before starting the modelling process, in order to validate the model. K-fold cross validation (about which we will learn more later) is another popular method.

- `scikit-learn` has inbuilt methods for variable selection which will take a lot of time, if done manually.

- Categorical variables can be included in the model by converting them into dummy variables.

- Some variables might need to be transformed before they are fit into a linear function. Sometimes, a variable might exhibit polynomial relationship with its predictor variable.

The linear regression is the simplest of all the predictive models. But after going through this chapter, we should be able to appreciate the complexities involved in the process. There can be multiple variations and the fine-tuning of the model is an elaborate process.

However, there's nothing to be worried about. We have gathered all the armor we need to implement a linear regression and understanding the model coefficients and parameters. The variations and kind of data shouldn't deter us in our endeavor. We need to fine tune the model using the methods discussed in this chapter.

6
Logistic Regression with Python

In the previous chapter, we learned about linear regression. We saw that linear regression is one of the most basic models that assumes that there is a linear relationship between a predictor variable and an output variable.

In this chapter, we will be discussing the details of logistic regression. We will be covering the following topics in this chapter:

- **Math behind logistic regression**: Logistic regression relies on concepts such as conditional probability and odds ratio. In this chapter, we will understand what they mean and how they are applied. We will also see how the odds ratio is transformed to establish a linear relationship with the predictor variable. We will analyze the final logistic regression equation and understand the meaning of each term and coefficient.

- **Implementing logistic regression with Python**: Similar to what we did in the last chapter, we will take a dataset and implement a logistic regression model on it to understand the various nuances of logistic regression. We will use both the `statsmodel.api` and `scikit-learn` modules for doing this.

- **Model validation**: The model, once developed, needs to be validated to assess the accuracy and efficiency of the model. We will see how a *k-fold cross validation* works to validate a model. We will also understand concepts such as Sensitivity, Specificity, and the **Receiver Operating Characteristic** (ROC) curve and see how they are used for model validation.

Linear regression versus logistic regression

One thing to note about the linear regression model is that the output variable is always a continuous variable. In other words, linear regression is a good choice when one needs to predict continuous numbers. However, what if the output variable is a discrete number. What if we want to classify our records in two or more categories? Can we still extend the assumptions of a linear relationship and try to classify the records?

As it happens, there is a separate regression model that takes care of a situation where the output variable is a binary or categorical variable rather than a continuous variable. This model is called logistic regression. In other words, logistic regression is a variation of linear regression where the output variable is a binary or categorical variable. The two regressions are similar in the sense that they both assume a linear relationship between the predictor and output variables. However, as we will see soon, the output variable needs to undergo some transformation in the case of logistic regression.

A few scenarios where logistic regression can be applied are as follows:

- To predict whether a random customer will buy a particular product or not, given his details such as income, gender, shopping history, and advertisement history

- To predict whether a team will win or lose a match, given the match and team details such as weather, form of players, stadium, and hours spent in training

   Note how the output variable in both the cases is a binary or categorical variable.

The following table contains a comparison of the two models:

	Linear regression	**Logistic regression**
Predictor variables	Continuous numeric/categorical	Continuous numeric/categorical
Output variables	Continuous numeric	Categorical
Relationship	Linear	Linear (with some transformations)

Before we delve into implementing and assessing the model, it is of critical importance to understand the mathematics that makes the foundation of the algorithm. Let us try to understand some mathematical concepts that make the backbone of the logistic regression model.

Understanding the math behind logistic regression

Imagine a situation where we have a dataset from a supermarket store about the gender of the customer and whether that person bought a particular product or not. We are interested in finding the chances of a customer buying that particular product, given their gender. What comes to mind when someone poses this question to you? Probability anyone? Odds of success?

What is the probability of a customer buying a product, given he is a male? What is the probability of a customer buying that product, given she is a female? If we know the answers to these questions, we can make a leap towards predicting the chances of a customer buying a product, given their gender.

Let us look at such a dataset. To do so, we write the following code snippet:

```
import pandas as pd
df=pd.read_csv('E:/Personal/Learning/Predictive Modeling Book/Book
Datasets/Logistic Regression/Gender Purchase.csv')
df.head()
```

	Gender	Purchase
0	Female	Yes
1	Female	Yes
2	Female	No
3	Male	No
4	Male	Yes

Fig. 6.1: Gender and Purchase dataset

The first column mentions the gender of the customer and the second column mentions whether that particular customer bought the product or not. There are a total of 511 rows in the dataset, as can be found out by typing `df.shape`.

Contingency tables

A contingency table is basically a representation of the frequency of observations falling under various categories of two or more variables. It comes in a matrix form and essentially contains the frequency of occurrences for the combination of categories of two or more variables.

Let us create a contingency table for the dataset we just imported and get a sense of how such a table actually looks. Creating a contingency table in Python is very simple and can be done in a single line using the `crosstab` method in the `pandas` library. One can actually create a `crosstab` object and use it for other purposes such as adding row/column sums. Here, we are creating a contingency table for the `Gender` and `Purchase` variables:

```
contingency_table=pd.crosstab(df['Gender'],df['Purchase'])
contingency_table
```

Purchase	No	Yes
Gender		
Female	106	159
Male	125	121

Fig. 6.2: Contingency table between Gender and Purchase variables

The interpretation of this table is simple. It implies that there are 106 females who didn't purchase that product, while 159 bought it. Similarly, 125 males didn't buy that particular product, but 121 did. Let us now find the total number of males and females for the purpose of calculating probabilities. The sum can be found out by simple manual addition. However, for the purpose of demonstrating how to do it in Python, let us do it using a code snippet:

```
contingency_table.sum(axis=1)
contingency_table.sum(axis=0)
```

```
Gender                          Purchase
Female     265                  No          231
Male       246                  Yes         280
dtype: int64                    dtype: int64
```

Calculating the total across gender (rows)   **Calculating the total across purchase (columns)**

Fig. 6.3: Totals across the rows and columns of the contingency table

Rather than calculating numbers, one can calculate the proportions as well. In our case, we will try to calculate the proportion of males and females who purchased and who didn't purchase a particular product. The whole calculation can be done programmatically also using the following code snippet:

```
contingency_table.astype('float').div(contingency_table.
sum(axis=1),axis=0)
```

The result of the snippet looks as follows:

Purchase	No	Yes
Gender		
Female	0.40000	0.60000
Male	0.50813	0.49187

Fig. 6.4: The contingency table for Gender and Purchase in percentage format

Creating a contingency table is a first step towards exploring the data that has a binary outcome variable and categorical predictor variable.

Conditional probability

Remember the questions we asked at the beginning of this section? What is the probability of a customer buying a product, given he is a male? What is the probability of a customer buying that product, given she is a female? These questions are the reasons behind something called **conditional probability**.

Conditional probability basically defines the probability of a certain event happening, given that a certain related event is true or has already happened. Look at the questions above. They perfectly fit the description for conditional probability. The conditional probability of a purchase, given the customer is male, is denoted as follows:

$$Probability(Purchase \backslash Male)$$

It is calculated by the following formula:

$$Probability(Purchase / Male) = \frac{Total\ number\ of\ purchases\ by\ males}{Total\ number\ of\ males\ in\ the\ group}$$

Now, when we know the required numbers and formulae, let us calculate the probabilities we were interested in before:

$$Probability\,(Purchase\,/\,Male) = 121\,/\,246 = 0.49$$
$$Probability\,(Not\,Purchase\,/\,Male) = 125\,/\,246 = 1 - 0.49 = 0.51$$
$$Probability\,(Purchase\,/\,Female) = 159\,/\,265 = 0.60$$
$$Probability\,(Not\,Purchase\,/\,Male) = 106\,/\,265 = 1 - 0.60 = 0.40$$

This concept comes in very handy in understanding many of the predictive models, as it is the building block of many of them.

Odds ratio

This is the correct time to introduce a very important concept called **odds ratio**. The odds ratio is a ratio of odds of success (purchase in this case) for each group (male and female in this case).

Odds of success for a group are defined as the ratio of probability of successes (purchases) to the probability of failures (non-purchases). In our case, the odds of the purchase for the group of males and females can be defined as follows:

$$Odds\,of\,purchase\,by\,males = P_m\,/\,(1 - P_m)$$
$$Odds\,of\,purchase\,by\,females = P_f\,/\,(1 - P_f)$$

Here, Pm=probability of purchase by males and Pf=probability of purchase by females.

For the preceding contingency table given:

$$P_m = 121\,/\,246, Pf = 159\,/\,265$$
$$Odds\,of\,purchase\,by\,males = (121\,/\,246)\,/\,(125\,/\,246) = 121\,/\,125$$
$$Odds\,of\,purchase\,by\,females = Pf\,/\,(1 - Pf) = (159\,/\,265)\,/\,(106\,/\,265) = 159\,/\,106$$

As it is obvious from the calculations above, the odds of the success for a particular group can easily be written as follows:

$$Odds\ of\ success\ for\ males = N_{sm} / N_{fm}$$

$$Odds\ of\ success\ for\ females = N_{sf} / N_{ff}$$

Here, Ns=number of successes in that group and Nf=number of failures in that group.

A few points to be noted about the odds of an event are as follows:

- If the odds of success for a group is more than 1, then it is more likely for that group to be successful. The higher the odds, the better the chances of success.

- If the odds of success is less than 1, then then it is more likely to get a failure. The lower the odds, the higher the chances of failure.

- The odds can range from 0 to infinity.

In our case, the odds of success is greater than 1 for females and less than 1 for males. Thus, we can conclude that females have a better chance of success (purchase), in this case, than males.

One better way to determine which group has better odds of success is by calculating odds ratios for each group. The odds ratio is defined as follows:

$$Odds\ ratio = Odd\ of\ success\ in\ Group\ 1 / Odds\ of\ success\ in\ group\ 2$$

$$Odds\ ratio = \frac{Pm / (1 - Pm)}{Pf / (1 - Pf)}$$

$$Odds\ ratio = \frac{Nsm / Nfm}{Nsf / Nff}$$

In the preceding example we have seen:

$$Odds\ ratio(for\ males) = Odds\ of\ success\ for\ males / Odds\ of\ success\ for\ females$$

$$= (121 / 125) / (159 / 106) = 0.64$$

$$Odds\ ratio(for\ males) = Odds\ of\ Purchase\ for\ female / Odds\ of\ purchase\ by\ males$$

$$= (159 / 106) / (121 / 125) = 1.54$$

Actually,

$$Odds\ ratio(for\ Group1) = 1 / Odds\ ratio\ (for\ Group\ 2)$$

There are a couple of important things to note about the odds ratio:

- The more the odds ratio, the more the chances of success from that group. In our case, the female group has an odds ratio of 1.54, which means that it is more probable to get success (purchase) from a female customer than a male customer.

- If the odds *ratio=1*, then there is no association between the two variables. If odds *ratio>1*, then the event is more likely to happen in *Group 1*. If the odds *ratio<1*, then the event is more likely to happen in *Group 2*.

- Also, the odds ratio for one group can be obtained by taking the reciprocal of the odds ratio of the other group.

Moving on to logistic regression from linear regression

If you remember, the equation for a simple linear regression model was as follows:

$$Y = a + b * X$$

In this case, Y was a continuous variable whose value can range from –infinity to +infinity. The X was either a continuous or a dummy categorical variable and hence it also ranged from –infinity to +infinity. So, the ranges of variables on both the sides of the equation matched.

However, when we move to logistic regression, the Y variable can take only discrete values, 0 or 1, as the outcome variable is a binary variable. However, predicting 0 or 1 using an equation similar to linear regression is not possible. What if we try to predict the probabilities associated with the two events rather than the binary outcomes? Predicting the probabilities will be feasible as their range spans from 0 to 1.

Earlier, we calculated the conditional probability of a customer purchasing a particular product, given he is male or female. These are the probabilities we are thinking of predicting. In the case demonstrated above, there was only one predictor variable, so it was very easy. However, as the number of predictor variables increase, these conditional probabilities will become more and more difficult to calculate. However, anyways, predicting probability is a better choice than predicting 0 or 1. Hence, for logistic regression, something like the following suits better:

$$P = a + b * X$$

Here P=conditional probability of success/failure given the X variable

Even with this new equation, the problem of non-matching ranges on both the sides of the equation persists. The P ranges from 0 to 1, while X ranges from –infinity to +infinity. What if we replace the P with odds, that is, $P/1$-P. We have seen earlier that the odds can range from 0 to +infinity. So, the proposed equation becomes:

$$P/1 - P = a + b * X$$

Where P=conditional probability of success/failure given the X variable

Still the LHS of the equation ranges from 0 to +infinity, while the RHS ranges from –infinity to +infinity. How to get rid of this? We need to transform one side of the equation so that the ranges on both the sides match. What if we take a natural logarithm of the odds (LHS of the equation)? Then, the range on the LHS also becomes –infinity to +infinity.

So, the final equation becomes as follows:

$$\log(P/1 - P) = a + b * X$$

Here, P=conditional probability of success/failure given the X variable.

The term log$_e$(Odds) is called **logit**.

 The base of the logarithm is e (e=2.73) as we have taken a natural logarithm.

The transformation can be better understood if we look at the plot of a logarithmic function. For a base greater than 1, the plot of a logarithmic function is shown as follows:

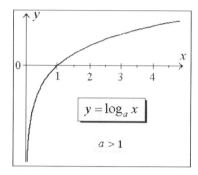

Fig. 6.5: The plot of a logarithmic curve for a base>1

The summary of the ranges of odds and the corresponding ranges of the loge(Odds) can be summarized as follows:

Range of Odds	Range of loge(Odds)
0 to 1	-infinity to 0
1 to +infinity	0 to +infinity

The evolution of the transformations that lead from linear to logistic regression can be summarized as follows. The range on the RHS of the equation is always –infinity to +infinity while we transform the LHS to match it:

Transformation (LHS)	Range of LHS	Range of LHS
Y	*Y= 0 or Y= 1*	*Infinity<X<+infinity*
P (Probability)	*0<P<1*	*Infinity<X<+infinity*
P/1-P (Odds)	*0<P/1-P<+infinity*	*Infinity<X<+infinity*
log(P/1-P)	*-infinity<log(P/1-P)<+infinity*	*Infinity<X<+infinity*

The final equation we have for logistic regression is as follows:

$$\log(P / 1 - P) = a + b * X$$

$$\frac{P}{1-P} = e^{a+b*X}$$

$$P = \frac{e^{a+b*X}}{1+e^{a+b*X}} = \frac{1}{1+e^{-(a+b*X)}}$$

The final equation can be used to calculate the probability, given the value of X, a, and b:

- If $a+b*X$ is very small, then P approaches 0
- If $a+b*X$ is very large, then P approaches 1
- If $a+b*X$ is), then $P=0.5$

For a multiple logistic regression, the equation can be written as follows:

$$\log(P/1-P) = a + b_1 * X_1 + b_2 * X_2 + b_3 * X_3 + \ldots\ldots\ldots\ldots\ldots + b_n * X_n$$

$$P = \frac{1}{1 + e^{-(a+b_1*X_1+b_2*X_2+b_3*X_3+\ldots+bn*Xn)}}$$

If we replace $(X1, X2, X3,\ldots,Xn)$ with Xi' and $(b1, b2, b3,----,bn)$ with bi', the equation can be rewritten as follows:

$$P = \frac{e^{a+b*Xi'}}{1+e^{a+b*Xi'}} = \frac{1}{1+e^{-(a+b*Xi')}}$$

Estimation using the Maximum Likelihood Method

The variables a and bi are estimated using the **Maximum Likelihood Method (MLE)**.

For a multivariate data having multiple variables and n observations, the **likelihood** (L) or the joint probability is defined as follows:

$$L = P_1 * P_3 * \ldots * P_n (1 - P_2)\ldots*(1-P_n)$$

$$= \prod_{i=1,y=1}^{n} Pi * \prod_{i=1,y=0}^{n}(1-Pi)$$

Here, Pi is the probability associated with the ith observation. When the outcome variable is positive (or 1), we take Pi for multiplying; when it is negative (or 0), we take $(1-Pi)$ for multiplying in the likelihood function:

As we have seen already, the defining equation for logistic regression is as follows:

$$Pi = \frac{e^{a+b*Xi}}{1+e^{a+b*Xi}} = \frac{1}{1+e^{-(a+b*Xi)}}$$

Also, assume that the output variable is Y1, Y2, Y3,…,Yn, all of which can take the value 0 or 1. For one predictor variable, the best estimate to predict the probability of the success is the mean value of all Yi's:

$$E\left[Y_i\right] = Y_m = P_i$$

Here, E[Yi] = Ym is the mean of Yi's.

Hence, the equation above can be rewritten as follows:

$$P_i = Y_m = \frac{e^{a+b*Xi}}{1+e^{a+b*Xi}} = \frac{1}{1+e^{-(a+b*X)}}$$

$$= \left(\sum_{i=1}^{n} Yi\right)/n = \frac{e^{a+b*Xi}}{1+e^{a+b*Xi}} = \frac{1}{1+e^{-(a+b*Xi)}}$$

Thus, the equation for Likelihood becomes as follows:

$$L = \prod_{i=1}^{n} \left(\frac{e^{a+b*Xi'} \sum_{i=1}^{n} Yi}{1+e^{a+b*Xi'}} \right) * \left(1 - \frac{e^{a+b*Xi'} \sum_{i=1}^{n} Yi}{1+e^{a+b*Xi'}} \right)$$

Taking log on both the sides:

$$logL = \sum_{i=1}^{n} \left[Yi * log\left(\frac{e^{a+b*Xi}}{1+e^{a+b*Xi}} \right) + \left(1 - Yi\right) * log\left(1 - \frac{e^{a+b*Xi}}{1+e^{a+b*Xi}} \right) \right]$$

To estimate the MLE of bi's, we equate the derivative of $logL$ to 0:

$$U = d(\log L) / dXi = 0$$

$d(logL)/dXi$ is the partial derivative of $logL$ with respect to each Xi (variable).

This equation is called the **Score** function and there would be as many such equations as there are variables in the dataset.

Another related calculation is that of the Fisher Information and it is given as the second derivative of $logL$:

$$Fischer\ Information = I = dU\ /\ dL$$

The Fisher Information is useful because its inverse gives the variance associated with the estimate of the bi. In the case of multiple variables, we will get a covariance matrix. It is also used to decide whether the values found with the help of setting the derivative to 0 were maxima or minima. These many equations will be difficult to solve analytically and there are numerical methods such as Newton-Raphson methods to do the same.

Let us go a little deeper into the mathematics behind calculating the coefficients using the maximum likelihood estimate. The following are the steps in this process:

1. Define a function that calculates the probability for each observation, given the data (predictor variables).

2. Define a likelihood function that multiplies Pi's and $(1-Pi)$'s for each observation, depending on whether the outcome is 1 or 0. Calculate the likelihood.

3. Use the Newton-Raphson method to calculate the roots. In the Newton-Raphson method, one starts with a value of the root and updates it using the following equation for a number of times until it stops improving:

$$Xn+1 = Xn - f(X) \backslash f'(X)$$

Likelihood function:

$$L(X|P) = \prod_{i=1, y_i=1}^{N} P(x_i) \prod_{i=1, y_i=0}^{N} (1 - P(x_i))$$

Log likelihood function:

$$L(X|P) = \sum_{i=1, y_i=1}^{N} \log P(x_i) + \sum_{i=0, y_i=0}^{N} \log(1 - P(x_i))$$

The derivative of the Log likelihood function is as follows:

$$\nabla_b L = \sum_{\substack{i=i \\ y_i=1}}^{N} \frac{P_i(1-p_i)}{P_i} x_i - \sum_{\substack{i=1 \\ y_i=0}}^{N} \frac{P_i(1-p_i)}{1-P_i} x_i$$

$$= \sum_{\substack{i=1 \\ y_i=1}}^{N} (1-p_i) x_i - \sum_{\substack{i=1 \\ y_i=0}}^{N} P_i x_i$$

$$= \sum_{i=1}^{N} \left[y_i(1-P_i) - (1-y_i)P_i \right] x_i$$

$$= \sum_{i=1}^{N} y_i x_i - P_i x_i = 0$$

The second derivative of the Log likelihood function is as follows:

$$H = \frac{\partial}{\partial b} \nabla_b L$$

$$= -\sum_{i=1}^{N} x_i \nabla_b P_i$$

$$= -\sum_{i=1}^{N} x_i P_i (1-P) x_i^T$$

$$= XWX^T$$

Partial derivatives have been taken with respect to the variable coefficients.

According to the Newton-Raphson method:

$$Xn+1 = Xn - f(X) f'(X)$$
$$\Delta X = f(X) f(X)$$

In this case, Newton-Raphson method translates to the following:

$$f(X) = first\ derivation\ of\ log\ likelihood\ function = X(Y - P)$$

$$f(X) = XWX^T$$

Here, W is a diagonal matrix containing the product of probabilities in the diagonal.

$$Hence, \Delta X = \left(XWX^T \right)^{-1} X(Y - P)$$

Here, we are solving for variable coefficients, that is, *a* and *b*. According to the Newton-Raphson method, if we calculate the multiplication above enough number of times, starting with an initial approximate value of variable coefficients (we assume 0 in this case), we will get the optimum values of coefficients. To help better understand the calculation behind the logistic regression, let us implement the mathematics behind the logistic regression using Python code. Let us build the logistic regression model from scratch.

Building the logistic regression model from scratch

The following are the steps to implement the mathematics behind the logistic regression. Before we start using the in-built methods in Python as a black box to implement logistic regression, let us create a code that can do all the computation and throw up coefficients and likelihoods as the results just the same way as a built in method in Python would. Each of the step has been defined as a separate Python function:

```
# Step 1: defining the likelihood function
def likelihood(y,pi):
    import numpy as np
    ll=1
    ll_in=range(1,len(y)+1)
    for i in range(len(y)):
        ll_in[i]=np.where(y[i]==1,pi[i],(1-pi[i]))
        ll=ll*ll_in[i]
    return ll
# Step 2: calculating probability for each observation
def logitprob(X,beta):
    import numpy as np
    rows=np.shape(X)[0]
    cols=np.shape(X)[1]
    pi=range(1,rows+1)
```

```
            expon=range(1,rows+1)
            for i in range(rows):
                expon[i]=0
                for j in range(cols):
                    ex=X[i][j]*beta[j]
                    expon[i]=ex+expon[i]
                with np.errstate(divide='ignore', invalid='ignore'):
                    pi[i]=np.exp(expon[i])/(1+np.exp(expon[i]))
            return pi
    # Step 3: Calculate the W diagonal matrix
    def findW(pi):
        import numpy as np
        W=np.zeros(len(pi)*len(pi)).reshape(len(pi),len(pi))
        for i in range(len(pi)):
            print i
            W[i,i]=pi[i]*(1-pi[i])
            W[i,i].astype(float)
        return W
    # Step 4: defining the logistic function
    def logistic(X,Y,limit):
        import numpy as np
        from numpy import linalg
        nrow=np.shape(X)[0]
        bias=np.ones(nrow).reshape(nrow,1)
        X_new=np.append(X,bias,axis=1)
        ncol=np.shape(X_new)[1]
        beta=np.zeros(ncol).reshape(ncol,1)
        root_diff=np.array(range(1,ncol+1)).reshape(ncol,1)
        iter_i=10000
        while(iter_i>limit):
            print iter_i, limit
            pi=logitprob(X_new,beta)
            print pi
            W=findW(pi)
            print W
            print X_new
            print (Y-np.transpose(pi))
            print np.array((linalg.inv(np.matrix(np.transpose(X_new))*np.
    matrix(W)*np.matrix(X_new)))*(np.transpose(np.matrix(X_new))*np.
    matrix(Y-np.transpose(pi)).transpose()))
            print beta
            print type(np.matrix(np.transpose(Y-np.transpose(pi))))
            print np.matrix(Y-np.transpose(pi)).transpose().shape
            print np.matrix(np.transpose(X_new)).shape
```

```
        root_diff=np.array((linalg.inv(np.matrix(np.transpose(X_
new))*np.matrix(W)*np.matrix(X_new)))*(np.transpose(np.matrix(X_
new))*np.matrix(Y-np.transpose(pi)).transpose()))
        beta=beta+root_diff
        iter_i=np.sum(root_diff*root_diff)
        ll=likelihood(Y,pi)
        print beta
        print beta.shape
    return beta
# Testing the model
import numpy as np
X=np.array(range(10)).reshape(10,1)
Y=[0,0,0,0,1,0,1,0,1,1]
bias=np.ones(10).reshape(10,1)
X_new=np.append(X,bias,axis=1)


# Running logistic Regression using our function
a=logistic(X,Y,0.000000001)
ll=likelihood(Y,logitprob(X,a))
Coefficient of X = 0.66 , Intercept = -3.69
# From stasmodel.api
import statsmodels.api as sm
logit_model=sm.Logit(Y,X_new)
result=logit_model.fit()
print result.summary()
Coefficient of X = 0.66, Intercept = -3.69
```

Isn't this cool?! We have been able to match the exact values for the variable coefficient and intercept. Run these codes in your Python IDE one by one and see what each snippet throws up as an output. Each of them is a separate function so you will have to give inputs to make them run. Compare it with the calculations performed above and see how the steps in the calculations have been implemented.

In Python, `scikit-learn` performs these calculations under the hood and throws up the estimates for the coefficients when asked to run a logistic regression.

Making sense of logistic regression parameters

As with the linear regression, there are various parameters that are thrown up by a logistic regression model, which can be assessed for variable selection and model accuracy.

Wald test

As in the case of linear regression, here also, we are estimating the values of the coefficients. There is a hypothesis test associated with each estimation. Here, we test the significance of the coefficients bi's:

$$Null\ Hypothesis : Ho : bi = 0$$

$$Alternate\ Hypothesis : Ha : bi <> 0$$

The Wald statistic is defined as follows:

$$Wald\ statistic = (b_{im} - 0) / sd(bi)$$

Here, bim=mean of bi and sd(bi)=standard error in estimation of bi.

The standard error comes from the Fisher Information covariance matrix. The Wald statistic assumes a standard normal distribution and, hence, we can perform a z-test over it. As we will see in the output of a logistic regression, there will be a p-value associated with the estimation of each bi. This p-value comes from this z-test. The smaller the p-value, the more the significance of that variable.

Likelihood Ratio Test statistic

The Likelihood Ratio Test statistic is the ratio of the (null) hypothesized value of the parameter to the MSE (alternate) values of the parameters.

The definition of the hypothesis test is the same as above:

$$Null\ Hypothesis : bi = 0$$

$$Alternate\ Hypothesis : bi <> 0$$

LR statistic is given by:

$$LR = -2\log(value\ of\ bi\ given\ Ho\ /\ value\ of\ bi\ given\ Ha)$$

$$= -2\log(bi\backslash Ho\ /\ bi\backslash Ha)$$

$$= -2\left[\left(log(bi\backslash Ho) - log\left(bi\backslash Ha\right)\right)\right]$$

To calculate the value of $bi \mid Ho$ and $bi \mid Ha$, we need to fit two different models and calculate the values of bi for each model.

If the proposed model is

$$log\left(P/1-P\right) = a + b_1 * X_1 + b_2 * X_2 + b_3 * X_3 + \ldots\ldots\ldots\ldots + b_n * X_n$$

If we are testing LR statistic for $b1$, then Ho would give rise to the following model:

$$Ho : log\left(P/1-P\right) = a + b_2 * X_2 + b_3 * X_3 + \ldots\ldots\ldots\ldots + b_n * X_n$$

Also, Ha would give rise to the following model:

$$Ha : log\left(P/1-P\right) = a + b_1 * X_1 + b_2 * X_2 + b_3 * X_3 + \ldots\ldots\ldots\ldots + b_n * X_n$$

The significance of the values of bi's is defined by the value of the LR statistic. The LR statistic follows a chi-square distribution with degrees of freedom equal to the difference in the degrees of freedom in two cases. If the p-value associated with this statistic is very small, then the alternate hypothesis is true, that is, the value of bi is significant and non-zero.

Both the models need to be fit and the MLE value of bi is calculated for bi from both the models. Then, a log of the ratio of the two values of bi gives the LR statistic.

Chi-square test

For large datasets (large n), a LR test reduces to a chi-square test with a degree of freedom equal to the number of parameters being estimated. This is the reason pairwise chi-square tests are often performed between the predictor and the outcome variable, in order to decide whether they are independent of each other or have some association. This is sometimes used for variable selection for the model. The variables for which there is an association between them and the outcome variable are better predictors of the outcome variable. If the null hypothesis for a predictor variable is rejected, then more often than not, it should be made a part of the model.

Implementing logistic regression with Python

We have understood the mathematics that goes behind the logistic regression algorithm. Now, let's take one dataset and implement a logistic regression model from scratch. The dataset we will be working with is from the marketing department of a bank and has data about whether the customers subscribed to a term deposit, given some information about the customer and how the bank has engaged and reached out to the customers to sell the term deposit.

Let us import the dataset and start exploring it:

```
import pandas as pd
bank=pd.read_csv('E:/Personal/Learning/Predictive Modeling Book/Book
Datasets/Logistic Regression/bank.csv',sep=';')
bank.head()
```

The dataset looks as follows:

	age	job	marital	education	default	housing	loan	contact	month	day_of_week	...	campaign	pdays	previous	poutcome	emp.var.l
0	30	blue-collar	married	basic.9y	no	yes	no	cellular	may	fri	..	2	999	0	nonexistent	-1.8
1	39	services	single	high.school	no	no	no	telephone	may	fri	..	4	999	0	nonexistent	1.1
2	25	services	married	high.school	no	yes	no	telephone	jun	wed	..	1	999	0	nonexistent	1.4
3	38	services	married	basic.9y	no	unknown	unknown	telephone	jun	fri	..	3	999	0	nonexistent	1.4
4	47	admin.	married	university.degree	no	yes	no	cellular	nov	mon	..	1	999	0	nonexistent	-0.1

Fig. 6.6: A glimpse of the bank dataset

There are 4119 records and 21 columns. The column names are as follows:

```
bank.columns.values
```

```
array(['age', 'job', 'marital', 'education', 'default', 'housing', 'loan',
       'contact', 'month', 'day_of_week', 'duration', 'campaign', 'pdays',
       'previous', 'poutcome', 'emp.var.rate', 'cons.price.idx',
       'cons.conf.idx', 'euribor3m', 'nr.employed', 'y'], dtype=object)
```

Fig. 6.7: The columns of the bank dataset

The details of each column are mentioned in the Data Dictionary file present in the Logistic Regression folder of the Google Drive folder. The type of the column can be found out as follows:

```
bank.dtypes
```

age	int64	duration	int64
job	object	campaign	int64
marital	object	pdays	int64
education	object	previous	int64
default	object	poutcome	object
housing	object	emp.var.rate	float64
loan	object	cons.price.idx	float64
contact	object	cons.conf.idx	float64
month	object	euribor3m	float64
day_of_week	object	nr.employed	float64
		y	object

Fig. 6.8: The column types of the bank dataset

Processing the data

The y column is the outcome variable recording yes and no. yes for customers who bought the term deposit and no for those who didn't. Let us start by converting yes-no to 0-1 so that they can be used in modelling. This can be done as follows:

```
bank['y']=(bank['y']=='yes').astype(int)
```

The preceding code snippet converts yes to 1 and no to 0. The astype method converts the True/False to integer (0/1).

The education column of the dataset has many categories and we need to reduce the categories for a better modelling. The education column has the following categories:

```
bank['education'].unique()
```

```
array(['basic.9y', 'high.school', 'university.degree',
       'professional.course', 'basic.6y', 'basic.4y', 'unknown',
       'illiterate'], dtype=object)
```

Fig. 6.9: The categories of the education column in the bank dataset

The basic category has been repeated three times probably to capture 4, 6, and 9 years of education. Let us club these three together and call them basic. Also, let us modify the categories so that they look better:

```
import numpy as np
bank['education']=np.where(bank['education'] =='basic.9y', 'Basic',
bank['education'])
bank['education']=np.where(bank['education'] =='basic.6y', 'Basic',
bank['education'])
bank['education']=np.where(bank['education'] =='basic.4y', 'Basic',
bank['education'])
```

```
bank['education']=np.where(bank['education'] =='university.degree',
'University Degree', bank['education'])
bank['education']=np.where(bank['education'] =='professional.course',
'Professional Course', bank['education'])
bank['education']=np.where(bank['education'] =='high.school', 'High
School', bank['education'])
bank['education']=np.where(bank['education'] =='illiterate',
'Illiterate', bank['education'])
bank['education']=np.where(bank['education'] =='unknown', 'Unknown',
bank['education'])
```

After the change, this is how the categories look:

```
['Basic',
 'High School',
 'University Degree',
 'Professional Course',
 'Unknown',
 'Illiterate']
```

Fig. 6.10: The column types of the bank dataset

Data exploration

First of all, let us find out the number of people who purchased the term deposit and those who didn't:

```
bank['y'].value_counts()
```

```
no        3668
yes        451
dtype: int64
```

Fig. 6.11: Total number of yes's and no's in the bank dataset

There are 3668 no's and 451 yes's in the outcome variables.

As you might have observed, there are many numerical variables in the dataset. Let us get a sense of the numbers across the two classes such as yes or no:

```
bank.groupby('y').mean()
```

	age	duration	campaign	pdays	previous	emp.var.rate	cons.price.idx	cons.conf.idx	euribor3m	nr.employed
y										
0	39.895311	219.40976	2.605780	982.763086	0.141767	0.240185	93.599677	-40.586723	3.802826	5175.502072
1	41.889135	560.78714	1.980044	778.722838	0.585366	-1.177384	93.417268	-39.786475	2.145448	5093.118625

Fig. 6.12: The mean of the numerical variables for yes's and no's

A few points to note from the preceding output are as follows:

- The average age of customers who bought the term deposit is higher than that of the customers who didn't.

- The *pdays* (days since the customer was last contacted) is understandably lower for the customers who bought it. The lower the *pdays*, the better the memory of the last call and hence the better chances of a sale.

- Surprisingly, campaigns (number of contacts or calls made during the current campaign) are lower for customers who bought the term deposit.

We can calculate categorical means for other categorical variables such as education and marital status to get a more detailed sense of our data. The categorical means for education looks as follows:

```
bank.groupby('education').mean()
```

	age	duration	campaign	pdays	previous	emp.var.rate	cons.price.idx	cons.conf.idx	euribor3m	nr.employed	y
education											
Basic	42.337124	253.898457	2.429732	978.815597	0.149472	0.237368	93.658600	-41.120552	3.775701	5174.133144	0.079610
High School	38.097720	258.534202	2.630836	958.022801	0.206298	-0.002497	93.564314	-40.995765	3.511732	5163.212595	0.105320
Illiterate	42.000000	146.000000	4.000000	999.000000	0.000000	-2.900000	92.201000	-31.400000	0.834000	5076.200000	0.000000
Professional Course	40.207477	278.816822	2.512150	958.211215	0.194393	0.163925	93.599630	-40.127664	3.701426	5167.595140	0.121495
University Degree	39.017405	247.707278	2.583070	947.900316	0.207278	-0.009731	93.499109	-39.830063	3.547132	5163.023180	0.130538
Unknown	42.826347	267.281437	2.538922	939.700599	0.263473	-0.074251	93.637455	-39.487425	3.410174	5151.260479	0.155689

Fig. 6.13: The mean of the numerical variables for different categories of education

Data visualization

Let us visualize our data to get a much clearer picture of the data and significant variables. Let us start with a histogram of education with separate bars for customers who bought the term deposit and the customers who didn't.

The tabular data for Education Level and whether they purchased the deposit or not would look like as follows:

y	0	1
education		
Basic	1133	98
High School	824	97
Illiterate	1	0
Professional Course	470	65
University Degree	1099	165
Unknown	141	26

Fig. 6.14: Tabular data for Education Level and Purchase

The same data can be plotted as a bar chart using the code snippet as follows:

```
%matplotlib inline
pd.crosstab(bank.education,bank.y).plot(kind='bar')
plt.title('Purchase Frequency for Education Level')
plt.xlabel('Education')
plt.ylabel('Frequency of Purchase')
```

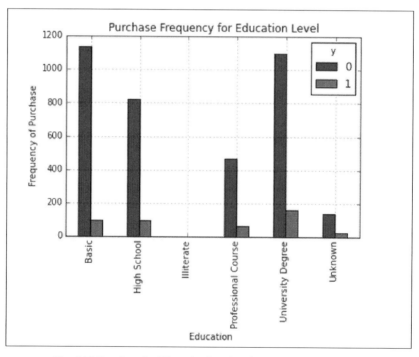

Fig. 6.15: Bar chart for Education Level and Frequency of Purchase

As is evident in the preceding plot, the frequency of purchase of the deposit depends a great deal on the Education Level. Thus, the Education Level can be a good predictor of the outcome variable.

Let us draw a stacked bar chart of the marital status and the purchase of term deposit. Basically, the chart will represent the proportion of the customers who bought the customers from each marital status. It looks as follows:

```
table=pd.crosstab(bank.marital,bank.y)
table.div(table.sum(1).astype(float), axis=0).plot(kind='bar',
stacked=True)
plt.title('Stacked Bar Chart of Marital Status vs Purchase')
plt.xlabel('Marital Status')
plt.ylabel('Proportion of Customers')
```

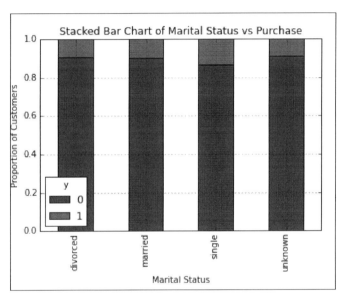

Fig. 6.16: The bar chart for the Marital Status and Proportion of Customers

The frequency of the purchase of the deposit is more or less the same for each marital status; hence, it might not be very helpful in predicting the outcome.

Let us plot the bar chart for the Frequency of Purchase against each day of the week to see whether this can be a good predictor of the outcome:

```
%matplotlib inline
import matplotlib.pyplot as plt
pd.crosstab(bank.day_of_week,bank.y).plot(kind='bar')
plt.title('Purchase Frequency for Day of Week')
plt.xlabel('Day of Week')
plt.ylabel('Frequency of Purchase')
```

The plot (the frequency of the positive outcomes) varies depending on the month of the year; hence, it might be a good predictor of the outcome:

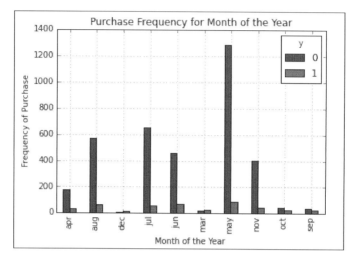

Fig. 6.17: The bar chart for Month of the Year and Frequency of Purchase

The `Histogram of Age` variable looks as follows, suggesting that the most of the customers of the bank in this dataset are in the age range of 30-40:

```
import matplotlib.pyplot as plt
bank.age.hist()
plt.title('Histogram of Age')
plt.xlabel('Age')
plt.ylabel('Frequency')
```

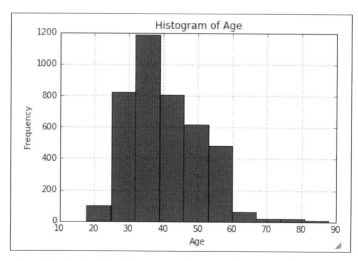

Fig. 6.18 The bar chart for customer's Age and Frequency of Purchase

Another bar chart of **Poutcome** and the frequency of purchase shows that the Poutcome might be an important predictor of the outcome:

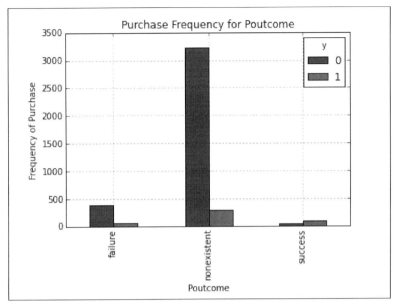

Fig. 6.19: The bar chart for Poutcome and Frequency of Purchase

Several other charts can be plotted to gauge which variables are more significant and which ones are not in order to predict the outcome variable.

Creating dummy variables for categorical variables

There are many categorical variables in the dataset and they need to be converted to dummy variables before they can be used for modelling. We know the process of converting a categorical variable into a dummy variable. However, since there are many categorical variables, it would be time-efficient to automate the process using a `for` loop. The following code snippet will create dummy variables for each categorical variables and join these dummy variables to the bank data frame:

```
cat_vars=['job','marital','education','default','housing','loan','cont
act','month','day_of_week','poutcome']
for var in cat_vars:
    cat_list='var'+'_'+var
    cat_list = pd.get_dummies(bank[var], prefix=var)
    bank1=bank.join(cat_list)
    bank=bank1
```

The actual categorical variable needs to be removed once the dummy variables have been created. We have done something like this earlier in this book:

```
cat_vars=['job','marital','education','default','housing','loan','cont
act','month','day_of_week','poutcome']
bank_vars=bank.columns.values.tolist()
to_keep=[i for i in bank_vars if i not in cat_vars]
```

Let us subset the bank data frame to keep only the columns present in the `to_keep` list:

```
bank_final=bank[to_keep]
bank_final.columns.values
```

```
array(['age', 'duration', 'campaign', 'pdays', 'previous', 'emp.var.rate',
       'cons.price.idx', 'cons.conf.idx', 'euribor3m', 'nr.employed', 'y',
       'job_admin.', 'job_blue-collar', 'job_entrepreneur',
       'job_housemaid', 'job_management', 'job_retired',
       'job_self-employed', 'job_services', 'job_student',
       'job_technician', 'job_unemployed', 'job_unknown',
       'marital_divorced', 'marital_married', 'marital_single',
       'marital_unknown', 'education_Basic', 'education_High School',
       'education_Illiterate', 'education_Professional Course',
       'education_University Degree', 'education_Unknown', 'default_no',
       'default_unknown', 'default_yes', 'housing_no', 'housing_unknown',
       'housing_yes', 'loan_no', 'loan_unknown', 'loan_yes',
       'contact_cellular', 'contact_telephone', 'month_apr', 'month_aug',
       'month_dec', 'month_jul', 'month_jun', 'month_mar', 'month_may',
       'month_nov', 'month_oct', 'month_sep', 'day_of_week_fri',
       'day_of_week_mon', 'day_of_week_thu', 'day_of_week_tue',
       'day_of_week_wed', 'poutcome_failure', 'poutcome_nonexistent',
       'poutcome_success'], dtype=object)
```

Fig. 6.20: Column names after creating dummy variables for categorical variables

The outcome variable is y and all the other variables are predictor variables. The X predictor and the Y outcome variable can be created using the code snippet as follows:

```
bank_final_vars=bank_final.columns.values.tolist()
Y=['y']
X=[i for i in bank_final_vars if i not in Y ]
```

Feature selection

Before implementing the model, let us perform a feature selection to decide the significant variables that can predict the outcome with great accuracy. We have the freedom to select as many as variables as we can. Let us select 12 columns. This can be done as follows, which is similar to that done in the chapter on linear regression:

```
from sklearn import datasets
from sklearn.feature_selection import RFE
from sklearn.linear_model import LogisticRegression

model = LogisticRegression()

rfe = RFE(model, 12)
rfe = rfe.fit(bank_final[X],bank_final[Y] )
print(rfe.support_)
print(rfe.ranking_)
```

The output of the preceding code snippet are two arrays. One contains the support and the other contains the ranking. The columns that have **True** in the support array are selected for the model, or the columns that have the value **1** in the rank array are selected for the model. If we want to include more (than 12) columns in the model, we can select the columns with the rank 2 onwards:

```
[False False False False  True False False False  True False False False
  True False False False  True False False False False False False False
 False False False False False False False False False False False False
 False False False False False False False False False  True  True  True
  True  True False  True False False False False False False  True False
  True False]
[34 43 18 46  1 14 27 25  1 40 22  3  1 36  2 38  1  5 30 32 12 48 19 44 31
 51 26 13 49 21 41  8 35 33 50 20  6 10 15  9 23 16  4 39 24  1  1  1  1  1
 17  1 47 37 28 42 29 11  1  7  1 45]
```

Fig. 6.21: The outcome of feature selection process. The columns with True/1 in the respective positions should be selected for the final model

The columns that are selected using this method are as follows:

```
'previous', 'euribor3m', 'job_entrepreneur', 'job_self-employed',
'poutcome_success', 'poutcome_failure', 'month_oct', 'month_
may','month_mar', 'month_jun', 'month_jul', 'month_dec'
```

Next, we will try to fit a logistic regression model using the preceding selected variables as predictor variables, with the y as the outcome variable:

```
cols=['previous', 'euribor3m', 'job_entrepreneur', 'job_self-
employed', 'poutcome_success', 'poutcome_failure', 'month_oct',
'month_may',
    'month_mar', 'month_jun', 'month_jul', 'month_dec']
X=bank_final[cols]
Y=bank_final['y']
```

Implementing the model

Let's first use the `stasmodel.api` method to run the logistic regression model as shown in the following code snippet:

```
import statsmodels.api as sm
logit_model=sm.Logit(Y,X)
result=logit_model.fit()
print result.summary()
```

```
                          Logit Regression Results
==============================================================================
Dep. Variable:                      y   No. Observations:                 4119
Model:                          Logit   Df Residuals:                     4107
Method:                           MLE   Df Model:                           11
Date:                Sun, 04 Oct 2015   Pseudo R-squ.:                   0.1918
Time:                        17:33:15   Log-Likelihood:                 -1149.9
converged:                       True   LL-Null:                        -1422.9
                                        LLR p-value:                  4.975e-110
==============================================================================
                      coef    std err          z      P>|z|      [95.0% Conf. Int.]
------------------------------------------------------------------------------------
previous            0.3493      0.141      2.475      0.013       0.073       0.626
euribor3m          -0.6253      0.026    -23.615      0.000      -0.677      -0.573
job_entrepreneur   -0.4842      0.382     -1.269      0.205      -1.232       0.264
job_self-employed  -0.4626      0.328     -1.413      0.158      -1.105       0.179
poutcome_success    0.7788      0.289      2.697      0.007       0.213       1.345
poutcome_failure   -1.0450      0.245     -4.260      0.000      -1.526      -0.564
month_oct           0.0707      0.270      0.262      0.793      -0.458       0.600
month_may          -1.0490      0.126     -8.302      0.000      -1.297      -0.801
month_mar           1.0612      0.315      3.367      0.001       0.443       1.679
month_jun           0.3431      0.169      2.031      0.042       0.012       0.674
month_jul           0.3280      0.184      1.781      0.075      -0.033       0.689
month_dec           0.7147      0.466      1.533      0.125      -0.199       1.628
==============================================================================
```

Fig. 6.22: The summary of the logistic regression model with selected variables

One advantage of this method is that p-values are calculated automatically in the result summary. The `scikit-learn` method doesn't have this facility, but is more powerful for calculation-intensive tasks such as prediction, calculating scores, and advanced functions such as feature selection. The `statsmodel.api` method can be used while exploring and fine-tuning the model, while the `scikit-learn` method can be used in the final model used to predict the outcome.

The summary of the model looks as shown in the preceding screenshot. For each variable, the coefficient value has been estimated, and corresponding to each estimation, there is a std error and p-value. This p-value corresponds to the hypothesis testing of the Wald statistics, and the lower the p-value, the more the significance of the variable in the model. For most of the variables in this model, the p-values are very less and, hence, most of them are significant to the model.

We will be using the `scikit-learn` method to fit the model as is shown in the following code snippet:

```
from sklearn import linear_model
clf = linear_model.LogisticRegression()
clf.fit(X, Y)
```

The accuracy of this model can be calculated as follows:

```
clf.score(X,Y)
```

The value comes out to be .902. The mean value of the outcome is .11, meaning that the outcome is positive (1) around 11% of the time and negative around 89% of the time. So, even by predicting 0 for all the rows, one could have achieved an accuracy rate of 89%. Our model takes this accuracy to 90.2. For a little bit of enhancement, maybe, we can try reducing the number of columns, training-testing split, and cross validation to increase this score.

For this method, one can get the value of the coefficients using the following code snippet:

```
import numpy as np
pd.DataFrame(zip(X.columns, np.transpose(clf.coef_)))
```

	0	1
0	previous	[0.379831612767]
1	euribor3m	[-0.502749071885]
2	job_entrepreneur	[-0.343066155911]
3	job_self-employed	[-0.335064163428]
4	poutcome_success	[1.07783253321]
5	poutcome_failure	[-0.753161867796]

6	month_oct	[0.411855746059]
7	month_may	[-0.743089631086]
8	month_mar	[1.27036122955]
9	month_jun	[0.50969498293]
10	month_jul	[0.382087449348]
11	month_dec	[0.873316799226]

Fig. 6.23: Coefficients for the variables in the model

The variable coefficients indicate the change in the log (odds) for a unit change in the variable. The coefficient for the previous variable is 0.37. This implies that, if the previous variable increases by 1, the log(odds) will increase by 0.37 and, hence, the probability of the purchase will change accordingly.

Model validation and evaluation

The preceding logistic regression model is built on the entire data. Let us now split the data into training and testing sets, build the model using the training set, and then check the accuracy using the testing set. The ultimate goal is to see whether it improves the accuracy of the prediction or not:

```
from sklearn.cross_validation import train_test_split
X_train, X_test, Y_train, Y_test = train_test_split(X, Y, test_
size=0.3, random_state=0)
```

The preceding code snippet creates testing and training datasets for a predictor and also outcome variables. Let us now build a logistic regression model over the training set:

```
from sklearn import linear_model
from sklearn import metrics
clf1 = linear_model.LogisticRegression()
clf1.fit(X_train, Y_train)
```

The preceding code snippet creates the model. If you remember the equation behind the model, you will know that the model predicts probabilities and not the classes (binary output, that is, 0 or 1). One needs to select a threshold over these probabilities to classify them into two categories. Something of this sort: if the probability is less than the threshold, then it is a 0 outcome, and if it is greater than the threshold, then it is a 1 outcome.

Let us see how we can get those probabilities and classifications:

```
probs = clf1.predict_proba(X_test)
```

This gives the probability of a negative and positive outcome for each row of the data:

```
[[ 0.93352157  0.06647843]
 [ 0.88259365  0.11740635]
 [ 0.93040666  0.06959334]
 ...,
 [ 0.73273217  0.26726783]
 [ 0.97862459  0.02137541]
 [ 0.24746608  0.75253392]]
```

Fig. 6.24: Predicted probability values for each observation

The second column provides the probability of a positive outcome (purchase of a deposit outcome in our case). By default, if this probability is more than 0.5, then the observation is categorized as a positive outcome, and as a negative outcome if it is less than that.

The default outcome for predicting the class can be found out using the following code snippet:

```
predicted = clf1.predict(X_test)
```

The output is an array consisting of 0 and 1. In the default case, it categorizes probabilities less than 0.5 as 0, and more than that as 1. One can use different cutoffs for this as well. One can change it to 0.15 or 0.20 depending upon the situation. In our case, we have seen that only 10% of the customers buy the product; hence, probability=0.10 can be a good threshold. If an observation has a probability of more than 0.10, we can classify it as a positive outcome (a customer will buy the product). An observation with the probability less than 0.10 will be classified as a negative outcome.

The changing of threshold values can be done using the following code snippet:

```
import pandas as pd
import numpy as np
prob=probs[:,1]
prob_df=pd.DataFrame(prob)
prob_df['predict']=np.where(prob_df[0]>=0.10,1,0)
prob_df.head()
```

The number of positive and negative responses will change with the threshold values. The percentage of positive outcomes with three different threshold probabilities are mentioned as follows:

Threshold	% Positive outcome
0.10	28%
0.15	18%
0.05	65%

Let us check the accuracy of this model using the following code snippet:

```
print metrics.accuracy_score(Y_test, predicted)
```

This model has the same accuracy of 90.21% as the previous model.

Cross validation

Cross validation is performed on a dataset while predicting to check how well the model will generalize its results on an independent dataset.

Cross validation is required to deal with an issue common with the predictive models. The models are developed based on one set of data, and most of the model parameters are calculated using the criterion of the most optimal fit with the data on which the model is being built. This leads to a problem called overfitting, wherein the model fits the given (training) data very well, but doesn't reproduce the good fitting with some other (testing) dataset. This problem is more severe in the case of datasets with less observations.

Splitting up a dataset in the training and testing dataset is the simplest way to do cross validation. This is called a holdout method, wherein the training set and testing set are randomly chosen.

The most popular way to perform a cross validation is using something called as k-fold cross validation. It is done as follows:

1. Divide the data set into k partitions.

2. One partition is used as the test set, while the other k-1 partitions together are used as the training set.

3. The process in (2) is repeated k times with a different partition as the testing dataset and the rest of them as the training dataset in each iteration.

4. For each iteration, the model accuracy is calculated and averaged out over the iterations. The averaged value is the value of the model accuracy.

5. If the accuracy of the model doesn't vary much and the average accuracy remains closer to the accuracy numbers calculated for the model before, then it can be confirmed that the model generalizes well.

Each observation gets to be part of the testing dataset exactly once, while each row becomes part of the training dataset exactly *k-1* times. One advantage of this method is that each of the observations get to be part of either testing or training dataset at least once; hence, it leads to a better generalization. *K=10* is generally the norm, but can be changed according to the situation. In scikit-learn, there is a separate method to perform cross validation which can be done very easily:

```
from sklearn.cross_validation import cross_val_score
scores = cross_val_score(linear_model.LogisticRegression(), X, Y,
scoring='accuracy', cv=8)
print scores
print scores.mean()
```

The preceding code snippet basically runs an 8-fold cross validation method and calculates the accuracy for each of the iterations. The average accuracy is also printed:

```
[ 0.91860465  0.90310078  0.89534884  0.90679612  0.89883268  0.89299611
  0.90466926  0.89883268]
0.902397639921
```

Fig. 6.25: The accuracy for each run (fold) of the model during cross validation

The average accuracy remains very close to the accuracy we have observed before; hence, we can conclude that the model generalizes well.

Model validation

Once the model has been built and evaluated, the next step is to validate the model. In the case of logistic regression models or classification models in general, we basically validate the model by comparing the actual class with the predicted class. There are various ways to do this, but the most famous and widely used is the **Receiver Operating Characteristic (ROC)** curve.

The ROC curve

An ROC curve is a graphical tool to understand the performance of a classification model. For a logistic regression model, a prediction can either be positive or negative. Also, this prediction can either be correct or incorrect.

There are four categories in which the predictions of a logistic regression model can fall:

Actual/predicted	Positive	Negative
Positive	**True Positive (TP):** • Correct positive prediction • Actually positive and prediction is also positive	**True Negative (TN):** • Correct negative prediction • Actually negative and prediction is also negative
Negative	**False Positive (FP):** • Incorrect positive prediction • Actually negative and prediction is positive	**False Negative (FN):** • Incorrect negative prediction • Actually positive and prediction is negative

So, True Positives are the ones that are actually positive, and the model has also predicted a positive outcome for them. False Positives are false successes. These are actually failures, but the model is predicting them as successes. False Negatives are actually successes, but the model predicts them as failures.

Let us state some totals in terms of these categories:

• The total number of actual positive = *TP+FN*

• The total number of actual negative = *TN+FP*

• The total number of correct predictions = *TP+TN*

• The total number of incorrect predictions = *FP+FN*

Aware of these terms, we can now understand the terms that are the constituents of a ROC curve. These terms are as follows:

Sensitivity (True Positive Rate): This is the proportion of the positive outcomes that are identified as such (as positives) by the model:

$$Sensitivity = TP / (TP + FN)$$

Specificity (True Negative Rate): This is the proportion of the negative outcomes that are identified as such (as negatives) by the model:

$$Specificity = TN / (TN + FP)$$

Sensitivity wards off against False Positive, while the Specificity does the same against False Negative. A perfect model will be 100% sensitive and also 100% specific.

An ROC curve is a plot of True Positive Rate vs False Positive Rate where *False Positive Rate=FP/(TN+FP) =1-Specificity*.

As we saw earlier, the number of positive and negative outcomes change as we change the threshold of probability values to classify a probability value as a positive or negative outcome. Thus, the Sensitivity and Specificity will change as well.

An ROC curve has the following important properties:

- Any increase in Sensitivity will decrease the Specificity
- The closer the curve is to the left and upper border of the quadrant, the better the model prediction
- The closer the curve is to the diagonal line, the worse the model prediction is
- The larger the area under the curve, the better the prediction

The following are the steps in plotting an ROC curve:

1. Define several probability thresholds and calculate Sensitivity and 1-Specificity for each threshold.
2. Plot Sensitivity and 1-Specificity points obtained in this way.

Let us plot the ROC curve for the model we built earlier in this chapter by following the steps described above. Later, we will see how to do it using the built-in methods in `scikit-learn`.

This is the model that we ran and calculated the probabilities for each observation:

```
from sklearn.cross_validation import train_test_split
from sklearn import linear_model
from sklearn import metrics
X_train, X_test, Y_train, Y_test = train_test_split(X, Y, test_
size=0.3, random_state=0)
clf1 = linear_model.LogisticRegression()
clf1.fit(X_train, Y_train)
probs = clf1.predict_proba(X_test)
```

Each probability value is then compared to a threshold probability, and categorized as 1 (positive outcome) if it is greater than threshold probability and 0 if less than threshold probability. It can be done using the following code snippet (we have chosen a threshold probability of 0.05 in this case):

```
prob=probs[:,1]
prob_df=pd.DataFrame(prob)
prob_df['predict']=np.where(prob_df[0]>=0.05,1,0)
prob_df['actual']=Y_test
prob_df.head()
```

The resulting data frame looks as follows:

	0	predict	actual
0	0.066478	1	0
1	0.117406	1	0
2	0.069593	1	0
3	0.062666	1	0
4	0.065086	1	0

Fig. 6.26: Predicted and actual outcomes for the bank dataset

Confusion matrix

The result of how many correct and incorrect predictions were made can be summarized using what is called a confusion matrix. A confusion matrix is just a tabular representation to state the number of TPs, TNs, FPs, and FNs. Once we have a data frame in such a format, we can calculate the confusion matrix using the `crosstab` statement as follows:

```
confusion_matrix=pd.crosstab(prob_df['actual'],prob_df['predict'])
confusion_matrix
```

The confusion matrix in this case is as follows:

At p=0.05:

Predict actual	0	1		TN 413	FP 701		Sensitivity	=107/ (107+15) =0.87
0	413	701		FN 15	TP 107		1-Specificity	=701/ (413+701) =0.62
1	15	107						

Fig. 6.27.1: Confusion matrix at p=0.05

At p=0.10:

Predict actual	0	1		TN 847	FP 267		Sensitivity	=76/ (76+46) =0.62
0	847	267		FN 46	TP 76		1-Specificity	=267/ (267+847) =0.23
1	46	76						

Fig. 6.27.2: Confusion matrix at p=0.10

The Sensitivity and Specificity are calculated at various other probability threshold levels and then the Sensitivity and (1-Specificity) are plotted against each other. The Sensitivity and (1-Specificity) or FPR at different threshold probability values are summarized as follows:

Threshold p	Sensitivity	(1-Specificity)
0.05	0.87	0.62
0.10	0.62	0.23
0.07	0.67	0.27
0.12	0.59	0.17
0.20	0.50	0.12
0.25	0.41	0.07
0.04	0.95	0.76

As one can observe, as the threshold of the probability increases, both the Sensitivity and the FPR (1-Specificity) decreases. Now, we have the Sensitivity and Specificity at different threshold probabilities. We can make use of this data to plot our ROC curve. A diagonal (*y=x*) line is a good benchmark for an ROC curve. If the ROC curve lies above the diagonal line, then the model is considered a better predictor than a random guess (represented by a diagonal line). An ROC curve lying below the diagonal line indicates that the model is a worse predictor compared to a random guess.

Let us plot our ROC curve and also the diagonal line and see whether the ROC curve lies above the diagonal line or below. This can be done using the following code snippet:

```
import matplotlib.pyplot as plt
%matplotlib inline
Sensitivity=[1,0.95,0.87,0.62,0.67,0.59,0.5,0.41,0]
FPR=[1,0.76,0.62,0.23,0.27,0.17,0.12,0.07,0]
plt.plot(FPR,Sensitivity,marker='o',linestyle='--',color='r')
x=[i*0.01 for i in range(100)]
y=[i*0.01 for i in range(100)]
plt.plot(x,y)
plt.xlabel('(1-Specificity)')
plt.ylabel('Sensitivity')
plt.title('ROC Curve')
```

The ROC curve looks as follows:

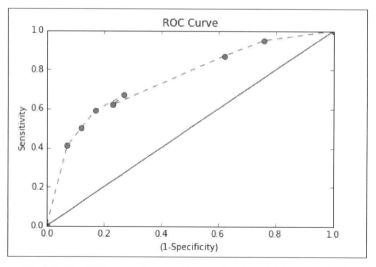

Fig. 6.28: The ROC curve drawn without using the scikit-learn methods

The curve in red is the ROC curve, while the blue line is the benchmark diagonal line. The ROC curve lies above the diagonal line and, hence, the model is a better predictor than a random guess. However, there can be many ROC curves lying above the diagonal line. How to determine one ROC curve is better than the other? This is determined by calculating the area enclosed under the ROC curves. The more the area enclosed by the ROC curve, the better it is. The area under the curve can lie between 0 and 1. The closer it is to 1, the better it is.

Let us now see how we can draw an ROC curve and calculate the area under the curve using the methods built in `scikit-learn`. This can be done using the following code snippet. Make sure you install the `ggplot` package before running this snippet:

```
from sklearn import metrics
from ggplot import *

prob = clf1.predict_proba(X_test)[:,1]
fpr, sensitivity, _ = metrics.roc_curve(Y_test, prob)

df = pd.DataFrame(dict(fpr=fpr, sensitivity=sensitivity))
ggplot(df, aes(x='fpr', y='sensitivity')) +\
    geom_line() +\
    geom_abline(linetype='dashed')
```

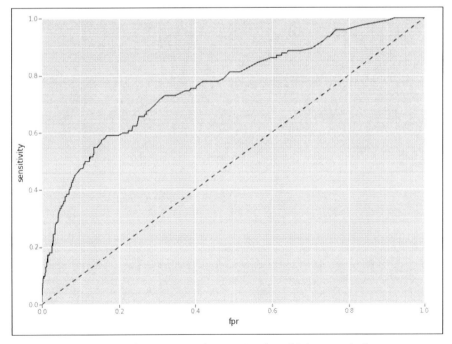

Fig. 6.29: The ROC curve drawn using the scikit-learn methods

The area under the curve can be found out as follows:

```
auc = metrics.auc(fpr,sensitivity)
auc
```

The area under the curve comes out to be 0.76, which is pretty good. The area under the curve can be plotted using the following code snippet:

```
ggplot(df, aes(x='fpr', ymin=0, ymax='sensitivity')) +\
    geom_area(alpha=0.2) +\
    geom_line(aes(y='sensitivity')) +\
    ggtitle("ROC Curve w/ AUC=%s" % str(auc))
```

The plot looks as follows:

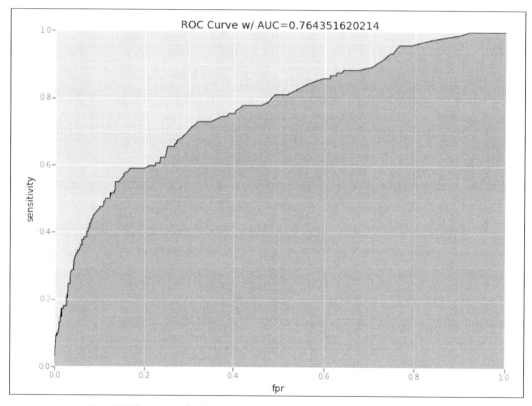

Fig. 6.30: The area under the ROC curve drawn using the scikit-learn methods

Summary

A logistic regression is a versatile technique used widely in the cases where the variable to be predicted is a binary (or categorical) variable. This chapter dives deep into the math behind the logistics regression and the process to implement it using the `scikit-learn` and `statsmodel api` modules. It is important to understand the math behind the algorithm so that the model is not used as a black box without knowing what is going on behind the hood. To recap, the following are the main takeaways from the chapter:

- Linear regression wouldn't be an appropriate model to predict binary variables as the predictor variables can range from -infinity to +infinity, while the binary variable would be 0 or 1.

- The odds of a certain event happening is the probability of that event happening divided by the probability of that event not happening. The higher the odds, the higher are the chances of the event happening. The odds can range from 0 to infinity.

- The final equation for the logistic regression is:

$$log(P/1-P) = a + b1 * X1 + b2 * X2 + b3 * X3 + \ldots\ldots\ldots\ldots + bn * Xn$$

- The variable coefficients are calculated using the maximum Log-likelihood estimate. The roots of the equation are often calculated using the Newton-Raphson method.

- Each coefficient estimate has a Wald statistic and p-value associated to it. The smaller the p-value, the more significant the variable coefficient is to the model.

- The model can be validated using the k-fold cross validation technique, wherein the logistic regression model is run k-times using the testing and training data derived from the overall dataset.

- The model predicts the probability for each observation. A threshold probability value is defined to categorize the probability values as 0 (failures) and 1 (successes).

- Sensitivity measures what proportion of successes were actually identified as successes, while Specificity measures what proportion of failures were actually identified as failures.

- An ROC curve is a plot of Sensitivity vs (1-Specificity). A diagonal ($y=x$) line is a good benchmark for the ROC curve. If the curve lies above the diagonal line, the model is better than a random guess. If the curve lies below, then the model is worse than a random guess.

It will do wonders for your understanding of logistic regression if you take a dataset and try implementing a logistic regression model on it. In the next chapter, we will learn about an unsupervised algorithm called **Clustering** or **Segmentation** that is used widely in marketing and natural sciences.

7
Clustering with Python

In the previous two chapters, we discussed and understood two important algorithms used in predictive analytics, namely, linear regression and logistic regression. Both of them are very widely used. They are supervised algorithms. If you stress your memory a tad bit and have thoroughly read the previous chapters of the book, you would remember that a supervised algorithm is one where the historical value of an output variable is known from the data. A supervised algorithm uses this value to train and build the model to forecast the value of an output variable for a dataset in future. An unsupervised algorithm, on the other hand, doesn't have the luxury or constraints (different perspectives of looking at it) of the output variable. It uses the values of the predictor variables instead to build a model.

Clustering—the algorithm that we are going to discuss in this chapter—is an unsupervised algorithm. Clustering or segmentation, as the name suggests, categorizes entries in clusters or segments in which the entries are more similar to each other than the entries outside the cluster. The properties of such clusters are then identified and treated separately. Once the clusters are defined, one can identify the properties of the cluster and define plans or strategy separately for each cluster. This results in efficient strategizing and planning for each cluster.

The broad focus of this chapter will be clustering and segmentation and by the end of this chapter, you would be able to learn the following:

- **Math behind the clustering algorithms**: This section will talk about the various kinds of measures of similarity or dissimilarity between observations. The similarity or dissimilarity is measured in something called distances. We will look at different types of distances and create distance metrics.

- **Different types of clustering algorithms**: This section has information about two kinds of clustering algorithms, namely, hierarchical clustering and k-means clustering. The details of the two algorithms will be illustrated using tables and code simulations.

- **Implementing clustering using Python**: This section will deal with implementing k-means clustering algorithm on a dataset from scratch, analyzing and making sense of the output, generating plots showing the clusters, and making contextual sense of the clusters.

- **Fine-tuning the clustering**: In this section, we will cover topics such as finding the optimum number of clusters and calculating a few statistics to check the efficiency of the clustering we performed.

Introduction to clustering – what, why, and how?

Now let us discuss the various aspects of clustering in greater detail.

What is clustering?

Clustering basically means the following:

- Creating a group with a high similarity among the members of clusters
- Creating a group with a significant distinction or dissimilarity between the members of two different clusters

The clustering algorithms work on calculating the similarity or dissimilarity between the observations to group them in clusters.

How is clustering used?

Let us look at the plot of **Monthly Income** and **Monthly Expense** for a group of 400 people. As one can see, there are visible clusters of people whose earnings and expenses are different from people from other clusters, but are very similar to the people in the cluster they belong to:

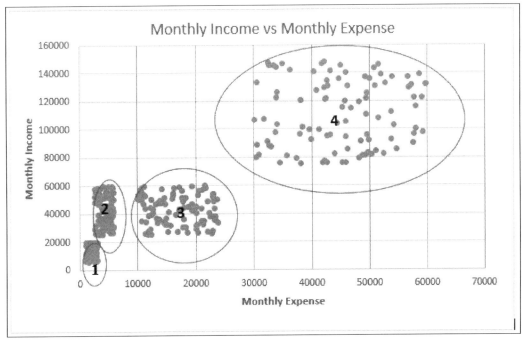

Fig. 7.1: Illustration of clustering plotting Monthly Income vs Monthly Expense

In the preceding plot, the visible clusters of the people can be identified based on their income and expense levels, as follows:

- 1 (low income, low expense): The cluster marked as 1 has low income and low expense levels

- 2 (medium income, less expense): The cluster marked as 2 has a medium level of income, but spend less — only a little higher than the people in the cluster 1 with low income

- 3 (medium income, medium or high expense): The cluster marked as 3 also has medium levels of income, almost the same range as cluster 2, but they spend more than cluster 2

- 4 (high income, high expense): The cluster marked as 4 has a high level of income and a high level of expense

This analysis can be very helpful if, let's say, an organization is trying to target potential customers for their different range of products. Once the clusters are known, the organization can target different clusters for different ranges of their products. Maybe, they can target the cluster 4 to sell their premium products and cluster 1 and 2 to sell their low-end products. This results in higher conversion rates for the advertisement campaigns.

This was one of the illustrations of how clustering can be advantageous. This was a very simple case with just the two attributes of the potential customers, and we were able to plot it on a 2D graph and look at the clusters. However, this is not the case for most of the time. We need to define some generalized metric for the similarity or dissimilarity of the observations. Also, we will discuss this in detail later in this chapter.

Some of the properties of a good cluster can be listed as follows:

- Clusters should be identifiable and significant in size so that they can be classified as one.

- Points within a cluster should be compactly placed within themselves and there should be minimum overlap with points in the other clusters.

- Clusters should make business sense. The observations in the same cluster should exhibit similar properties when it comes to the business context.

Why do we do clustering?

Clustering can have a variety of applications. The following are some of the cases where clustering is used:

- Clustering and segmentation are the bread and butter of the marketing professionals. The advent of digital marketing has made clustering indispensable. The goal here is to find customers who think, behave, and make decisions on similar lines and reach out to them and persuade them in a fashion tailor-made for them. Think of Facebook and sponsored posts. How do they use the demography, age group, and your preferences data to show you the most relevant posts?

- Remember those taxonomy charts in Biology books from high school? Well, that is one of the most widely used applications of clustering—a particular type called hierarchical clustering. The clustering, in this case, happens on the basis of the similarity between sequences of amino acids between the two genus/species.

- Clustering is used in seismology to find the expected epicenter of earthquakes and identify earthquake-prone zones.

- Clustering is also used to impute values to the missing elements in a dataset. Remember that we imputed the missing values with the mean of the rest of the observations. To start with, some forms of clustering require calculating or assuming the centroid of the clusters. These can be used to impute missing values.

- Clustering is used in urban planning to group together houses according to their geography, value, and amenities. It can also be used to identify a spot for public amenities such as public transport stops, mobile signal towers, and so on.

Mathematics behind clustering

Earlier in this chapter, we discussed how a measure of similarity or dissimilarity is needed for the purpose of clustering observations. In this section, we will see what those measures are and how they are used.

Distances between two observations

If we consider each observation as a point in an n-dimensional space, where n is the number of columns in the dataset, one can calculate the mathematical distance between the points. The lesser the distance, the more similar they are. The points that are less distant to each other will be clubbed together.

Now, there are many ways of calculating distances and different algorithms use different methods of calculating distance. Let us see the different methods with a few examples. Let us consider a sample dataset of 10 observations with three variables, each to illustrate the distance better. The following dataset contains percentage marks obtained by 10 students in English, Maths, and Science:

Student	English	Maths	Science
1	0.12	0.49	0.21
2	0.21	0.81	0.79
3	0.73	0.30	0.99
4	0.55	0.03	0.17
5	0.15	0.83	0.25
6	0.24	0.37	0.63
7	0.20	0.82	0.85
8	0.17	0.92	0.45
9	0.26	0.16	0.31
10	0.15	0.47	0.23

Table 7.1: Percentage marks obtained by 10 students in English, Maths, and Science

Euclidean distance

This is the most commonly used definition of the distance. Let us denote each observation as Xi. Then, the Euclidean distance between the two points, Xi and Xj, for a dataset having n-columns, is defined as follows:

$$D_{i,j} = \sqrt{\left(X_{i,1} - X_{j,1}\right)^2 + \left(X_{i,2} - X_{j,2}\right)^2 + \ldots\ldots + \left(X_{i,n} - X_{j,n}\right)^2}$$

For our dataset, the Euclidean distance between the student 1 and 2 is calculated as follows:

$$S_{1,2} = \sqrt{\left(0.12 - 0.21\right)^2 + \left(0.49 - 0.81\right)^2 + \ldots\ldots + \left(0.21 - 0.79\right)^2} = 0.67$$

Thus, the Euclidian distance between the student 1 and 2 comes out to be 0.67.

Manhattan distance

Manhattan distance is defined as follows:

$$D_{i,j} = \left(| X_{i,1} - X_{j,1} | + | X_{i,2} - X_{j,2} | + \ldots\ldots + | X_{i,n} - X_{j,n} |\right)$$

Minkowski distance

Minkowski distance is defined as follows:

$$D_{i,j} = \left(\left(| X_{i,1} - X_{j,1} |\right)^P + \left(| X_{i,2} - X_{j,2} |\right)^P + \ldots\ldots + \left(| X_{i,n} - X_{j,n} |\right)^P\right)1/p$$

where p>=1

The distance matrix

Once we have defined the distance between the two points, we can calculate the distance between any two points and store them as a matrix. This matrix representing the distance between any two points (observations) in the dataset is called a distance matrix. A distance matrix has certain properties as follows:

- All the diagonal elements in a distance matrix have a value 0 as they represent the distance of the point from itself, that is, $D_{i,i}=0$ for all i's.

- For a dataset with *n* observations, we get a *nxn* distance matrix.
- A distance matrix is a symmetric matrix as the distance between the two points is the same, irrespective of the order of the points. The distance between point 1 and point 2 is the same as the difference between point 2 and point 1. This implies $D_{i,j} = D_{j,I}$ for all *i*'s and *j*'s.

For our dataset containing information about the marks of 10 students, it would be a 10x10 matrix. If we decide to calculate the matrix for Euclidean distances, the distance matrix will look as follows:

	1	2	3	4	5	6	7	8	9	10
1	0.00	0.67	1.01	0.63	0.33	0.45	0.72	0.49	0.37	0.04
2	0.67	0.00	0.76	1.06	0.55	0.47	0.06	0.36	0.81	0.66
3	1.01	0.76	0.00	0.88	1.08	0.62	0.76	1.00	0.84	0.97
4	0.63	1.06	0.88	0.00	0.89	0.65	1.10	1.01	0.35	0.60
5	0.33	0.55	1.08	0.89	0.00	0.60	0.60	0.23	0.68	0.35
6	0.45	0.47	0.62	0.65	0.60	0.00	0.50	0.58	0.38	0.41
7	0.72	0.06	0.76	1.10	0.60	0.50	0.00	0.41	0.85	0.71
8	0.49	0.36	1.00	1.01	0.23	0.58	0.41	0.00	0.78	0.50
9	0.37	0.81	0.84	0.35	0.68	0.38	0.85	0.78	0.00	0.34
10	0.04	0.66	0.97	0.60	0.35	0.41	0.71	0.50	0.34	0.00

Table 7.2: Distance matrix for marks information for 10 students

Each element of this matrix has been calculated in the same way as we calculated $S_{1,2}$, only that the different rows are used for calculation. One can observe that these two properties stated above are satisfied. The diagonal elements are all 0. Interpreting a distance matrix is simple. The value in the 2nd row and the 1st column gives the distance between the 2nd and the 1st student (or the 1st and the 2nd student), and so on. So, $D_{1,3}=1.01$, $D_{2,5} = 0.55$, $D_{6,8} = 0.58$, and so on.

Normalizing the distances

These distances can sometimes be misleading if the variables are not in the same numerical range. What happens in such cases is that the variables having larger numerical values start influencing the distance more than the variables having smaller numerical values. This gives undue importance to the variables with large numerical values and subdues the importance of the ones with small numerical values.

The following dataset has the data of the **Monthly Income, Monthly Expense,** and **Education Level** for 10 customers. Look at the **1** and **9** customers. The difference in their monthly income is 1758. The difference in the monthly expense is 7707. Also, the difference in the education level is just 3. The contribution of the education level in distance becomes insignificant compared to the contribution of the other two variables even though, actually, the difference of 3 in the education level might matter more. This creates a problem as the distance is not a reliable measure of similarity anymore and can give rise to incorrect clustering.

Let us look at the following datasheet:

Customer	Monthly Expense	Monthly Income	Education Level
1	4319	28799	5
2	4513	20282	2
3	2959	28743	3
4	4315	28570	3
5	2706	20234	1
6	3794	21981	5
7	2923	24780	4
8	3645	28487	5
9	2561	21092	2
10	4794	22153	5

Fig. 7.2: Monthly Income, Monthly Expense and Education Levels

The solution to this problem is normalizing the values of the variables to bring them in the same numerical range. The normalization entails the numerical transformation of each value so that they come in the same numerical range. The following method is used to normalize values. This method uses the min and max values and the transformation is defined as follows:

$$Z_i = \left(X_i - X_{min} \right) / \left(X_{max} - X_{min} \right)$$

Note that Xi is the value of the variables, $Xmin$ is the minimum value of the variable, $Xmax$ is the maximum value of the variable, and Zi is the normalized value of the variable.

The preceding dataset shows us how to normalize using the preceding equation; the datasheet looks as shown:

Customer	Monthly Expense	Monthly Income	Education Level
1	0.79	1.00	1.00
2	0.87	0.01	0.25
3	0.18	0.99	0.50
4	0.79	0.97	0.50
5	0.06	0.00	0.00
6	0.55	0.20	1.00
7	0.16	0.53	0.75
8	0.49	0.96	1.00
9	0.00	0.10	0.25
10	1.00	0.22	1.00

Fig. 7.3: Monthly Income, Monthly Expense, and Education Levels after normalization

Linkage methods

While clustering the observations using the distances, one needs to link two or more points or clusters to form a new cluster or grow an already existing cluster. The distance between two clusters can be defined in many ways; for example, it can be the minimum distance between two points in two clusters, the maximum distance between two such points, or the distance between the centroids of the two clusters. The two clusters having the minimum distance between each other are clubbed together. Corresponding to each definition of the distance between the two clusters, there is a linkage method. Some of these linkage methods are shown in the following sections.

Single linkage

- The distance between two clusters is the minimum distance between a point in cluster 1 and cluster 2

- Two clusters having the smallest distance between them are combined as follows:

$$d(Cm, Cn) = min(d(i, j))$$

Here, *Cm* and *Cn* are two clusters; i and j are are points in the m and n clusters.

Compete linkage

- The distance between two clusters is the maximum distance between a point in cluster 1 and cluster 2

- Two clusters having the smallest distance between them are combined as follows:

$$d\left(Cm, Cn\right) = max\left(d\left(i, j\right)\right)$$

Here, *Cm* and *Cn* are two clusters; i and j are points in the m and n clusters.

Average linkage

- The distance between two clusters is the average distance between a point in cluster 1 and cluster 2

- Two clusters having the smallest distance between them are combined as follows:

$$d\left(Cm, Cn\right) = avg\left(d\left(i, j\right)\right)$$

Here, *Cm* and *Cn* are two clusters; *i* and *j* are points in the m and n clusters.

Centroid linkage

- The distance between two clusters is the distance between the centroid (mean) of all the points in cluster 1 and the centroid (mean) of all the points in cluster 2

- Two clusters having the smallest distance between them are combined as follows:

$$d\left(Cm, Cn\right) = d\left(centroid\left(Cm\right), centroid\left(Cn\right)\right)$$

Here, *Cm* and *Cn* are two clusters.

Ward's method

A cluster that minimizes the increase in the combined error sum of the square of ANOVA is joined to an already existing cluster to form a new joined cluster. ANOVA is a statistical method to check whether there is more variation within the cluster or in the overall dataset. The smallest increase in the ANOVA error term shows that the elements of the newly joined clusters are more similar to each other than elements in other clusters.

Hierarchical clustering

Hierarchical clustering is an agglomerative method of clustering, wherein we start with each point as a separate cluster and then agglomerate them in a single cluster based on the similarity between observations.

For a dataset with N observations and NxN distance matrix, a hierarchical cluster can be created using the following steps:

1. Start with each observation as a cluster so that you have N clusters to start with.

2. Find the smallest distance in the distance matrix. Join the two observations having the smallest distance to form a cluster.

3. Recompute the distances between all the old clusters and the new clusters. If one follows a single linkage method, the distance between two clusters is the minimum distance between two points on the two clusters.

4. Repeat the steps 2 and 3 until you are left with a single cluster of all the N observations.

Let us take the distance matrix we created earlier in this chapter and follow the above steps to create a hierarchical cluster. The distance matrix, as we have seen before, looks like this:

	1	2	3	4	5	6	7	8	9	10
1	0	0.67	1.01	0.63	0.33	0.45	0.72	0.49	0.37	0.04
2	0.67	0	0.76	1.06	0.55	0.47	0.06	0.36	0.81	0.66
3	1.01	0.76	0	0.88	1.08	0.62	0.76	1	0.84	0.97
4	0.63	1.06	0.88	0	0.89	0.65	1.1	1.01	0.35	0.6
5	0.33	0.55	1.08	0.89	0	0.6	0.6	0.23	0.68	0.35
6	0.45	0.47	0.62	0.65	0.6	0	0.5	0.58	0.38	0.41
7	0.72	0.06	0.76	1.1	0.6	0.5	0	0.41	0.85	0.71
8	0.49	0.36	1	1.01	0.23	0.58	0.41	0	0.78	0.5
9	0.37	0.81	0.84	0.35	0.68	0.38	0.85	0.78	0	0.34
10	0.04	0.66	0.97	0.6	0.35	0.41	0.71	0.5	0.34	0

Fig. 7.4: Distance matrix for the students' marks

Iteration 1:

	1|10	2	3	4	5	6	7	8	9
1|10	0	0.66	0.97	0.6	0.33	0.41	0.71	0.49	0.34
2	0.66	0	0.76	1.06	0.55	0.47	0.06	0.36	0.81
3	0.97	0.76	0	0.88	1.08	0.62	0.76	1	0.84
4	0.6	1.06	0.88	0	0.89	0.65	1.1	1.01	0.35
5	0.33	0.55	1.08	0.89	0	0.6	0.6	0.23	0.68
6	0.41	0.47	0.62	0.65	0.6	0	0.5	0.58	0.38
7	0.71	0.06	0.76	1.1	0.6	0.5	0	0.41	0.85
8	0.49	0.36	1	1.01	0.23	0.58	0.41	0	0.78
9	0.34	0.81	0.84	0.35	0.68	0.38	0.85	0.78	0

Fig. 7.5: The first iteration of clustering

Iteration 2:

	1|10	2|7	3	4	5	6	8	9
1|10	0	0.66	0.97	0.6	0.33	0.41	0.49	0.34
2|7	0.66	0	0.76	1.06	0.55	0.47	0.36	0.81
3	0.97	0.76	0	0.88	1.08	0.62	1	0.84
4	0.6	1.06	0.88	0	0.89	0.65	1.01	0.35
5	0.33	0.55	1.08	0.89	0	0.6	0.23	0.68
6	0.41	0.47	0.62	0.65	0.6	0	0.58	0.38
8	0.49	0.36	1	1.01	0.23	0.58	0	0.78
9	0.34	0.81	0.84	0.35	0.68	0.38	0.78	0

Fig. 7.6: The second iteration of clustering

Iteration 3:

	1|10	2|7	5|8	3	4	6	9
1|10	0	0.66	0.33	0.97	0.6	0.41	0.34
2|7	0.66	0	0.36	0.76	1.06	0.47	0.81
5|8	0.33	0.36	0	1	0.89	0.58	0.68
3	0.97	0.76	1	0	0.88	0.62	0.84
4	0.6	1.06	0.89	0.88	0	0.65	0.35
6	0.41	0.47	0.58	0.62	0.65	0	0.38
9	0.34	0.81	0.68	0.84	0.35	0.38	0

Fig. 7.7: The third iteration of clustering

Iteration 4:

	1|10|5|8	**2|7**	**3**	**4**	**6**	**9**
1|10|5|8	0	0.36	0.97	0.6	0.41	0.34
2|7	0.36	0	0.76	1.06	0.47	0.81
3	0.97	0.76	0	0.88	0.62	0.84
4	0.6	1.06	0.88	0	0.65	0.35
6	0.41	0.47	0.62	0.65	0	0.38
9	0.34	0.81	0.84	0.35	0.38	0

Fig. 7.8: The fourth iteration of clustering

Next, iterations can be performed in a similar manner. Here we used a single linkage method. If we use a different linkage method, the clustering would take a different shape. The hierarchical clusters can be best understood using a hierarchical tree depicting when and where the two or more points/clusters joined to form a bigger cluster.

For the distance matrix used above and the single method of linkage, one would get the following tree structure:

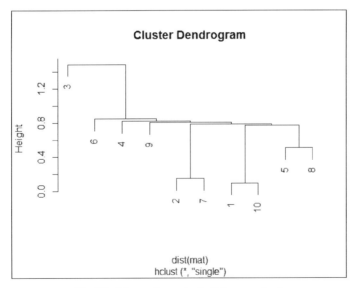

Fig. 7.9: A tree using a single linkage method

While using Ward's method, one gets a tree as shown in the following figure:

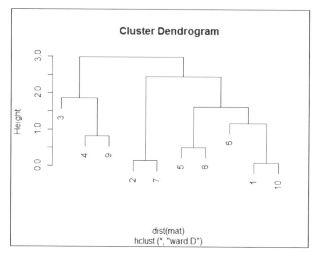

Fig. 7.10: A tree using Ward's linkage method

The tree formed using a single linkage can be interpreted as follows:

- The #1 and #10 observations are joined to form a cluster at first, followed by a cluster formed by #2 and #7.

- The #5 and #8 observations form a different cluster that later joins the cluster formed by #1 and #10.

- This bigger cluster containing #1, #10, #5, and #8 is joined by the cluster containing #2 and #7, and so on

- The observations that joined earlier to form a cluster are more similar to each other. So, (#1, #10), (#2, #7), and (#5, #8) are similar to each other.

Hierarchical clusters produce efficient and analyzable results when the number of observations in the dataset is relatively less. As the number of observations increase, the trees resulting from the hierarchical clusters become messier and more difficult to analyze. In such cases, it is better to try another method of clustering.

K-means clustering

K-means clustering is another unsupervised algorithm to cluster a number of observations. It is different from the hierarchical cluster in the sense that here the number of desired clusters and the centroid of the clusters need to be defined prior to the model formation. The centroid of the clusters keep updating based on the observations assigned to that cluster. The output consists of an array containing the cluster number to which each observation belongs to.

A step-by-step detail of the k-means clustering algorithm is as follows:

1. Decide the number of clusters and assign the cluster centroid for each cluster. The number of clusters can be decided based on the business context. The cluster centroids can be passed manually (based on the business context or some prior information), or the randomly chosen observations can serve as the cluster centroids to start with.

2. Calculate the distance of each observation from each cluster. Assign the observation to the cluster from which its distance is the least. The distance of an observation from a cluster is defined.

3. Recalculate the cluster centroid using the mean of the observations in the cluster. The following formula defines the update of the cluster centroids:

$$vi = \frac{1}{ci} \sum_{m=1}^{ci} Xm$$

Here, *ci=number* of observations in the clusters, and *Xm=observation* vector whose length is equal to the number of columns in the observation. A cluster centroid is also as long as the observation vector or the number of columns in the observation.

4. Repeat the steps starting from step 2.

5. Stop if none of the observations were reassigned from one cluster to another.

   None of the observations are being reassigned; that means that all the observations are already in the correct clusters and their distance to a cluster centroid can't be reduced further.

The goal of this algorithm is to attain a configuration of cluster centers and cluster observation so that the overall *J* squared error function or *J*-score is minimized:

$$J = \sum_{i=1}^{c} \sum_{j=1}^{ci} (Xj - Vi)^2$$

Here, c=number of clusters, ci=number of points in the cluster, and Vi=centroid of the ith cluster.

The *J* squared error function can be understood as the sum of the squared distance of points from their respective cluster centroids. A smaller value of *J* squared function implies tightly packed and homogeneous clusters. This also implies that most of the points have been placed in the right clusters.

Let us try the k-means clustering algorithm for clustering some random numbers between 0 and 1. The Python library and Scipy have some inbuilt methods to perform the algorithm and return a list defining which observation belongs to which cluster:

1. Define a set of observations consisting of random numbers ranging from 0 to 1. In this case, we have defined an observation set of 30x3:

    ```
    Import numpy as np
    obs=np.random.random(90).reshape(30,3)
    obs
    ```

    The output of the code looks as follows:

    ```
    array([[ 0.57661327,  0.57228436,  0.09121444],
           [ 0.57243857,  0.50374038,  0.56191463],
           [ 0.6331554 ,  0.31386819,  0.18356078],
           [ 0.86898774,  0.0403591 ,  0.86725316],
           [ 0.2607788 ,  0.59915679,  0.90926909],
           [ 0.58096358,  0.5744143 ,  0.82951824],
           [ 0.84253324,  0.69768867,  0.04050713],
           [ 0.62160337,  0.97374147,  0.83282739],
           [ 0.74153731,  0.38723477,  0.11345058],
           [ 0.39491075,  0.56146279,  0.23015805],
    ```

    Fig. 7.11: A 30x3 array of random numbers between 0 and 1

2. Decide that we want two clusters (no hard and fast rule, you can try with three clusters also). Select two observations at random to make them cluster centroids:

    ```
    c1=np.random.choice(range(len(obs)))
    c2=np.random.choice(range(len(obs)))
    clust_cen=np.vstack([obs[c1],obs[c2]])
    clust_cen
    ```

    The output of the code looks as follows:

    ```
    array([[ 0.47184647,  0.89249612,  0.73130458],
           [ 0.28342103,  0.64640709,  0.24428166]])
    ```

    Fig. 7.12: Selecting two rows (out of 30) at random to be initial cluster centers

    The two rows in the `clust_cen` array correspond to the two cluster centroids.

3. With the number of clusters and cluster centroids defined, one is ready to implement the k-means clustering. This can be done using the `cluster` method of Scipy:

    ```
    from scipy.cluster.vq import vq
    vq(obs,clust_cen)
    ```

```
(array([1, 0, 1, 0, 0, 0, 1, 0, 1, 1, 0, 1, 1, 0, 1, 0, 1, 1, 0, 1, 1, 0, 0,
        0, 1, 0, 0, 1, 0, 1], dtype=int64),
 array([ 0.33894755,  0.43582422,  0.48639827,  0.94991615,  0.40282613,
         0.35032629,  0.59729417,  0.19833007,  0.54236297,  0.14087217,
         0.19110092,  0.34641348,  0.        ,  0.25230902,  0.87490428,
         0.27554023,  0.5590402 ,  0.25151793,  0.28609226,  0.77169955,
         0.72043438,  0.        ,  0.44381884,  0.68654886,  0.80043611,
         0.33197907,  0.37141823,  0.5703176 ,  0.45580223,  0.77236007]))
```

Fig. 7.13: Cluster label and distance from cluster centers for each observation

The first array gives us the information as to which cluster the observation belongs to. The first observation belongs to cluster c2, the second observation belongs to c1, the third belongs to c2, the fourth to c1, and so on.

The second array gives the distance of the observation from the final cluster centroid. Hence, the first observation is at a distance of 0.33 units from the centroid of the cluster c2, the second observation is at a distance of 0.43 from the centroid of the cluster c1, and so on.

4. Find the cluster centroid for the two clusters. This is done using the kmeans method in Scipy:

```
from scipy.cluster.vq import kmeans
kmeans(obs,clust_cen)
```

The output of the code looks as follows:

```
(array([[ 0.52471403,  0.83763873,  0.67613882],
        [ 0.6133091 ,  0.34955296,  0.35004751]]), 0.35108732217332617)
```

Fig. 7.14: The final cluster centers and the value of the squared error function or J-score

The two rows in the array correspond to the two final cluster centroids. The centroid of the first cluster is at (0.524, 0.837, 0.676). The number at the end is the value of the squared error function or J-score, which we seek to minimize. Its value comes out to be 0.35.

K-means also works if one provides just the number of required clusters and not the cluster centroids. If only the required number of clusters is provided, then the method will randomly select that many observations at random from the observation set to become a cluster centroid. Thus, we could have also written the following:

```
from scipy.cluster.vq import kmeans
kmeans(obs,2)
```

Implementing clustering using Python

Now, as we understand the mathematics behind the k-means clustering better, let us implement it on a dataset and see how to glean insights from the performed clustering.

The dataset we will be using for this is about wine. Each observation represents a separate sample of wine and has information about the chemical composition of that wine. Some wine connoisseur painstakingly analyzed various samples of wine to create this dataset. Each column of the dataset has information about the composition of one chemical. There is one column called quality as well, which is based on the ratings given by the professional wine testers.

The prices of wines are generally decided by the ratings given by the professional testers. However, this can be very subjective and certainly there is a scope for a more logical process to wine prices. One approach is to cluster them based on their chemical compositions and quality and then price the similar clusters together based on the desirable components present in the wine clusters.

Importing and exploring the dataset

Let us import and have a look at this dataset:

```
import pandas as pd
df=pd.read_csv('E:/Personal/Learning/Predictive Modeling Book/Book
Datasets/Clustering/wine.csv',sep=';')
df.head()
```

The output looks as follows:

	fixed acidity	volatile acidity	citric acid	residual sugar	chlorides	free sulfur dioxide	total sulfur dioxide	density	pH	sulphates	alcohol	quality
0	7.4	0.70	0.00	1.9	0.076	11	34	0.9978	3.51	0.56	9.4	5
1	7.8	0.88	0.00	2.6	0.098	25	67	0.9968	3.20	0.68	9.8	5
2	7.8	0.76	0.04	2.3	0.092	15	54	0.9970	3.26	0.65	9.8	5
3	11.2	0.28	0.56	1.9	0.075	17	60	0.9980	3.16	0.58	9.8	6
4	7.4	0.70	0.00	1.9	0.076	11	34	0.9978	3.51	0.56	9.4	5

Fig. 7.15: The first few observations of the wine dataset

As one can observe, it has 12 columns as follows:

```
array(['fixed acidity', 'volatile acidity', 'citric acid',
       'residual sugar', 'chlorides', 'free sulfur dioxide',
       'total sulfur dioxide', 'density', 'pH', 'sulphates', 'alcohol',
       'quality'], dtype=object)
```

Fig. 7.16: The column names of the wine dataset

There are 1599 observations in this dataset.

Let us focus on the quality variable for a while and plot a histogram to see the number of wine samples in each quality type:

```
import matplotlib.pyplot as plt
% matplotlib inline
plt.hist(df['quality'])
```

The code shows the following output:

Fig. 7.17: The histogram of wine quality. The majority of samples have been rated 6 or 7 for quality

As it is evident from the plot, more than 75% of the samples were assigned the quality of **5** and **6**. Also, let's look at the mean of the various chemical compositions across samples for the different groups of the wine quality:

```
df.groupby('quality').mean()
```

The code shows the following output:

	fixed acidity	volatile acidity	citric acid	residual sugar	chlorides	free sulfur dioxide	total sulfur dioxide	density	pH	sulphates	alcohol
quality											
3	8.360000	0.884500	0.171000	2.636000	0.122500	11.000000	24.900000	0.997464	3.398000	0.570000	9.955000
4	7.779245	0.693962	0.174151	2.694340	0.090679	12.264151	36.245283	0.996542	3.381509	0.596415	10.265094
5	8.167254	0.577041	0.243686	2.528855	0.092736	16.983847	56.513950	0.997104	3.304949	0.620969	9.899706
6	8.347179	0.497484	0.273824	2.477194	0.084956	15.711599	40.869906	0.996615	3.318072	0.675329	10.629519
7	8.872362	0.403920	0.375176	2.720603	0.076588	14.045226	35.020101	0.996104	3.290754	0.741256	11.465913
8	8.566667	0.423333	0.391111	2.577778	0.068444	13.277778	33.444444	0.995212	3.267222	0.767778	12.094444

Fig. 7.18: The mean values of all the numerical columns for each value of quality

Some observations based on this table are as follows:

- The lesser the **volatile acidity** and **chlorides**, the higher the wine quality
- The more the **sulphates** and **citric acid** content, the higher the wine quality
- The **density** and **pH** don't vary much across the wine quality

Next, let's proceed with clustering these observations using k-means.

Normalizing the values in the dataset

As discussed above, normalizing the values is important to get the clustering right. This can be achieved by applying the following formula to each value in the dataset:

$$Z_i = \left(X_i - X_{min} \right) / \left(X_{max} - X_{min} \right)$$

To normalize our dataset, we write the following code snippet:

```
df_norm = (df - df.min()) / (df.max() - df.min())
df_norm.head()
```

This results in a data frame with normalized values for entire data frame as follows:

	fixed acidity	volatile acidity	citric acid	residual sugar	chlorides	free sulfur dioxide	total sulfur dioxide	density	pH	sulphates	alcohol	quality
0	0.247788	0.397260	0.00	0.068493	0.106845	0.140845	0.098940	0.567548	0.606299	0.137725	0.153846	0.4
1	0.283186	0.520548	0.00	0.116438	0.143573	0.338028	0.215548	0.494126	0.362205	0.209581	0.215385	0.4
2	0.283186	0.438356	0.04	0.095890	0.133556	0.197183	0.169611	0.508811	0.409449	0.191617	0.215385	0.4
3	0.584071	0.109589	0.56	0.068493	0.105175	0.225352	0.190813	0.582232	0.330709	0.149701	0.215385	0.6
4	0.247788	0.397260	0.00	0.068493	0.106845	0.140845	0.098940	0.567548	0.606299	0.137725	0.153846	0.4

Fig. 7.19 Normalized wine dataset

Hierarchical clustering using scikit-learn

Hierarchical clustering or agglomerative clustering can be implemented using the `AgglomerativeClustering` method in scikit-learn's cluster library as shown in the following code. It returns a label for each row denoting which cluster that row belongs to. The number of clusters needs to be defined in advance. We have used the `ward` method of linkage:

```
from sklearn.cluster import AgglomerativeClustering
ward = AgglomerativeClustering(n_clusters=6, linkage='ward').fit(df_norm)
md=pd.Series(ward.labels_)
```

We can plot a histogram of cluster labels to get a sense of how many rows belong to a particular cluster:

```
import matplotlib.pyplot as plt
% matplotlib inline
plt.hist(md)
plt.title('Histogram of Cluster Label')
plt.xlabel('Cluster')
plt.ylabel('Frequency')
```

The plot looks as follows. The observations are more uniformly distributed across the cluster except Cluster 2 that has more observations than the others:

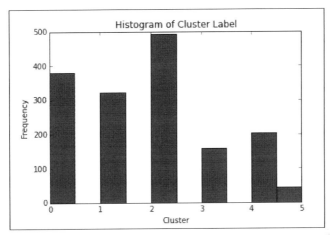

Fig. 7.20: The histogram of Cluster Labels. Samples are more-or-less uniformly distributed across clusters

It also outputs the children for each non-leaf node. This would be an array with the shape (number of non-leaf nodes, 2) as there would be two immediate children for any non-leaf node:

```
ward.children_
```

The code shows the following output:

```
array([[1592, 1596],
       [1579, 1581],
       [1564, 1567],
       ...,
       [3179, 3191],
       [3192, 3193],
       [3194, 3195]], dtype=int64)
```

Fig. 7.21: The child array containing two child elements for each non-leaf node

K-Means clustering using scikit-learn

Let us randomly choose 6 as the required number of clusters for now as there were that many groups of quality in the dataset. Then, to cluster the observations, one needs to write the following code snippet:

```
from sklearn.cluster import KMeans
from sklearn import datasets
model=KMeans(n_clusters=6)
model.fit(df_norm)
```

The preceding snippet fits the k-means clustering model to the wine dataset. To know which observation belongs to which of the clusters, one can call the `labels_` parameter of the `model`. It returns an array depicting the cluster the row belongs to:

```
model.labels_
```

The output of the code is as follows:

```
array([2, 2, 2, ..., 5, 5, 3])
```

Fig. 7.22: Cluster labels for each row

For better observation, let us make this array part of the data frame so that we can look at the cluster each row belongs to, in the same data frame:

```
md=pd.Series(model.labels_)
df_norm['clust']=md
df_norm.head()
```

The output of the code shows the following datasheet:

	fixed acidity	volatile acidity	citric acid	residual sugar	chlorides	free sulfur dioxide	total sulfur dioxide	density	pH	sulphates	alcohol	quality	clust
0	0.247788	0.397260	0.00	0.068493	0.106845	0.140845	0.098940	0.567548	0.606299	0.137725	0.153846	0.4	2
1	0.283186	0.520548	0.00	0.116438	0.143573	0.338028	0.215548	0.494126	0.362205	0.209581	0.215385	0.4	2
2	0.283186	0.438356	0.04	0.095890	0.133556	0.197183	0.169611	0.508811	0.409449	0.191617	0.215385	0.4	2
3	0.584071	0.109589	0.56	0.068493	0.105175	0.225352	0.190813	0.582232	0.330709	0.149701	0.215385	0.6	1
4	0.247788	0.397260	0.00	0.068493	0.106845	0.140845	0.098940	0.567548	0.606299	0.137725	0.153846	0.4	2

Fig. 7.23: The wine dataset with a clust column depicting the cluster the row belongs to

The last column **clust** of the data frame denotes the cluster to which that particular observation belongs. The 1st, 2nd, 3rd, and 5th observations belong to the 3rd cluster (counting starts from 0), while the 4th observation belongs to the 2nd cluster.

The final cluster's centroids for each cluster can be found out as follows:

```
model.cluster_centers_
```

Note that each cluster centroid would have 12 coordinates as there are 12 variables in the dataset.

The dataset is as follows:

```
array([[ 0.31657408,  0.27714878,  0.30457413,  0.15202455,  0.12698872,
         0.38048163,  0.29785645,  0.5390477 ,  0.43592737,  0.17890402,
         0.21400954,  0.45615142],
       [ 0.57666747,  0.20368051,  0.50645914,  0.131816  ,  0.1305873 ,
         0.13722804,  0.09139157,  0.6528223 ,  0.3351512 ,  0.22556444,
         0.29055173,  0.54941634],
       [ 0.26395373,  0.35904298,  0.12348425,  0.09132645,  0.12283596,
         0.14482367,  0.10768343,  0.49211153,  0.48648397,  0.1554293 ,
         0.22016455,  0.43976378],
       [ 0.36290046,  0.15975098,  0.42329457,  0.10547414,  0.10543412,
         0.16350038,  0.08386063,  0.40849071,  0.41863517,  0.23557536,
         0.49129398,  0.69689922],
       [ 0.32987489,  0.28412848,  0.48758621,  0.07416155,  0.54953658,
         0.21369597,  0.2114049 ,  0.51240569,  0.23486288,  0.59281437,
         0.16127321,  0.46896552],
       [ 0.17610619,  0.32432996,  0.08913043,  0.09416319,  0.09608042,
         0.24856093,  0.12292211,  0.32587627,  0.57733653,  0.18516011,
         0.48637681,  0.61043478]])
```

Fig. 7.24: Cluster centroids for each of the six clusters

The *J*-score can be thought of as the sum of the squared distance between points and cluster centroid for each point and cluster. For an efficient cluster, the *J*-score should be as low as possible. The value of the *J*-score can be found as follows:

```
model.inertia_
```

The value comes out to be 186.56.

Let us plot a histogram for the `clust` variable to get an idea of the number of observations in each cluster:

```
import matplotlib.pyplot as plt
% matplotlib inline
plt.hist(df_norm['clust'])
plt.title('Histogram of Clusters')
plt.xlabel('Cluster')
plt.ylabel('Frequency')
```

The code shows the following output:

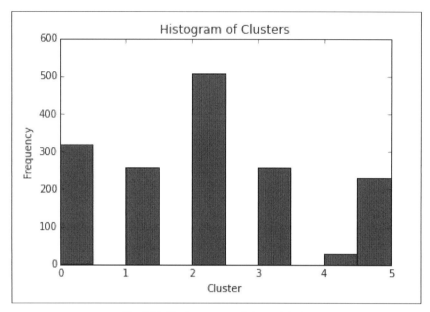

Fig. 7.25: The histogram of cluster labels

As can be observed, the number of wine samples is more uniformly (or rather normally) distributed in this case when compared to the distribution based on the wine quality. This is an improvement from the classification based on the wine quality as it provides us with better segregated and identifiable clusters.

Interpreting the cluster

This clustering can be used to price the wine samples in the same cluster similarly and target the customers who prefer the particular ingredient of wine by marketing them as a different brand having that ingredient as its specialty.

Let us calculate the mean of the composition for each cluster and each component. If you observe the output table, it is exactly similar to the six cluster centroids observed above. This is because the cluster centroids are nothing but the mean of the coordinates of all the observations in a particular cluster:

```
df_norm.groupby('clust').mean()
```

	fixed acidity	volatile acidity	citric acid	residual sugar	chlorides	free sulfur dioxide	total sulfur dioxide	density	pH	sulphates	alcohol	quality
clust												
0	0.316574	0.277149	0.304574	0.152025	0.126989	0.380482	0.297856	0.539048	0.435927	0.178904	0.214010	0.456151
1	0.576667	0.203681	0.506459	0.131816	0.130587	0.137228	0.091392	0.652822	0.335151	0.225564	0.290552	0.549416
2	0.263954	0.359043	0.123484	0.091326	0.122836	0.144824	0.107683	0.492112	0.486484	0.155429	0.220165	0.439764
3	0.362900	0.159751	0.423295	0.105474	0.105434	0.163500	0.083861	0.408491	0.418635	0.235575	0.491294	0.696899
4	0.329875	0.284128	0.487586	0.074162	0.549537	0.213696	0.211405	0.512406	0.234863	0.592814	0.161273	0.468956
5	0.176106	0.324330	0.089130	0.094163	0.096080	0.248561	0.122922	0.325876	0.577337	0.185160	0.486377	0.610435

Fig. 7.26: The mean of all the numerical columns for different clusters

The wine quality and taste mainly depends on the quantity of acid, alcohol, and sugar. A few examples of how the information on clustering can be used for efficient marketing and pricing are as follows:

- People from cooler regions prefer wines with higher volatile acid content. So, clusters 2 and 5 can be marketed in cooler (temperature-wise) markets.

- Some people might prefer wine with higher alcohol content, and the wine samples from clusters 3 and 5 can be marketed to them.

- Some connoisseurs trust others' judgment more and they might like to go with professional wine testers' judgments. These kinds of people should be sold the wine samples from clusters 3 and 5 as they have high mean quality.

More information from the wine industry can be combined with this result to form a better marketing and pricing strategy.

Fine-tuning the clustering

Deciding the optimum value of K is one of the tough parts while performing a k-means clustering. There are a few methods that can be used to do this.

The elbow method

We earlier discussed that a good cluster is defined by the compactness between the observations of that cluster. The compactness is quantified by something called intra-cluster distance. The intra-cluster distance for a cluster is essentially the sum of pair-wise distances between all possible pairs of points in that cluster.

If we denote intra-cluster distance by W, then for a cluster k intra-cluster, the distance can be denoted by:

$$Wk = \sum_{i=1}^{ck} \sum_{j=1}^{ck} \left(Xi - Xj \right)^2$$

$$Wk = 2Nk \sum_{i=1}^{ck} \left(Xi - Mk \right)^2$$

Generally, the normalized intra-cluster distance is used, which is given by:

$$Wk' = \sum_{i=1}^{ck} \frac{1}{2Nk} * Wk$$

Here Xi and Xj are points in the cluster, Mk is the centroid of the cluster, Nk is the number of points in the centroid, and K is the number of clusters.

Wk' is actually a measure of the variance between the points in the same cluster. Since it is normalized, its value would range from 0 to 1. As one increases the number of clusters, the value of Wk' increases marginally until a certain point post of this marginal increase stops. At this point, we get an elbow in the curve and this gives us the correct number of the cluster as shown in the following graph:

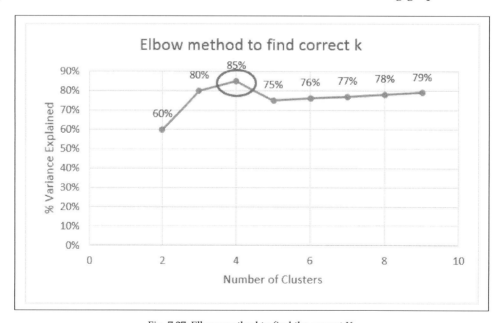

Fig. 7.27: Elbow method to find the correct K

As shown in the preceding plot for a hypothetical dataset, the percentage variance explained by the clusters peaks at *k=4*, post which the marginal increase stops. This encircled point in the preceding graph is called the elbow that gives the name to the method. The correct number of clusters in this case is then 4.

Silhouette Coefficient

Silhouette Coefficient for an observation in the dataset quantifies how tightly the point is bound to the other points in the same cluster and how loosely the point is bound to points in the nearest neighbor cluster. The Silhouette Coefficient is calculated using the mean intra-cluster distance (*b*) and the mean nearest-cluster distance (*a*) for each sample:

$$Silhouette\,coefficient\,(S) = (b-a)\,/\,max\,(a,b)$$

Let us have a look at the following example to understand the concept of the Silhouette Coefficient better:

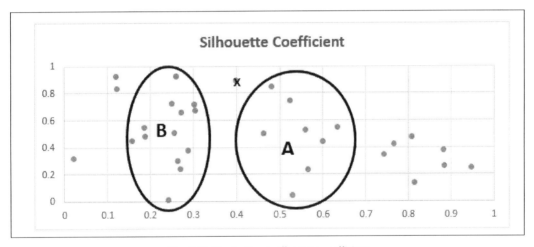

Fig. 7.28: Illustrating a silhouette coefficient

Let us look at the preceding situation for the point (observation) marked **X**. It has two nearby clusters, **A** and **B**; A being relatively closer to X than B. The mean intra-cluster distance of X from the points in A is denoted by *a*. The mean intra-cluster distance of X from the points in the next nearest cluster (B in this case) is denoted by *b*. The intra-cluster distance is simply defined as the sum of the distances of the point marked X from all the points in a given cluster.

The Silhouette Coefficient, S, can be rewritten as follows:

$$\frac{1-(a/b), if\ a<b}{S=0, if\ a=b}$$
$$(b/a)-1, if\ a>b$$

The value of the Silhouette Coefficient ranges from -1 to 1. A value close to -1 means that a is (very) large than b implying that the point is more similar to the neighboring cluster (B) than the current cluster (A) and is wrongly placed in the current cluster. A value close to 1 means that a is (very) smaller than b and hence a point is placed in the correct cluster.

Overall the silhouette coefficient of the entire dataset is a mean of the silhouette coefficients of each sample. The value of the Silhouette Coefficient is affected by the number of clusters. The Silhouette Coefficients can be used to decide the optimum number of clusters as follows:

1. Start with two clusters. Calculate the mean silhouette coefficient for each cluster.

2. Calculate the mean silhouette coefficients of the entire dataset (average over all the clusters).

3. Check whether the mean silhouette coefficient of any of the clusters is less than the overall mean silhouette coefficient of the dataset. If this is the case, the number of clusters is suboptimal or a bad pick. If it is not the case, then it is a potential candidate for being the optimum number of clusters.

4. Repeat the steps 1 to 3 for different numbers of clusters (untill $n=6$ to 10 or a suitable number derived from the context or elbow method).

5. Decide on one of the potential candidates identified in the steps 3 and 4 to be the optimum number of clusters.

The elbow method and silhouette coefficients can be used to fine-tune the clustering once it has been run assuming some arbitrary number of clusters. The actual clustering can then be performed once the optimum number of clusters is known. The results from these methods coupled with the business context should give an idea about the number of clusters to be used.

Summary

In this chapter, we learned the following:

- Clustering is an unsupervised predictive algorithm to club similar data points together and segregate the dissimilar points from each other. This algorithm finds the usage in marketing, taxonomy, seismology, public policy, and data mining.

- The distance between two observations is one of the criteria on which the observations can be clustered together.

- The distance between all the points in a dataset is best represented by an *nxn* symmetric matrix called a distance matrix.

- Hierarchical clustering is an agglomerative mode of clustering wherein we start with *n* clusters (equal to the number of points in the dataset) that are agglomerated into a lesser number of cluster based on the linkages developed over distance matrix.

- K-means clustering algorithm is a widely used mode of clustering wherein the number of clusters need to be stated in advance before performing the clustering. K-means clustering method outputs a label for each row of data depicting the cluster it belongs to. It also outputs the cluster centers. K-means method is easier to analyze and make sense of.

- Deciding the number of clusters (k) for the k-means clustering is an important task. The elbow method and silhouette coefficient method are some of the methods that can help us to decide the optimum number of k.

In the current chapter, we dealt with an unsupervised algorithm that is very widely used. Next, we will learn about a classification supervised algorithm. It is called a decision tree. It is a great set of algorithms to classify and predict data.

8
Trees and Random Forests
with Python

Clustering, discussed in the last chapter, is an unsupervised algorithm. It is now time to switch back to a supervised algorithm. Classification is a class of problems that surfaces quite frequently in predictive modelling and in various forms. Accordingly, to deal with all of them, a family of classification algorithms is used.

A decision tree is a supervised classification algorithm that is used when the target variable is a discrete or categorical variable (having two or more than two classes) and the predictor variables are either categorical or numerical variables. A decision tree can be thought of as a set of if-then rules for a classification problem where the target variables are discrete or categorical variables. The if-then rules are represented as a tree.

A decision tree is used when the decision is based on multiple-staged criteria and variables. A decision tree is very effective as a decision making tool as it has a pictorial output that is easier to understand and implement compared to the output of the other predictive models.

Decision trees and related classification algorithms will be the theme running throughout this chapter. At the end of this chapter, the reader will be able to get a basic understanding of the concept of a decision tree, the mathematics behind it, the implementation of decision trees and Python, and the efficiency of the classification performed through the model.

We will cover the following topics in depth:

- Introducing decision trees
- Understanding the mathematics behind decision trees
- Implementing a decision tree
- Understanding and implementing regression trees
- Understanding and implementing random forests

Introducing decision trees

A tree is a data structure that might be used to state certain decision rules because it can be represented in such a way as to pictorially illustrate these rules. A tree has three basic elements: nodes, branches, and leaves. Nodes are the points from where one or more branches come out. A node from where no branch originates is a leaf. A typical tree looks as follows:

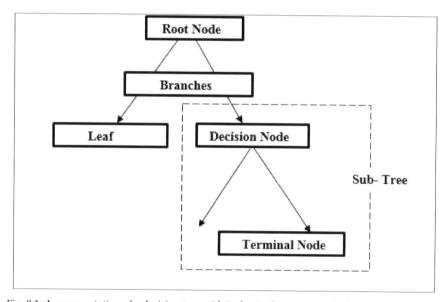

Fig. 8.1: A representation of a decision tree with its basic elements—node, branches, and leaves

A tree, specifically a decision tree, starts with a root node, proceeds to the decision nodes, and ultimately to the terminal nodes where the decision rules are made. All nodes, except the terminal node, represent one variable and the branches represent the different categories (values) of that variable. The terminal node represents the final decision or value for that route.

A decision tree

To understand what decision trees look like and how to make sense of them, let us consider an example. Consider a situation where one wants to predict whether a particular Place will get a Bumper, Moderate, or a Meagre Harvest of a crop based on information about the Rainfall, Terrain, availability of groundwater, and usage of fertilizers. Consider the following dataset for that situation:

Place	Rainfall	Terrain	Fertilisers	Groundwater	Harvest
P1	High	Plains	Yes	Yes	Bumper
P2	Low	Hills	No	Yes	Meagre
P3	Low	Plateau	No	Yes	Moderate
P4	High	Plateau	No	Yes	Moderate
P5	High	Plains	Yes	No	Bumper
P6	Low	Hills	No	No	Meagre
P7	Low	Plateau	No	No	Meagre
P8	Mild	Plateau	No	No	Meagre
P9	High	Hills	Yes	Yes	Moderate
P10	Mild	Plateau	Yes	Yes	Bumper
P11	High	Plateau	Yes	No	Bumper
P12	Mild	Plateau	Yes	No	Moderate
P13	High	Hills	Yes	No	Moderate
P14	Low	Plains	Yes	Yes	Moderate
P15	Mild	Plains	Yes	No	Moderate
P16	Low	Plains	No	No	Meagre
P17	Low	Hills	Yes	No	Meagre
P18	Mild	Plateau	No	No	Meagre
P19	High	Plains	No	Yes	Moderate
P20	Mild	Hills	Yes	Yes	Moderate

Fig. 8.2 A simulated dataset containing information about the Harvest type and conditions such as the Rainfall, Terrain, Usage of Fertilizers, and Availability of Groundwater

For a while, let us forget how these trees are constructed and focus on interpreting a tree and how it becomes handy in classification problems. For illustrative purposes, let us assume that the final decision tree looks as follows (we will learn the mathematics behind it later):

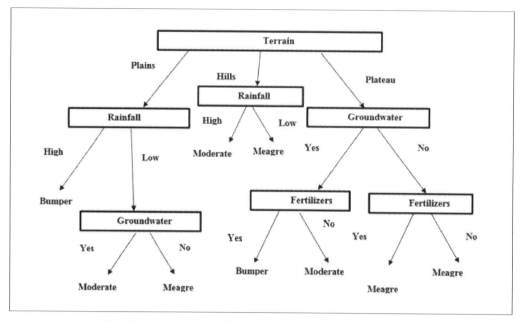

Fig. 8.3: A representational decision tree based on the above dataset

There are multiple decisions one can make using this decision tree:

- If Terrain is Plain and Rainfall is High, then the harvest will be Bumper
- If Terrain is Plain, Rainfall is Low, and Groundwater is Yes (present), then the harvest will be Moderate
- If Terrain is Plain, Rainfall is Low, and Groundwater is No (present), then the harvest will be Meagre
- If Terrain is Hills and Rainfall is High, then the harvest will be Moderate
- If Terrain is Hills and Rainfall is Low, then the harvest will be Meagre
- If Terrain is Plateau, Groundwater is Yes, and Fertilizer is Yes (present), then the harvest will be Bumper
- If Terrain is Plateau, Groundwater is Yes, and Fertilizer is No (present), then the harvest will be Moderate

- If Terrain is Plateau, Groundwater is No, and Fertilizer is Yes (present), then the harvest will be Meagre

- If Terrain is Plateau, Groundwater is No, and Fertilizer is No (present), then the harvest will be Meagre

A decision tree, or the decisions implied by it, can also be represented as disjunction statements. For example, the conditions for the harvest being *Bumper* can be written as a combination of AND and OR operators (or disjunctions), as follows:

$$Harvest == 'Bumper'$$

$$(Terrain == 'Plains' \cap Rainfall == 'High')$$

$$\cup (Terrain == 'Plateau' \cap Groundwater == 'Yes' \cap Fertilizers == 'Yes')$$

In the same way, the conditions for a *Moderate* harvest can be summarized using disjunctions as follows:

$$Harvest == 'Moderate'$$

$$(Terrain == 'Plains' \cap Rainfall == 'Low' \cap Groundwater == 'Yes')$$

$$(\cup (Terrain == 'Hills' \cap Rainfall == 'High')$$

$$\cup (Terrain == 'Plateau' \cap Groundwater == 'Yes' \cap Fertilizers == 'No')$$

In the preceding example, we have used only categorical variables as the predictor variables. However, there is no such restriction. The numerical variables can very well be used as predictor variables. However, the numerical variables are not the most preferred variables for a decision tree, as they lose some information while they are categorized into groups to be used in a decision tree algorithm.

A decision tree is advantageous because it is easier to understand and doesn't require a lot of data cleaning in the sense that it is not influenced by missing values and outliers that much.

Understanding the mathematics behind decision trees

The main goal in a decision tree algorithm is to identify a variable and classification on which one can give a more homogeneous distribution with reference to the target variable. The homogeneous distribution means that similar values of the target variable are grouped together so that a concrete decision can be made.

Homogeneity

In the preceding example, the first goal would be to find a parameter (out of four: Terrain, Rainfall, Groundwater, and Fertilizers) that results in a better homogeneous distribution of the target variable within those categories.

Without any parameter, the count of harvest type looks as follows:

Bumper	Moderate	Meagre
4	9	7

Let us calculate, for each parameter, how the split on that parameter affects the homogeneity of the target variable split:

Rainfall

Rainfall	Bumper	Meagre	Moderate
High	3 (43%)	0 (0%)	4 (57%)
Low	0 (0%)	5 (71%)	2 (29%)
Mild	1 (17%)	2 (33%)	3 (50%)

Terrain

Terrain	Bumper	Meagre	Moderate
Hills	0 (0%)	3 (50%)	3 (50%)
Plains	2 (33%)	1 (17%)	3 (50%)
Plateau	2 (25%)	3 (37.5%)	3 (37.5%)

Fertilizers

Fertilizers	Bumper	Meagre	Moderate
No	0 (0%)	6 (67%)	3 (33%)
Yes	4 (36%)	1 (9%)	6 (55%)

Groundwater

Groundwater	Bumper	Meagre	Moderate
No	2 (18%)	6 (55%)	3 (27%)
Yes	2 (22%)	1 (11%)	6 (67%)

Fig. 8.4: Splitting the predictor and the target variables into categories to see their effect on the homogeneity of the dataset

If one observes carefully, the classification done on the Rainfall parameter is more homogeneous than that done on the Terrain parameter. Homogeneity means more similar things together or, in other words, fewer dissimilar things together. Homogeneity can be understood as follows: for Low rainfall, the harvest is distributed as 0%, 71%, and 29% across Bumper, Meagre, and Moderate, and it is a more homogeneous classification than 0% (Bumper), 50% (Meagre), and 50% (Moderate) for hilly terrains. This is because Low rainfall was able to group more of the Meagre rainfall (71%) together than the classes in the Terrain parameter. For the Fertilizers and Groundwater parameters, the highest homogeneity that can be achieved is 67%. Thus, the rainfall is the most suited to classify the target variable; that is, the Harvest type. This can be refined more as we add more variables (parameters) for the classification.

To understand it even better, let us look at the following pictures. Which one is more homogeneous? Which one can represent a node where a concrete decision (about the type of dot: bold or normal) can be made? Definitely **C**, because it has only one type of dot. **B** is the next best choice as, in this case, the decision of the dot type is skewed more towards the bold dots (compared to **A**) than the normal dots.

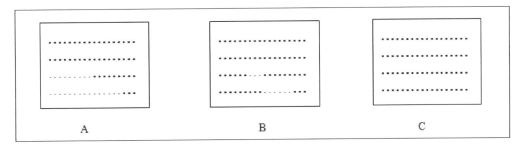

Making these classifications more and more homogeneous, so that they can be identified as concrete decisions, is the ultimate goal in decision tree algorithms. Identifying the variable that results in the best homogeneous classification can be done in many ways. There are multiple algorithms available to do this. Let us take a look at some of them.

Entropy

The entropy technique takes cues from information theory. The premise is that more homogeneous or pure nodes require less information to be represented. One example of information can be an encrypted signal that has to be transmitted. If the constituents of the message are more homogeneous, it will consume fewer bits. The configuration that requires less information is always preferred.

The impurity or heterogeneity of a node can be measured using something called **entropy**. One interpretation of entropy (from information theory) is the minimum number of bits required to encode the classification of an arbitrary member of the set. The change (reduction) in non-desirable entropy can be measured with information gain. In the case of a decision tree, the nodes whose addition results in information gain should be added to the configuration.

Entropy is defined as follows:

$$Entropy(S) = \sum -p_i log_2 p_i$$

Here, the summation is over different categories of the target variable. *Pi* is the proportion (over the total number of observations) of the ith particular category of the target variable.

Entropy ranges from 0 to log_2c, c being the number of categories present in the target variable. The entropy will be 0 when the observations are perfectly homogeneous, while it will be log_2c when the observations are perfectly heterogeneous. The entropy reaches the maximum value (log_2c) when all the *pi*'s are equal. The entropy reaches the minimum value (0) when one pi is equal to 1 and all the others are 0. If *pi=1*, the receiver of the information will know with certainty what classification an arbitrary member should belong to, so that there will be no information required and, thus, the entropy will be 0.

In the preceding example, we have three categories of target variables; hence, the entropy can range from 0 to $log_2 3$ (1.58). We have three categories of the target variable, namely, Bumper, Meagre, and Moderate with proportions 4/20, 9/20, and 7/20. Thus, the entropy can be calculated as follows:

$$S = -((4/20) * Log_2(4/20) + (9/20) * Log_2(9/20) + (7/20) * Log_2(7/20)$$
$$= -(-0.46 - 0.51 - 0.53) = 1.5$$

When the target variables are perfectly homogeneously distributed, the entropy will be 0. Suppose that all the observations had Bumper, Meagre, or Moderate as a target variable, then the entropy would be as follows:

$$S = -((20/20) * log_2(20/20) + (0) * log_2(0/20) + (0) * log_2(0/20) = 0(remember\ log_2 1 = 0)$$

On the other hand, if the classification is perfectly heterogeneous (that is, when each category of the target variable has equal number of observations) then the entropy reaches its maximum value.

A plot of entropy versus pi takes up the shape of an inverted U with a maxima in the middle. A plot of entropy versus the pi for a binary classification looks as follows:

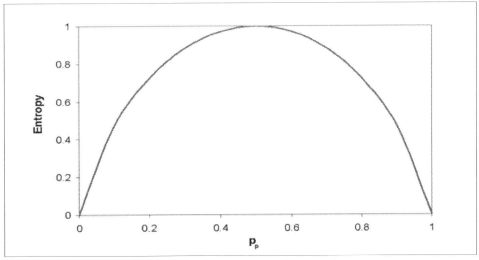

Fig. 8.5: A plot of entropy versus the proportions

As you can see in the preceding picture, the entropy increases with an increase in *pi*, reaches a maximum at the point where all the *pi*'s are equal, and then starts decreasing as the *pi* increases after that.

Information gain

The entropy (*S=1.5*) we calculated is the entropy of the system at the beginning. This reduces as we introduce variables as nodes in the system. This reduction reflects as an *Information Gain*. Let us see how information gains are calculated for different variables. The information gain for a particular variable *V* is defined as follows:

$$information\ Gain\,(S,V) = S_v - \sum(V_c\,/\,V).Entropy(V_c)$$

S_v is the total entropy for the node variable *V*, *c* stands for the categories in the node variable, V_c is the number of total observation with the category c of the node variable, *V* is the total number of observations, and Entropy(V_c) is the entropy of the system having observations with the category *c* of the node variable. Summation is over the categories of the variable.

Let us calculate the information gain based on using the Terrain variable as a node.

For this, let us calculate the entropy for different categories of the Terrain variable. Entropy is always calculated keeping the target variable in mind. For each category of the particular variable, we need to count how many target variables of each kind are present:

$$Terrain = Plains \rightarrow 2\,Bumper, 1\,Meagre, 3\,Moderate$$

$$S_{plains} = -((2/6) * Log_2(2/6) + (1/6) * Log_2(1/6) + (3/6) * Log_2(3/6) = 1.45$$

$$Terrain = Plateau \rightarrow 2\,Bumper, 3\,Meagre, 3\,Moderate$$

$$S_{Plateau} = -((2/8) * Log_2(2/8) + (3/8) * Log_2(3/8) + (3/8) * Log_2(3/8) = 1.56$$

$$Terrain = Hills \rightarrow 2\,Bumper, 1\,Meagre, 3\,Moderate$$

$$S_{Hills} = -((0/6) * Log_2(0/6) + (3/6) * Log_2(3/6) + (3/6) * Log_2(3/6) = 1$$

Now, we can calculate the information gain as follows:

$$Information\,Gain(S,V) = 1.5 - \left[(6/20) * S_{Plain} + (8/20) * S_{Plateau} + *S_{Hills} \right]$$

$$= 1.5 - \left[(6/20) * 1.45 + (8/20) * 1.56 + (6/20) * 1 \right] = 1.5 - 1.36 = 0.14$$

The preceding calculation can be summarized in a tree-branch as follows:

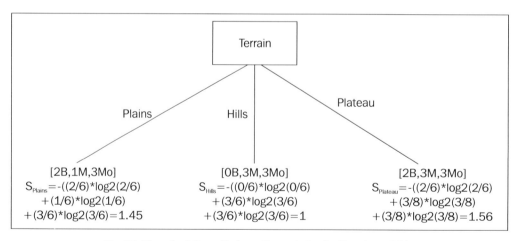

Fig. 8.6: The calculation of information gain for the Terrain variable

Similarly, the information gain for the Rainfall variable can be calculated as 0.42, that for the Fertilizers variable can be calculated as 0.36, and that for Groundwater can be calculated as 0.16:

Parameter	Information Gain
Terrain	0.14
Rainfall	0.42
Fertilizers	0.36
Groundwater	0.16

The variable that provides the maximum information gain is chosen to be the node. In this case, the Rainfall variable is chosen as it results in the maximum information gain of 0.42.

ID3 algorithm to create a decision tree

The tree keeps growing by selecting the next variable that results in the maximum information gain as a subnode branching out from this node (Rainfall in this case). A node should be chosen separately for each branch of the previous node. The variables already used for the split still qualify to be considered for being a node. It is a recursive process that stops when the node is totally homogeneous (pure), or it reaches the maximum possible depth (the number of observations in the dataset) of the tree.

This algorithm using entropy and information gain is called ID3 algorithm, and can be summarized as follows:

1. Calculate the initial entropy of the system based on the target variable.
2. Calculate the information gains for each candidate variable for a node. Select the variable that provides the maximum information gain as a decision node.
3. Repeat step 2 for each branch (value) of the node (variable) identified in step 2. The newly identified node is termed as leaf node.
4. Check whether the leaf node classifies the entire data perfectly. If not, repeat the steps from step 2 onwards. If yes, stop.

Apart from the ID3 algorithm involving entropy and information gain, there are other algorithms that can be used to decide which variable should be chosen as a subnode. Some of them are Gini index method, **Chi-Square Automatic Interaction Detector (CHAID)** method, and **Reduction in Variance** method. All these algorithms are useful and might give better results than the others in specific scenarios. A summary of all these methods is available in the following table:

Method	Properties
Gini index	This can be used only if the target variable is a binary variable. **Classification and Regression Trees (CART)**, a famous classification technique, uses Gini index method.
CHAID	This uses the chi-square statistic to find the statistical significance of the difference between a parent node and a subnode. It can handle more than two categories of the target variable.
Reduction in Variance	This is used to handle a continuous numerical variable as the target variable in decision tree creation. It calculates the variance at each node and takes a weighted average of the variances to decide the subnode.

To give an idea about the nitty-gritty of these methods, a couple of them such as Gini index and Reduction in Variance have been explained in detail.

Gini index

Gini method works only when the target variable is a binary variable. This method is used by the famous CART algorithm.

Gini is defined as the sum of the square of proportions of categories of the target variable for the particular category of the node variable. Suppose the node variable, for which we are trying to look for a subnode, has two categories *C1* and *C2*. *C1* has 2 *yes*'s and 8 *no*'s (out of the total 10 observations with *C1* as the value of the node variable), while *C2* has 6 *yes*'s and 4 *no*'s (the total of 8 *yes*'s and 12 *no*'s). Gini for each category is calculated as follows:

$$Gini_{C1} = (0.2)^2 + (0.8)^2 = 0.68$$
$$Gini_{C2} = (0.6)^2 + (0.4)^2 = 0.52$$

Then, Gini index for a variable is calculated by taking a weighted average over the categories:

$$Gini\ index = (10/20)*0.68 + (10/20)*0.52 = 0.60$$

Gini index is calculated for all the candidate variables. A variable with a higher Gini index is selected to create the subnode.

Reduction in Variance

In the Reduction in Variance method, the target variable is supposed to be a numerical variable. Let's consider the same example that we considered for understanding the Gini index method. To convert the target variable (*yes* and *no*) to a numerical variable, let's transform *yes* to 1 and *no* to 0 (resulting in 8 1's and 12 0's).

$$Mean\ for\ root\ node = (8*1+12*0)/20 = 0.4$$

$$Variance\ for\ root\ node = \left[8*(1-0.4)^2 + 12*(0-0.4)^2\right]/20 = 0.24$$

$$Mean\ for\ category\ C1\ of\ variable = (1*2+8*0)/10 = 0.2$$

$$Variance\ for\ category\ C1\ of\ variable = \left[2*(1-0.2)^2 + 8*(0-0.2)^2\right]/10 = 0.16$$

$$Mean\ for\ category\ C2\ of\ variable = (1*6+4*0)/10 = 0.6$$

$$Variance\ for\ category\ C2\ of\ variable = \left[6*(1-0.6)^2 + 4*(0-0.6)^2\right]/10 = 0.24$$

$$Weighted\ variance\ for\ the\ variable = (10/20)*0.16 + (10/20)*0.24 = 0.20$$

The weighed variance is calculated for each variable. The variable with the smallest weighted variance is chosen to be the node.

Pruning a tree

As we have seen earlier, a decision tree keeps growing by adding subnodes to the parent node until the data is perfectly classified or totally homogeneous. An extreme case is that of a decision tree that has as many nodes as there are observations in the dataset. This happens rarely, but a more common phenomenon is over-fitting, where the tree over-learns a given training dataset, but doesn't perform that well with other similar datasets. A small tree will lose out on accuracy as it might miss out on some important variables, decreasing its accuracy.

A common strategy to overcome this situation is to first allow the tree to grow until the nodes have the minimum number of instances under them and then prune the tree to remove the branches or nodes that don't provide a lot of classification power to the tree. This procedure is called pruning a decision tree and can be done in both a bottom-up and top-down fashion. The following are a few methods that are used to do this:

- **Reduced error pruning**: It is a naïve top-down approach for pruning a tree. Starting from the terminal nodes or the leaves, each node is replaced with its most popular category. If the accuracy of the tree is not affected, the replacements are put into effect.

- **Cost complexity pruning**: This method generates a set of trees, $T0, T1,...,Tn$, where $T0$ is the unpruned tree and Tn is just the root node. The Ti tree is created by replacing a subtree of the $Ti-1$ tree with one of the leaf nodes (selecting the leaf node is done using either of the algorithms explained above). The subtree to be replaced is chosen as follows:

  1. Define an error rate for a decision tree T over a dataset D as $err(T,D)$.

  2. The number of terminal nodes or leaves in a decision tree T is given by leaves (T). A decision tree T from which a subtree t has been pruned is denoted by $prune(T,t)$.

  3. Define a function M, where $M=[err(prune(T,t),D)-err(T,D)]/[\,|leaves(T)|-|leaves(prune(T,t))|\,]$.

  4. Calculate M for all the candidate subtrees.

  5. The subtree that minimizes the M is chosen for removal.

Handling a continuous numerical variable

Earlier in the discussion, we mentioned that continuous numerical variables can also be used as a predictor variable while creating a decision tree. However, the algorithms we have discussed to choose a subnode and grow the tree, all require a categorical variable. How do we then use continuous numerical variables to create a decision tree?

The answer is by defining thresholds for the continuous numerical variable, based on which the variable will be categorized in several classes dynamically. How do we define such a threshold for a numerical variable? To answer these questions, let us suppose that the harvest dataset used earlier has the information about Temperature, as well. Let us look at the first 10 observations for such a dataset (showing only the Temperature and Harvest variables):

Temp(⁰C)	35	27	12	51	46	38	4	22	29	17
Harvest	Bumper	Moderate	Meagre	Meagre	Meagre	Bumper	Meagre	Moderate	Moderate	Meagre

To find the appropriate thresholds that can be used to divide Temperature into categories for the sake of creating a decision tree, the following steps can be performed:

1. Sort the dataset based on Temperature (the numerical variable) in ascending order. The sorted dataset will look as shown in the following table:

Temp(⁰C)	4	12	17	22	27	29	35	38	35	46	51
Harvest	Meagre	Meagre	Meagre	Moderate	Moderate	Moderate	Bumper	Bumper	Bumper	Meagre	Meagre

2. Mark the Temperature ranges where the Harvest type transitions from one category to another. For example, in the 17-22 range, the Harvest type changes from Meagre to Moderate. Similarly, in the 29-35 range, the Harvest type transitions from Moderate to Bumper, and in the 35-46 range, Harvest transitions from Bumper to Meagre.

3. Corresponding to each transition in Harvest, there will be one threshold. In this case, there are three transitions so there will be three thresholds. Let us call these c_1, c_2, and c_3.

4. The thresholds of Temperature for these transitions are nothing but the average of the Temperature range over which the transition occurs. Thus, $c_1=(17+22)/2=19.5$, $c_2=(29+35)/2=32$, and $c_3=(35+46)/2=40.5$.

5. Corresponding to each of the thresholds, there will be a separate category of Temperature. Thus, the 3 categories of the Temperature will be as follows: *Temperature>19.5*, *Temperature>32*, and *Temperature>40.5*.

This method works because it has already been proved that such ranges where the target variable transitions from one category to an other provide the thresholds for continuous numerical variables that maximize the information gain.

Handling a missing value of an attribute

One of the advantages of using a decision tree is that it can handle missing values of an attribute. In many situations in real life where decision trees are used, one faces a situation where the data points of an attribute are missing. For example, consider a situation where one wants to predict a patient condition based on a number of laboratory results. What if some of the laboratory results of some of the tests are not available for some of the patients? How do we handle such a situation?

Let us consider the first 10 observations of the dataset we used above, albeit with a few missing values:

Place	Rainfall	Terrain	Fertilizers	Groundwater	Harvest
P1	High	Plains	Yes	Yes	Bumper
P2	Low		No	Yes	Meagre
P3	Low	Plateau	No	Yes	Moderate
P4	High	Plateau	No	Yes	Moderate
P5	High	Plains	Yes	No	Bumper
P6	Low	Hills	No	No	Meagre
P7	Low	Plateau	No	No	Meagre
P8	Mild	Plateau	No	No	Meagre
P9	High	Hills	Yes	Yes	Moderate
P10	Mild		Yes	Yes	Bumper

Some of the approaches that can be used to handle the missing values while creating a decision tree are as follows:

- Assign the most common (highest frequency) category of that variable to the missing value. In the preceding case, the Terrain variable has a missing value. The most common category of the Terrain variable is Plateau. So, the missing value will be replaced by Plateau.

- Assign the most common (highest frequency) category of that variable among all the observations that have the same class of the target variable to the missing value. For the first blank Harvest class is Meagre. The most common class for the *Harvest==Meagre* is Plateau. So, we will replace the blank with Plateau. For the second blank, the Harvest type is Bumper. The most common class for the *Harvest==Bumper* is Plain. So, we will replace the blank with Plain.

Once the missing values have been replaced, the usual decision tree algorithms can be applied steadfastly.

Implementing a decision tree with scikit-learn

Now, when we are sufficiently aware of the mathematics behind decision trees, let us implement a simple decision tree using the methods in scikit-learn. The dataset we will be using for this is a commonly available dataset called the iris dataset that has information about flower species and their petal and sepal dimensions. The purpose of this exercise will be to create a classifier that can classify a flower as belonging to a certain species based on the flower petal and sepal dimensions.

To do this, let's first import the dataset and have a look at it:

```
import pandas as pd
data=pd.read_csv('E:/Personal/Learning/Predictive Modeling Book/My
Work/Chapter 7/iris.csv')
data.head()
```

The datasheet looks as follows:

	Sepal.Length	Sepal.Width	Petal.Length	Petal.Width	Species
0	5.1	3.5	1.4	0.2	setosa
1	4.9	3.0	1.4	0.2	setosa
2	4.7	3.2	1.3	0.2	setosa
3	4.6	3.1	1.5	0.2	setosa
4	5.0	3.6	1.4	0.2	setosa

Fig. 8.7: The first few observations of the iris dataset

Sepal-length, Sepal-width, Petal-length, and Petal-width are the dimensions of the flower while the Species denotes the class the flower belongs to. There are actually three classes of species here that can be looked at as follows:

```
data['Species'].unique()
```

The output will be three categories of the species as follows:

```
array(['setosa', 'versicolor', 'virginica'], dtype=object)
```

Fig. 8.8: The categories of the species in the iris dataset

The purpose of this exercise will be to classify the flowers as belonging to one of the three species based on the dimensions. Let us see how we can do this.

Let us first get the predictors and the target variables separated:

```
colnames=data.columns.values.tolist()
predictors=colnames[:4]
target=colnames[4]
```

The first four columns of the dataset are termed predictors and the last one, that is, species is termed as the target variable.

Next, let's split the dataset into training and testing data:

```
Import numpy as np
data['is_train'] = np.random.uniform(0, 1, len(data) <= .75
train, test = data[data['is_train']==True], data[data['is_
train']==False]
```

In the first line, we are basically creating as many uniformly distributed random numbers between 0 and 1 as there are observations in the dataset. If the random number is less than or equal to .75, that observation goes to the training dataset; otherwise the observation goes to the testing dataset.

We have everything ready to create a decision tree now. As we have seen earlier, there are several methods to create nodes and subnodes. This method can be specified while invoking the DecisionTreeClassifier method of the sklearn library:

```
from sklearn.tree import DecisionTreeClassifier
dt = DecisionTreeClassifier(criterion='entropy',min_samples_split=20,
random_state=99)
dt.fit(train[predictors], train[target])
```

The `min_samples_split` specifies the minimum number of observations required to split a node into a subnode. By default, it is set to **2**, which can be troublesome and can lead to over-fitting as a tree in such case can keep growing until it can find at least two observations. In this case, we have specified it to be **20**. Our decision tree is now ready. Let us now test the result of our decision tree by using it for prediction over the testing dataset:

```
preds=dt.predict(test[predictors])
pd.crosstab(test['Species'],preds,rownames=['Actual'],colnames=['Pred
ictions'])
```

In the first line of the preceding code snippet, the decision tree is used to predict the class (species) for the flowers in the test dataset using the flower dimensions. The second line creates a table comparing the Actual species and the Predicted species. The table looks as follows:

Predictions	setosa	versicolor	virginica
Actual			
setosa	11	0	0
versicolor	0	11	2
virginica	0	1	11

Fig. 8.9: Comparing the Actual and Predicted categories

This table can be interpreted as follows: all the actual setosas were actually classified correctly as setosas. Out of the total 13 versicolors, 11 were classified correctly and 2 were classified wrongly as virginicas. Out of the total 12 virginicas, 11 were classified correctly while 1 was classified wrongly as versicolor. This accuracy rate is pretty good.

Visualizing the tree

In `scikit-learn`, there are the following four steps to visualize a tree:

1. Creating a `.dot` file from the Decision Tree Classifier model that is fit for the data.

2. In Python, this can be done using the `export_graphviz` module in the `sklearn` package. A `.dot` file contains information necessary to draw a tree. This information includes the entropy value (or Gini) at that node, the number of observations in that node, the condition referring to that node, and the node number pointing to another node number denoting which node is connected next to which one. For example, 2->3 and 3->4 means that node 2 is connected to 3, 3 is connected to 4, and so on. You can specify the directory name where you want to create the `.dot` file:

```
from sklearn.tree import export_graphviz
with open('E:/Personal/Learning/Predictive Modeling Book/My Work/
Chapter 7/dtree2.dot', 'w') as dotfile:
    export_graphviz(dt, out_file = dotfile, feature_names =
predictors)
dotfile.close()
```

3. Take a look at the `.dot` file after it is created to have a better idea. It looks as follows:

```
digraph Tree {
0 [label="Petal.Length <= 2.4500\nentropy = 1.58496250072\nsamples =
150", shape="box"] ;
1 [label="entropy = 0.0000\nsamples = 50\nvalue = [ 50.   0.   0.]",
shape="box"] ;
0 -> 1 ;
2 [label="Petal.Width <= 1.7500\nentropy = 1.0\nsamples = 100",
shape="box"] ;
0 -> 2 ;
3 [label="Petal.Length <= 4.9500\nentropy = 0.445064857051\nsamples =
54", shape="box"] ;
2 -> 3 ;
4 [label="Petal.Width <= 1.6500\nentropy = 0.14609425012\nsamples = 48",
shape="box"] ;
3 -> 4 ;
5 [label="entropy = 0.0000\nsamples = 47\nvalue = [  0.  47.   0.]",
shape="box"] ;
```

Fig. 8.10: Information inside a .dot file

4. Rendering a `.dot` file into a tree:

This can be done using the `system` module of the `os` package that is used to run the `cmd` commands from within Python. This is done as follows:

```
from os import system
system("dot -Tpng /E:/Personal/Learning/Predictive Modeling Book/
My Work/Chapter 7/dtree2.dot -o /E:/Personal/Learning/Predictive
Modeling Book/My Work/Chapter 7/dtree2.png")
```

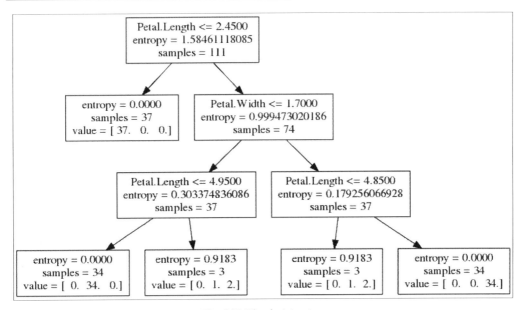

Fig. 8.11: The decision tree

This is how the tree looks like. The left arrow from the node ascribes to **True** and the right arrow to **False** for the condition given in the node. Each node has several important pieces of information such as the entropy at that node (remember, the less, the better), the number of samples (observations) at that node, and the number of samples in each species flower (under the heading value).

The tree is read as follows:

- If *Petal Length*<=2.45, then the flower species is setosa.
- If *Petal Length*>2.45, then check Petal Width. If *Petal Length*<=4.95, then the species is versicolor. If *Petal Length* > 4.95, then there is 1 versicolor and 2 virginica, and further classification is not possible.
- If *Petal Length*>2.45, then check Petal Width. If *Petal Length*<=4.85, then there is 1 versicolor and 2 virginica, and further classification is not possible. If *Petal Length*>4.85, then the species is virginica.

Some other observations from the tree are as follows:

- The maximum depth (the number of levels) of the tree is 3. In 3 leaves, the tree has been able to identify categories, which will make the dataset homogeneous.
- Sepal dimensions don't seem to be playing any role in the tree formation or, in other words, in the classification of these flowers into one of the species.

- There is a terminal node at the 1st level itself. If *Petal Length<=2.45*, one gets only the setosa species of flowers.

- The value in each node denotes the number of observations belonging to the three species (setosa, versicolor, and virginica in that order) at that node. Thus, the terminal node in the 1st level has 34 setosas, 0 versicolors, and 0 virginicas.

Cross-validating and pruning the decision tree

The tree might have grown very complex even after putting the `min_samples_split` of 20. There is a parameter of `DecisionTreeClassifier` that can be used to check the maximum depth to which the tree grows. This is called `max_depth`. Let us use this parameter and also the cross validation accuracy score to get an optimum depth of the tree. We are actually pruning the tree to get to an optimum depth where it neither overfits nor underfits the dataset.

We will do cross validation over the entire dataset. If you remember, cross validation splits the dataset into training and testing sets on its own and does this a number of times to generalize the results of the model.

Let us cross validate our decision tree:

```
X=data[predictors]
Y=data[target]
dt1.fit(X,Y)
dt1 = DecisionTreeClassifier(criterion='entropy',max_depth=5, min_
samples_split=20, random_state=99)
```

In these lines, we just assigned predictor variables to *X* and the target variable to *Y*. We have created a new decision tree that is very similar to the tree we created previously, except that it has an additional parameter, namely, `max_depth=5`.

The next step is to import the cross validation methods in `sklearn` and perform the cross validation:

```
from sklearn.cross_validation import KFold
crossvalidation = KFold(n=X.shape[0], n_folds=10, shuffle=True,
random_state=1)
from sklearn.cross_validation import cross_val_score
score = np.mean(cross_val_score(dt1, X, Y, scoring='accuracy',
cv=crossvalidation, n_jobs=1))
score
```

We have chosen to do a 10-fold cross validation, and the score is the mean of the accuracy score obtained from each fold. The score in this comes out to be 0.933. This score signifies the accuracy of the classification.

If we vary the `max_depth` from 1 to 10, this is how the mean accuracy score varies:

max_depth	score		max_depth	score
1	0.566		6	0.9335
2	0.920		7	0.9335
3	0.940		8	0.9335
4	0.933		9	0.9335
5	0.9335		10	0.9335

As you can observe, for `max_depth => 4`, the score remains almost constant. The maximum score is obtained when `max_depth = 3`. Hence, we will choose to grow our tree to only three levels from the root node.

Let us now do a feature importance test to determine which of the variables in the preceding dataset are actually important for the model. This can be easily done as follows:

```
dt1.feature_importances_
```

```
array([ 0.        ,  0.        ,  0.66869158,  0.33130842])
```

Fig. 8.12: Feature importance scores of the variables in the iris dataset

The higher the values, the higher the feature importance. Hence, we conclude that the Petal width and Petal length are important features (in ascending order of importance) to predict the flower species using this dataset.

Understanding and implementing regression trees

An algorithm very similar to decision trees is regression tree. The difference between the two is that the target variable in the case of a regression tree is a continuous numerical variable, unlike decision trees where the target variable is a categorical variable.

Regression tree algorithm

Regression trees are particularly useful when there are multiple features in the training dataset that interact in complicated and non-linear ways. In such cases, a simple linear regression or even the linear regression with some tweaks will not be feasible or produces a very complex model that will be of little use. An alternative to non-linear regression is to partition the dataset into smaller nodes/local partitions where the interactions are more manageable. We keep partitioning until the point where the non-linear interactions are non-existent or the observations in that partition/node are very similar to each other. This is called recursive partition.

A regression tree is similar to a decision tree because the algorithm behind them is more or less the same; that is, the node is split into subnodes based on certain criteria. The criterion of a split, in this case, is the maximum Reduction in Variance; as we discussed earlier, this approach is used when the target variable is a continuous numerical variable. The nodes are partitioned based on this criterion unless met by a stopping criterion. This process is called recursive partitioning. One of the common stopping criteria is the one we described above for the decision tree. The depth (level of nodes) after which the accuracy of the model stops improving is generally the stopping point for a regression tree. Also, the predictor variables that are continuous numerical variables are categorized into classes using the approach described earlier.

Once a leaf (terminal) node is decided, a local model is fit for all the observations falling under that node. The local model is nothing but the average of the output values of all the observations falling under that leaf node. If the observations (x_1, y_1), (x_2, y_2), (x_3, y_3), ..., and (x_n, y_n) fall under the leaf node l, then the output value, y, for this node is given by:

$$y = (1/n) * \sum y_i$$

A stepwise summary of the regression tree algorithm is as follows:

1. Start with a single node, that is, all the observations, calculate the mean, and then the variance of the target variable.

2. Calculate the reduction in variance caused by each of the variables that are potential candidates for being the next node, using the approach described earlier in this chapter. Choose the variable that provides the maximum reduction in the variance as the node.

3. For each leaf node, check whether the maximum reduction in the variance provided by any of the variables is less than a set threshold, or the number of observations in a given node is less than a set threshold. If one of these criterions is satisfied, stop. If not, repeat step 2.

Some advantages of using the regression tree are as follows:

- It can take care of non-linear and complicated relations between predictor and target variables. Non-linear models often become difficult to comprehend, while the regression trees are simple to implement and understand.

- Even if some of the attributes of an observation or an entire observation is missing, the observation might not be able to reach a leaf node, but we can still get an output value for that observation by averaging the output values available at the terminal subnode of the observation.

- Regression trees are also very useful for feature selection; that is, selecting the variables that are important to make a prediction. The variables that are a part of the tree are important variables to make a prediction.

Implementing a regression tree using Python

Let us see an implementation of the regression trees in Python on a commonly used dataset called `Boston`. This dataset has information about housing and median prices in `Boston`. Most of the predictor variables are continuous numerical variables. The target variable, the median price of the house, is also a continuous numerical variable. The purpose of fitting a regression tree is to predict these prices:

Let us take a look at the dataset and then see what the variables mean:

```
import pandas as pd
data=pd.read_csv('E:/Personal/Learning/Predictive Modeling Book/My
Work/Chapter 7/Boston.csv')
data.head()
```

	crim	zn	indus	chas	nox	rm	age	dis	rad	tax	ptratio	black	lstat	medv
0	0.00632	18	2.31	0	0.538	6.575	65.2	4.0900	1	296	15.3	396.90	4.98	24.0
1	0.02731	0	7.07	0	0.469	6.421	78.9	4.9671	2	242	17.8	396.90	9.14	21.6
2	0.02729	0	7.07	0	0.469	7.185	61.1	4.9671	2	242	17.8	392.83	4.03	34.7
3	0.03237	0	2.18	0	0.458	6.998	45.8	6.0622	3	222	18.7	394.63	2.94	33.4
4	0.06905	0	2.18	0	0.458	7.147	54.2	6.0622	3	222	18.7	396.90	5.33	36.2

Fig. 8.13: A look at the Boston dataset

Here is a brief data dictionary describing the meaning of all the columns in the dataset:

- **CRIM**: This is the per-capita crime rate by town
- **ZN**: This is the proportion of residential land zoned for lots over 25,000 sq.ft
- **INDUS**: This is the proportion of non-retail business acres per town
- **CHAS**: The is the Charles River dummy variable (1 if the tract bounds river; 0 otherwise)
- **NOX**: This is the nitric oxide concentration (parts per 10 million)
- **RM**: This is the average number of rooms per dwelling
- **AGE**: This is the proportion of owner-occupied units built prior to 1940
- **DIS**: This is the weighted distance to five Boston employment centers
- **RAD**: This is the index of accessibility to radial highways
- **TAX**: This is the full-value property tax rate per $10,000
- **PTRATIO**: This is the pupil-teacher ratio by town
- **B**: *1000(Bk - 0.63)^2*: Here, Bk is the proportion of blacks by town
- **LSTAT**: This is the % of lower status of the population
- **MEDV**: This is the median value of owner-occupied homes in $1000s

Let us perform the required preprocessing before we build the regression tree model. In the following code snippet, we just assign the first 13 variables of the preceding dataset as predictor variables and the last one (MEDV) as the target variable:

```
colnames=data.columns.values.tolist()
predictors=colnames[:13]
target=colnames[13]
X=data[predictors]
Y=data[target]
```

Let us now build the regression tree model:

```
from sklearn.tree import DecisionTreeRegressor
regression_tree = DecisionTreeRegressor(min_samples_split=30,min_
samples_leaf=10,random_state=0)
regression_tree.fit(X,Y)
```

The `min_samples_split` specifies the minimum number of observations required in a node for it to be qualified for a split. The `min_samples_leaf` specifies the minimum number of observations required to classify a node as a leaf.

Let us now use the model to make some predictions on the same dataset and see how close they are to the actual value of the target variable:

```
reg_tree_pred=regression_tree.predict(data[predictors])
data['pred']=reg_tree_pred
cols=['pred','medv']
data[cols]
```

	pred	medv
0	22.840000	24.0
1	22.840000	21.6
2	35.247826	34.7
3	35.247826	33.4
4	35.247826	36.2
5	24.058621	28.7
6	20.811111	22.9

Fig. 8.14: Comparing the actual and predicted values of the target variable

One point to observe here is that many of the observations have the same predicted values. This was expected because, if you remember, the output of a regression model is nothing but an average of the output of all the observations falling under a particular node. Thus, all the observations falling under the same node will have the same predicted output value.

Let us now cross-validate our model and see how accurate the cross-validated model is:

```
from sklearn.cross_validation import KFold
from sklearn.cross_validation import cross_val_score
import numpy as np
crossvalidation = KFold(n=X.shape[0], n_folds=10,shuffle=True, random_
state=1)
score = np.mean(cross_val_score(regression_tree, X, Y,scoring='mean_
squared_error', cv=crossvalidation,n_jobs=1))
score
```

In this case, the score we are interested in looking at is the mean squared error. A mean of the score in this comes out to be 20.10. The `cross_val_predict` module can be used, just like the `cross_val_score` module, to predict the values of the output variable from the cross-validated model.

Let us now have a look at the other outputs of the regression tree that can be useful. One important attribute of a regression tree is the feature importance of various variables. The importance of a feature is measured by the total reduction it has brought to the variance. The feature importance for the variables of a regression tree can be calculated as follows:

```
regression_tree.feature_importances_
```

```
array([ 0.03421203,  0.         ,  0.00116059,  0.         ,  0.01856163,
        0.6308568 ,  0.01725115,  0.00137451,  0.         ,  0.00236983,
        0.00933325,  0.         ,  0.28488021])
```

Fig. 8.15: Feature importance scores for regression tree on the Boston dataset

The higher the value of the feature importance for a variable, the more important it is. In this case, the three most important variables are `age`, `lstat`, and `rm`, in ascending order of importance.

A regression tree can be drawn in the same way as the decision tree to understand the results and predictions better.

Understanding and implementing random forests

Random forests is a predictive algorithm falling under the ambit of ensemble learning algorithms. Ensemble learning algorithms consist of a combination of various independent models (similar or different) to solve a particular prediction problem. The final result is calculated based on the results from all these independent models, which is better than the results of any of the independent models.

There are two kinds of ensemble algorithm, as follows:

- Averaging methods: Several similar independent models are created (in the case of decision trees, it can mean trees with different depths or trees involving a certain variable and not involving the others, and so on.) and the final prediction is given by the average of the predictions of all the models.

- Boosting methods: The goal here is to reduce the bias of the combined estimator by sequentially building it from the base estimators. A powerful model is created using several weak models.

Random forest, as the name implies, is a collection of classifier or regression trees. A random forest algorithm creates trees at random and then averages the predictions (random forest is an averaging method of ensemble learning) of these trees.

Random forest is an easy-to-use algorithm for both classification and regression prediction problems and doesn't come with all the prerequisites that other algorithms have. Random forest is sometimes called the leatherman of all algorithms because one can use it to model any kind of dataset and find a decent result.

Random forest doesn't need a cross-validation. Instead, it uses something called **Bagging**. Suppose we want n observations in our training dataset T. Also, let's say there are m variables in the dataset. We decide to grow S trees in our forest. Each tree will be grown from a separate training dataset. So, there will be S training datasets. The training datasets are created by sampling n observations randomly with a replacement (n times). So, each dataset can have duplicate observations as well, and some of the observations might be missing from all the S training datasets. These datasets are called bootstrap samples or simply bags. The observations that are not part of a bag are out of the bag observation for that bag or sample.

The random forest algorithm

The following is a stepwise algorithm for a random forest:

1. Take a random sample of size n with a replacement.

2. Take a random sample of the predictor variables without a replacement.

3. Construct a regression tree using the predictors chosen in the random sample in step 2. Let it grow as much as it can. Do not prune the tree.

4. Pass the outside of the bag observations for this bootstrap sample through the current tree. Store the value or class assigned to each observation through this process.

5. Repeat steps 1 to 4 for a large number of times or the number of times specified (this is basically the number of trees one wants in the forest).

6. The final predicted value for an observation is the average of the predicted values for that observation over all the trees. In the case of a classifier, the final class will be decided by a majority of votes; that is, the class that gets predicted by the maximum number of trees gets to be the final prediction for that observation.

Implementing a random forest using Python

Let us fit a random forest on the same dataset and see whether there is some improvement in the error rate of the prediction:

```
from sklearn.ensemble import RandomForestRegressor
rf = RandomForestRegressor(n_jobs=2,oob_score=True,n_estimators=10)
rf.fit(X,Y)
```

The parameters in `RandomForestRegressor` have their significance. The `n_jobs` is used to specify the parallelization of the computing and signifies the number of jobs running parallel for both fit and predict. The `oob_score` is a binary variable. Setting it to `True` means that the model has done an out-of-the-box sampling to make the predictions. The `n_estimators` specifies the number of trees our random forest will have. It has been chosen to be 10 just for illustrative purposes. One can try a higher number and see whether it improves the error rate or not.

The predicted values can be obtained using the `oob_prediction` attribute of the random forest:

```
rf.oob_prediction_
Let us now make the predictions a part of the data frame and have a
look at it.
data['rf_pred']=rf.oob_prediction_
cols=['rf_pred','medv']
data[cols].head()
```

The output of the preceding code snippet looks as follows:

	rf_pred	medv
0	27.700000	24.0
1	24.933333	21.6
2	37.600000	34.7
3	36.640000	33.4
4	34.880000	36.2

Fig. 8.16: Comparing the actual and predicted values of the target variable

The next step is to calculate a mean squared error for the prediction. For a regression tree, we specified the cross-validation scoring method to be a mean squared error; hence, we were able to obtain a mean squared error for the regression tree from the cross-validation score. In the case of random forest, as we noted earlier, a cross validation is not needed. So, to calculate a mean squared error, we can use the oob predicted values and the actual values as follows:

```
data['rf_pred']=rf.oob_prediction_
data['err']=(data['rf_pred']-data['medv'])**2
sum(data['err'])/506
```

The mean squared error comes out to be 16.823, which is less than 20.10 obtained from the regression tree with cross-validation.

Another attribute of the random forest regressor is oob_score, which is similar to the coefficient of the determination (or R^2) used in the linear regression.

The oob_score for a random forest can be obtained by writing the following one liner: rf.oob_score_

The oob_score for this random forest comes out at 0.83.

Why do random forests work?

Random forests do a better job of making predictions because they average the outputs from an ensemble of trees. This maximizes the variance reduction. Also, taking a random sample of the predictors to create a tree makes the tree independent of the other trees (as they are not necessarily using the same predictors, even if using similar datasets).

Random forest is one of the algorithms where all the variables of a dataset are optimally utilized. In most machine learning algorithms, we select a bunch of variables that are the most important for an optimal prediction. However, in the case of random forest, because of the random selection of the variables and also because the final outputs in a tree are calculated at the local partitions where some of the variables that are not important globally might become significant, each variable is utilized to its full potential. Thus, the entire data is more optimally used. This helps in reducing the bias arising out of dependence on only a few of the predictors.

Important parameters for random forests

The following are some of the important parameters for random forests that help in fine-tuning the results of the random forest models:

- **Node size**: The trees in random forests can have very few observations in their leaf node, unlike the decision or regression trees. The trees in a random forest are allowed to grow without pruning. The goal is to reduce the bias as much as possible. This can be specified by the `min_samples_leaf` parameter of the `RandomForestRegressor`.

- **Number of trees**: The number of trees in a random forest is generally set to a large number around 500. It also depends on the number of observations and columns in the dataset. This can be specified by the `n_estimators` parameter of the `RandomForestRegressor`.

- **Number of predictors sampled**: This is an important tuning parameter determining how the tree grows independently and unbiased. Generally, it should range between 2 to 5.

Summary

In this chapter on the decision trees, we first tried to understand the structure and the meaning of a decision tree. This was followed by a discussion on the mathematics behind creating a decision tree. Apart from implementing a decision tree in Python, the chapter also discussed the mathematics of related algorithms such as regression trees and random forests. Here is a brief summary of the chapter:

- A decision tree is a classification algorithm used when the predictor variables are either categorical or continuous numerical variables.

- Splitting a node into subnodes so that one gets a more homogeneous distribution (similar observations together), is the primary goal while making a tree.

- There are various methods to decide which variable should be used to split the node. These methods include information gain, Gini, and maximum reduction in variance methods.

- The method of building a regression tree is very similar to a decision tree. However, the target variable in the case of a regression tree is a continuous numerical variable, unlike the decision tree where it is a categorical variable.

- Random forest is an algorithm coming under the ambit of ensemble methods. In ensemble methods, a lot of models are fitted over the same dataset. The final prediction is a combination (average or maximum votes) of the outputs from these models.

- In the case of random forests, the models are all decision or regression trees. A random forest is more accurate than a single decision or a regression tree because the averaging of outputs maximizes the variance reduction.

In the next and final chapter, we will go through some best practices in predictive modeling to get optimal results.

9

Best Practices for Predictive Modelling

As we have seen in all the chapters on the modelling techniques, a predictive model is nothing but a set of mathematical equations derived using a few lines of codes. In essence, this code together with a slide-deck highlighting the high-level results from the model constitute a project. However, the user of our solution is more interested in finding a solution for the problem he is facing in the business context. It is the responsibility of the analyst or the data scientist to offer the solution in a way that is user-friendly and maximizes output or insights.

There are some general guidelines that can be followed for the optimum results in a predictive modelling project. As predictive modelling comprises a mix of computer science techniques, algorithms, statistics, and business context capabilities, the best practices in the predictive modelling are a total of the best practices in the aforementioned individual fields.

In this chapter, we will be learning about the best practices adopted in the field of predictive modelling to get the optimum results. The major headings under which all the best practices in the field of predictive analytics/modelling can be clubbed are as follows:

- **Code**: This makes the code legible, reproducible, elegant, and parametric.

- **Data handling**: This makes sure the data is read correctly without any loss. Also, it makes preliminary guesses about the data.

- **Algorithms**: This explains the math underlying the selected algorithm in a lucid manner and illustrates how the selected algorithm fits the best for the problem in the business context. In brief, it answers as to why this is the most suited algorithm for the given problem.

- **Statistics**: This applies the statistical tests relevant to the business context and interprets their result; it interprets the statistical output parameters of the algorithms or models and documents their implications in the business context.

- **Business context/communication**: This clearly states the key insights unearthed from the analysis, the improvement or change the model has brought and what are its implications in the business context, and the key action items for the business.

The following are some of the best practices or conventional wisdom amassed over the decade-long existence of predictive modelling.

Best practices for coding

When one uses Python for predictive modelling, one needs to write small snippets of code. To ensure that one gets the maximum out of their code snippets and that the work is reproducible, one should be aware of and aspire to follow the best practices in coding. Some of the best practices for coding are as follows.

Commenting the codes

There is a tradeoff between the elegance and understandability of a code snippet. As a code snippet becomes more elegant, its understandability by a new user (other than the author of the snippet) decreases. Some of the users are interested only in the end results, but most of the users like to understand what is going on behind the hood and want to have a good understanding of the code.

For the code snippet to be understandable by a new person or the user of the code, it is a common practice to comment on the important lines, if not all the lines, and write the headings for the major chunks of the code. Some of the properties of a comment are as follows:

- The code should be succinct, brief, and preferably a one-liner.
- The comment should be part of the code, but shouldn't be executable unlike the other parts of the code. In Python, a line can be commented by appending a hash # in front of the line.

Some of the reasons to prefer a commented code are as follows:

- Commenting can also be used for testing the code and trying small modifications in a considerably large code snippet.
- Transferring the understanding of the code to a new person is an integral part of the process of knowledge transfers in the project management.

The following is an example of a well-commented code snippet clearly stating the objective of the code in the header and the purpose of each line in the comments. This code has already been used in the *Chapter 3, Data Wrangling*. You can revisit this for more context and then try to understand the code with comments. Most likely, it would be easier to understand with the comments:

```python
# appending 333 similar datasets to form a bigger dataset

import pandas as pd            # importing pandas library
filepath='E:/Personal/Learning/Predictive Modeling Book/Book Datasets/
Merge and Join/lotofdata' # defining filepath variable as the folder
# which has all the small datasets
data_final=pd.read_csv('E:/Personal/Learning/Predictive Modeling Book/
Book Datasets/Merge and Join/lotofdata/001.csv') # initialising the
# data-final data frame with the first dataset of the lot
data_final_size=len(data_final)    # initializing the data_final_size
variable which counts the number of rows in the data_final data frame
for i in range(1,333):             # defining a loop over all the 333
files
    if i<10:
        filename='0'+'0'+str(i)+'.csv' # the files are named as 001.
csv, 101.csv etc. Accordingly, 3 conditions arise for the filename
        # variable. i<10 requires appending 2 zeros at the beginning.
    if 10<=i<100:
        filename='0'+str(i)+'.csv' # i<100 requires appending 1 zeros
at the beginning.
    if i>=100:
        filename=str(i)+'.csv'     # i>=100 requires appending no
zeros at the beginning.

    file=filepath+'/'+filename     # defining the file variable by
appending filepath and filename variable. file variable contains a new
    # file in every iteration
    data=pd.read_csv(file)         # file is read as data frame called
data
    data_final_size+=len(data)     # data_final_size variable is
updated by adding the length of the currently read file


    data_final=pd.concat([data_final,data],axis=0)  # concatanating/
appending data to the data_final data frame on the axis=0 i.e. on rows
print data_final_size                         # printing the
final_data_size variable containing the number of rows in the final
# data frame
```

The same code looks as follows in the *IPython Notebook*:

```
# appending 333 similar datasets to form a bigger dataset

import pandas as pd          # importing pandas library
filepath='E:/Personal/Learning/Predictive Modeling Book/Book Datasets/Merge and Join/lotofdata' # defining filepath variable as the folder
# which has all the small datasets
data_final=pd.read_csv('E:/Personal/Learning/Predictive Modeling Book/Book Datasets/Merge and Join/lotofdata/001.csv') # initialising the
# data-final data frame with the first dataset of the lot
data_final_size=len(data_final)    # initialising the data_final_size variable which counts the number of rows in the data_final data frame
for i in range(1,333):             # defining a loop over all the 333 files
    if i<10:
        filename='0'+'0'+str(i)+'.csv' # the files are named as 001.csv, 101.csv etc. Accordingly, 3 conditions arise for the filename
        # variable. i<10 requires appending 2 zeros at the beginning.
    if 10<=i<100:
        filename='0'+str(i)+'.csv' # i<100 requires appending 1 zeros at the beginning.
    if i>=100:
        filename=str(i)+'.csv'     # i>=100 requires appending no zeros at the beginning.

    file=filepath+'/'+filename     # defining the file variable by appending filepath and filename variable. file variable contains a new
    # file in every iteration
    data=pd.read_csv(file)         # file is read as data frame called data
    data_final_size+=len(data)     # data_final_size variable is updated by adding the length of the currently read file

    data_final=pd.concat([data_final,data],axis=0)  # concatanating/appending data to the data_final data frame on the axis=0 i.e. on rows
print data_final_size                               # printing the final_data_size variable containing the number of rows in the final
# data frame
```

Fig. 9.1: An example of a well-commented code

Defining functions for substantial individual tasks

Any code implements a set of tasks. Many of these talks are an important part of the overall task at hand, but can be segregated from the main code. These tasks can be defined separately as functions parameterizing all the possible inputs required for the particular task. These functions can then be used with the particular inputs, and the output can be used in the implementation of the main task.

The functions are useful because of a variety of reasons, as follows:

- Functions are also useful when the same task needs to be performed a large number of times with just a minor change in the inputs.

- Defining separate functions makes the code legible and easier to understand and follow. In the absence of a function, the code becomes cluttered and difficult to follow.

- If the task performed by the function is a calculation, transformation, or aggregation, then it can be easily applied across columns using the `apply` method.

- Debugging also becomes difficult if they are not present. These functions can be tested on their own. If they work fine, then we know that the error is somewhere else.

Let us now see a few examples of a function defined to implement small tasks.

Example 1

This function takes a positive integer greater than 2 as an input and creates a Fibonacci sequence with as many members in the sequence as the positive integer:

```
def fib(n):
a,b=1,2
count=3
fib_list=[1,2]
while(count<=n):
    a,b=b,a+b
    count=count+1
    fib_list.append(b)
return fib_list
```

Example 2

This function calculates the distance of a particular place (defined by latitude and longitude) from a list of possible stations and finds the station that is the closest to the given place. This function can take an array consisting of latitude and longitude and calculate the distances from possible stations for each location. It can also be applied to a column of data consisting of latitude and longitude in each row to find the closest station for each location (defined by latitude and longitude):

```
def closest_station(lat, longi,stations):
    loc = np.array([lat, longi])
    deltas = stations - loc[None, :]
    dist2 = (deltas**2).sum(1)
    return np.argmin(dist2)
```

An example of the list of stations can be a list of two possible stations containing the latitude and longitudes for both the stations as follows:

```
stations = np.array([[41.995, -87.933],
                    [41.786, -87.752]])
```

Example 3

A function can work without any input as well. These functions will perform some task, but will not necessarily return an output. They perform some sort of transformation or manipulation. Functions can also be defined to implement several repetitive tasks at once; for example, applying the same conversion to all the columns of a dataset.

One example of defining such a function is to define a function to convert several columns of a dataset at once to a desired data type. This is a very common and widely used data preparation step used in almost all the predictive modelling projects because the data type of some of the columns need to be changed to facilitate a particular operation or calculation in the business context.

In the following example, a hypothetical dataset called `datafile` is opened as a dictionary so that it can be read line by line and sub settled easily over columns. The dataset has columns `Date`, `Latitude`, `Longitude`, `NumA1`, and `NumA2` that need to be converted to `date`, `float`, `float`, `int`, and `int` data types, respectively. A dictionary consisting of the column names and the required data type of the column name is defined. Each column is then converted to the required data type and the resultant line is appended to the final dataset called data:

```
def load_data():
    data = []
    for line in csv.DictReader(open("..../datafile.csv")):
        for name, converter in {"Date" : date,
                                "Latitude" : float, "Longitude" :
float,
                                "NumA1" : int, "NumA2" : int}.items():
            line[name] = converter(line[name])
        data.append(line)
    return data
```

As one can see, these small tasks are significant on their own so that they are identified as a separate subtask, but in the larger picture, they are a part of the larger task and can be used later for further analyses.

Avoid hard-coding of variables as much as possible

One of the most essential guidelines to follow while writing a legible and an easy-to-debug code is to create variables and avoid hard-coding as much as possible.

Some of the benefits of avoiding hard-coding can be listed as follows:

- Hard-coding makes it difficult to spot the error and debug the code. If a variable is created, one needs to check for the error at just one place, that is, the place where the variable has been defined. If not, one has to go through the entire code, spot the places where the hard-coding has been used and check for error at all those places.

- Also, once defined, a variable can be used at multiple places in the code. Making a change in the script also becomes easier as the variable-related change needs to be done only once if the variable is defined.

The following code is one example of defining a variable and avoiding hard-coding. Here, we are defining a variable for a particular directory path and a couple of files. We can use these variables for subsequent usage such as reading one of the files. If one of the inputs, such as the directory path, needs to be changed, it can be done by making a change only at one place, that is, where it is defined:

```
import pandas as pd
import os
filepath='E:\Personal\Learning\Predictive Modeling Book\Book Datasets\
Interesting Datasets'
filename1='chopstick-effectiveness.csv'
filename2='pigeon-racing.csv'

df1=pd.read_csv(os.path.join(filepath,filename1))
df2=pd.read_csv(os.path.join(filepath,filename2))

df1.head()
df2.head()
```

Some parameters, which need to be changed regularly, should always be defined as a variable. Some codes need to be run repeatedly with a change only in one of the variables. In such cases also, defining a variable comes in very handy.

Version control

While developing the code, the changes and improvements are suggested phase-wise and not all at once. It is not possible to write in one sitting, a perfectly working code with no scope for improvement. However, the intermediate code might be used for demonstrative (the proof of concept or POC; before a project starts officially, evidence is needed to prove that the concept can be put into reality) and testing purposes. Hence, there is a need to follow a version control.

It essentially means saving a copy of the old code, making a copy of it, renaming it, and making changes to the new copy. The new copy is the new version of the code. This new copy can be released as the latest production version once it is tested after making the changes and has started running without error. Until then, the latest but one version of the code should be used as the production version. Version control can be done manually or by using version controlling tools such as GitHub and so on.

Using standard libraries, methods, and formulas

As far as possible, try to use a function or method, if it already exists, to perform a particular task in the production version of the code. For better understanding of how the method works, one can deconstruct the method and try building it up from scratch (as we have done for the logistic regression algorithm in this book) on their own, but this should be a part of the exploratory work. In the production version, already existing methods should be used.

For example, to calculate correlation, one should use the already existing formula and not reinvent the wheel from scratch. Another example is the `groupby` functionality in `pandas` to split the dataset into groups based on the different categories of a categorical variable. This saves time and also increases the elegance of the code snippet. There are an ample number of libraries to choose from to perform tasks in Python. One should choose a library that performs well and is stable over a range of IDEs, interpreters, and OSs.

Best practices for data handling

Data cleaning and manipulation constitutes the framework of any analytics project. To ensure that this important step is executed efficiently, the following best practices should be executed:

- After importing the dataset, one should ensure that the dataset (all the variables and rows) has been read correctly. This means reading all the variables in their correct or required format. Sometimes, due to some limitation on the data or the IDE side, some variables are read wrongly and they need to be formatted to the correct format.

- For example, if a variable reports some numerical ID (let's say 10-digits long), many a times it would be read and displayed in a scientific notation. However, this would be wrong as it is an ID and shouldn't be displayed in a scientific notation. Sometimes, a variable containing long strings are truncated. These issues should be taken care of before performing any operation on the data.

- After every data manipulation step such as transposing a dataset, creating and joining dummy variables to the dataset, merging two datasets, creating a new variable, or changing the format type of a variable, one should look at the resultant dataset to see whether the manipulation has taken place correctly or not.

- As far as possible, data shouldn't be deleted from a dataset. This should be kept in mind while dealing with missing values. If some of the values in a row are missing, imputing values should be the preferred choice. Deleting the entire row should be avoided.

- Basic plots, namely, histograms and scatter plots should be created for all the numerical variables to see the general outlook and behavior of that variable. This helps in spotting some obvious trends, outliers, potential modifications, and so on. The pair-wise scatter plot of all the numerical variables can also be tried if the number of variables is manageable. This plot is called scatter plot matrix and is very useful to spot relationships, if any, among any two variables. Category-wise histograms are also used to get a good sense of distribution of a variable over different categories.

Best practices for algorithms

The choice of which algorithm to deploy to answer a business question depends on a variety of parameters, and there is no one good answer. The choice of algorithm generally depends on the nature of the predictor and output variables; also, the overarching nature of the business problem at hand—whether it is a numerical prediction, classification, or an aggregation problem. Based on these preliminary criteria, one can shortlist a few existing methods to apply on the dataset.

Each method will have its own pros and cons, and the final decision should be taken keeping in mind the business context. The decision for the best-suited algorithm is usually taken based on the following two requirements:

- Sometimes, the user of the result is interested only in the accuracy of the results. In such cases, the choice of the algorithm is done based on the accuracy of the algorithms. All the qualifying models are run and the one with the maximum accuracy is finalized.

- At other times, the user is interested in knowing the details of the algorithms as well. In such cases, the complexity of the algorithm also becomes a concern. The selected algorithms shouldn't be too complex to explain to the user and should also be decently accurate.

The following table summarizes the algorithms that should be chosen depending upon the type of predictor and outcome variables and the question needed to be answered in the business context:

Type of variables	Business contexts/questions	Algorithm/Model
A continuous numerical variable as an output variable; a mix of categorical and numerical variables as predictor variables.	To answer quantifiable questions such as how many, how much, and so on.	Linear regression, polynomial regression, and regression tree.
A binary or categorical variable as an output variable; a mix of categorical and numerical variables as predictor variables.	Classification problems. To answer questions with yes/no, fail/success, and 0/1 answers.	Logistic regression.
No output variable; a mix of categorical and numerical variables as predictor variables.	Grouping/aggregation and targeted marketing. To answer what data points are similar to each other? How many such groups can be created? These groups are earlier non-existent.	Clustering and segmentation.
A categorical or numerical variable as an output variable; a mix of categorical and numerical variables as predictor variables.	Classification problems. Classifying data points into already existing groups.	Decision Trees, k-Nearest Neighbor, Bayes' Classifier, Support Vector Machines, and so on.

Best practices for statistics

Statistics are an integral part of any predictive modelling assignment. Statistics are important because they help us gauge the efficiency of a model. Each predictive model generates a set of statistics, which suggests how good the model is and how the model can be fine-tuned to perform better. The following is a summary of the most widely reported statistics and their desired values for the predictive models described in this book:

Algorithms	Statistics/Parameter	The desired value of statistics
Linear regression	R^2, p-values, F-statistic, and Adj. R^2	High Adj. R^2, low F-statistic, and low p-value
Logistic regression	Sensitivity, specificity, **Area Under the Curve** (**AUC**), and KS statistic	High AUC (proximity to 1)
Clustering	Intra-cluster distance and silhouette coefficient	High intra-cluster distance and high silhouette coefficient (proximity to 1)
Decision trees (classification)	AUC and KS statistics	High AUC (proximity to 1)

While reporting the results of a predictive model, the value of these statistics and its meaning in the business context should be stated explicitly. A brief and lucid explanation of the relevance and significance of the statistic is appreciated. Report the best values (most optimum value attainable) of these statistics. The model should be fine-tuned based on the value of these statistics until the point that they can't be further improved.

Apart from these statistics, there are various statistical tests that can be performed over the dataset to test certain hypothesis about the data before fitting any predictive model to it. These tests include **Z-test**, **t-test**, **chi-square test**, **ANOVA**, and so on. If such tests have been performed, the results (value and significance) and their implications should be clearly stated.

Best practices for business contexts

This is the meatiest part of the report created for a predictive modeling project. Some users of the report will navigate directly to this section as they are primarily interested in the overall effect of the project. Thus, it is imperative to mention the highlights and most important findings of the project in this section. This is different from reporting the statistics, which is in a way the raw output of the predictive model. In this section, we will focus on the following:

- Findings and insights of the analyses
- Major problems identified
- Major results from the model
- The accuracy or efficiency of the model
- Action steps for the user to solve the business problem, and so on

If it is a customer segmentation problem, mention the names and characteristics of the segments identified along with the statistical summary for each segment. Recommend a plan to maximize sales and revenue (or whatever the business objective might be) for each of the segments.

If it is a regression/prediction/forecasting problem, mention the accuracy of the results along with a summary of the results. For example, the expected number of house sales in the coming year is around **t** (say 900K), according to the model. The accuracy of the model is **a**% (say 98.5%).

Don't write in paragraphs. Write in bullet points. Add relevant plots and graphs to summarize the results.

Tables are a great way to summarize a lot of information in a small space. Use a lot of them. Screenshots are also a great way to show results as they are quite widely used. Assumptions, if any, should be clearly stated.

Summary

What are the do's and don'ts of a predictive modelling project? This chapter dealt with these pressing questions and listed a number of best practices to make a predictive modelling project successful. Following are the important points:

- Codes should be well-commented, modular, version-controlled, generalized, and not have hard-coded values.

- Data should be observed carefully after every import and manipulation in order to check for any errors that might creep in while performing these operations.

- The choice of the algorithm is guided by the nature of the predictor and outcome variable. The ultimate selection of the algorithm depends upon whether the user prioritizes accuracy or the understandability of the algorithm.

- While reporting the results of a predictive model, the most optimum value of the important statistics and their relevance should be clearly stated.

- Main business questions should be clearly answered. Major finding should be reported clearly. Some actionable recommendations for the findings should be given. All the assumptions should be stated.

As a practitioner of any discipline, one should strive to follow the best practices, to get the best result and impact. The same stands true for predictive modelling as well.

A List of Links

The following is a list of links that have been referenced throughout the chapters in this book:

- Link to the datasets used in the book:
  - https://goo.gl/zjS4C6

- Info on predictive modelling:
  - http://aci.info/2014/07/12/the-data-explosion-in-2014-minute-by-minute-infographic/
  - http://www.bbc.com/news/business-26383058

- UCI Machine Learning Library of datasets:
  - http://archive.ics.uci.edu/ml/

- Scikit-learn official website:
  - http://scikit-learn.org/stable/

- Pandas documentation:
  - http://pandas.pydata.org/pandas-docs/stable/tutorials.html

- An Introduction to Statistical Learning:
  - http://www-bcf.usc.edu/~gareth/ISL/ISLR%20First%20Printing.pdf

- Analytics Vidhya blog:
  - http://www.analyticsvidhya.com/

- Kaggle blog:
  - http://blog.kaggle.com/

- Hierarchical clustering PPT, San Jose State University:
  - ○ `http://goo.gl/p4kSxv`

- Decision tree learning material, Carnegie Mellon University:
  - ○ `http://www.cs.cmu.edu/afs/cs/project/theo-20/www/mlbook/ch3.pdf`

- Biostatistics Course BIOST 515, Washington University:
  - ○ `http://courses.washington.edu/b515/l13.pdf`
  - ○ `http://courses.washington.edu/b515/l12.pdf`

- Scipy documentation:
  - ○ `http://www.scipy.org/docs.html`

- Matplotlib documentation:
  - ○ `http://matplotlib.org/`

Index

G

guidelines, for selecting predictor variables
F-statistic 171
p-values 171
R2 171
RSE 171
VIF 171

H

Harvard Business Review (HBR) 2
heteroscedasticity 194
hierarchical clustering 251-254
histograms
about 48
plotting 48
hypothesis testing
about 119
confidence intervals 121, 122
example 126, 127
left-tailed 124
null hypothesis, versus alternate
hypothesis 119
p-values 123
right-tailed 124
significance levels 121, 122
step-by-step guide 125
t-statistic 120
two-tailed 125
types 123
Z-statistic 119

I

IDEs, for Python
about 18
IDLE 18
IPython Notebook 18
Spyder 19
IDLE
about 18
features 18
Inner Join
about 108

characteristics 108
example 111
Inter Quartile Range(IQR) 192
intra-cluster distance 265
IPython
about 17
URL 17
IPython Notebook
about 18
features 18
issues handling, in linear regression
about 173
categorical variables, handling 175-181
outliers, handling 187-191
variable, transforming to fit
non-linear relations 181-187

J

joins
summarizing 113

K

Kaggle blog
reference 317
k-means clustering 254-257
knowledge matrix, predictive modelling 6

L

Left Join
about 108
characteristics 108
example 112
left-tailed test 124
Likelihood Ratio Test statistic 214
linear regression
about 141
assumptions 192-194
considerations 192-194
issues, handling 173, 174
versus logistic regression 198
**linear regression, implementing
with Python**
about 156

imputation 41-44
  propagating 41
  treating 41
model validation
  about 168, 232
  data split, testing 168-170
  data split, training 168-170
  feature selection, with scikit-learn 172, 173
  guidelines, for selecting variables 171
  linear regression with scikit-learn 171, 172
  models, summarizing 170
Monte-Carlo simulation
  for finding value of pi 73
multi-collinearity 166

N

normal distribution 70-73
null hypothesis
  versus alternate hypothesis 119
NumPy
  about 16
  URL 16

O

outliers
  about 187
  handling 187-191

P

pandas
  about 16
  URL 16
parameters, random forest
  node size 302
  number of predictors sampled 302
  number of trees 302
pip
  installing 13-15
predictive analytics 2
predictive modelling
  about 1
  applications and examples 8

business context 5, 6
historical data 4
knowledge matrix 6
mathematical function 5
scope 3
statistical algorithms 3
statistical tools 4
task matrix 7, 8
predictor variables
  about 160
  backward selection approach 161
  forward selection approach 161
probability density function 66
probability distributions
  about 66
  cumulative density function 66
  probability density function 66
p-values 153, 154
Python packages
  about 11
  Anaconda 11
  installing 13
  installing, with pip 15, 16
  Standalone Python 12
Python packages, for predictive modelling
  about 16
  IPython 17
  matplotlib 17
  NumPy 16
  pandas 16
  scikit-learn 17

R

random forest
  about 298, 299
  features 301
  implementing, using Python 300, 301
  parameters 302
random forest algorithm 299
random numbers
  about 62
  generating 62
  generating, following probability
     distributions 66

use cases, read_csv method
  .txt dataset, reading with comma
      delimiter 29
  about 28
  dataset column names, specifying
      from list 29, 30
  directory address and filename, passing as
      variables 28, 29

V

value of pi
  calculating 74-76
Variance Inflation Factor (VIF) 167

W

Wald test 214

Z

Z-statistic 119
Z-test 315
Z- test (normal distribution) 120

About Packt Publishing

Packt, pronounced 'packed', published its first book, *Mastering phpMyAdmin for Effective MySQL Management*, in April 2004, and subsequently continued to specialize in publishing highly focused books on specific technologies and solutions.

Our books and publications share the experiences of your fellow IT professionals in adapting and customizing today's systems, applications, and frameworks. Our solution-based books give you the knowledge and power to customize the software and technologies you're using to get the job done. Packt books are more specific and less general than the IT books you have seen in the past. Our unique business model allows us to bring you more focused information, giving you more of what you need to know, and less of what you don't.

Packt is a modern yet unique publishing company that focuses on producing quality, cutting-edge books for communities of developers, administrators, and newbies alike. For more information, please visit our website at www.packtpub.com.

About Packt Open Source

In 2010, Packt launched two new brands, Packt Open Source and Packt Enterprise, in order to continue its focus on specialization. This book is part of the Packt Open Source brand, home to books published on software built around open source licenses, and offering information to anybody from advanced developers to budding web designers. The Open Source brand also runs Packt's Open Source Royalty Scheme, by which Packt gives a royalty to each open source project about whose software a book is sold.

Writing for Packt

We welcome all inquiries from people who are interested in authoring. Book proposals should be sent to author@packtpub.com. If your book idea is still at an early stage and you would like to discuss it first before writing a formal book proposal, then please contact us; one of our commissioning editors will get in touch with you.

We're not just looking for published authors; if you have strong technical skills but no writing experience, our experienced editors can help you develop a writing career, or simply get some additional reward for your expertise.

Learning Predictive Analytics with R

ISBN: 978-1-78216-935-2   Paperback: 332 pages

Get to grips with key data visualization and predictive analytic skills using R

1. Acquire predictive analytic skills using various tools of R.

2. Make predictions about future events by discovering valuable information from data using R.

3. Comprehensible guidelines that focus on predictive model design with real-world data.

Learning IPython for Interactive Computing and Data Visualization

ISBN: 978-1-78216-993-2   Paperback: 138 pages

Learn IPython for interactive Python programming, high-performance numerical computing, and data visualization

1. A practical step-by-step tutorial which will help you to replace the Python console with the powerful IPython command-line interface.

2. Use the IPython notebook to modernize the way you interact with Python.

3. Perform highly efficient computations with NumPy and Pandas.

Please check **www.PacktPub.com** for information on our titles

Learning Python Data Visualization

ISBN: 978-1-78355-333-4   Paperback: 212 pages

Master how to build dynamic HTML5-ready SVG charts using Python and the pygal library

1. A practical guide that helps you break into the world of data visualization with Python.

2. Understand the fundamentals of building charts in Python.

3. Packed with easy-to-understand tutorials for developers who are new to Python or charting in Python.

Mastering Predictive Analytics with R

ISBN: 978-1-78398-280-6   Paperback: 414 pages

Master the craft of predictive modeling by developing strategy, intuition, and a solid foundation in essential concepts

1. Grasp the major methods of predictive modeling and move beyond black box thinking to a deeper level of understanding.

2. Leverage the flexibility and modularity of R to experiment with a range of different techniques and data types.

3. Packed with practical advice and tips explaining important concepts and best practices to help you understand quickly and easily.

Please check **www.PacktPub.com** for information on our titles

Made in the USA
Lexington, KY
29 April 2017